COPYRIGHTS AND COPYWRONGS

SIVA VAIDHYANATHAN

COPYRIGHTS AND COPYWRONGS

*The Rise of Intellectual Property and How It
Threatens Creativity*

New York University Press • *New York and London*

NEW YORK UNIVERSITY PRESS
New York and London

Library of Congress Cataloging-in-Publication Data
Vaidhyanathan, Siva.
Copyrights and copywrongs : the rise of intellectual property and
how it threatens creativity / Siva Vaidhyanathan.
p.   cm.
Includes bibliographical references and index.
ISBN 0-8147-8806-8 (alk. paper)
1. Copyright—Social aspects—United States. 2. Copyright—United
States—History. 3. United States—Cultural policy.   I. Title.
Z642 .V35 2001
346.7304'82—dc21   2001002178

New York University Press books are printed on acid-free paper,
and their binding materials are chosen for strength and durability.

Manufactured in the United States of America

10   9   8   7   6   5   4   3   2   1

Contents

Acknowledgments

My greatest debt is to Shelley Fisher Fishkin. She has been an ideal mentor throughout my brief career and will continue to inspire my explorations for years to come. As Professor Fishkin exemplifies, there is no warmer social and intellectual support system than the circle of Mark Twain scholars around the world. Victor Doyno and Robert Hirst enthusiastically encouraged me to pursue Twain's interest in copyright, and each opened up many invaluable opportunities. Louis J. Budd and David E. E. Sloane were early and constant supporters of my interests in American humor. Joe Alvarez, Gregg Camfield, Andrew Hoffman, Michael Kiskis, McAvoy Layne, Bruce Michelson, R. Kent Rasmussen, Taylor Roberts, Laura Skandera-Trombley, David L. Smith, Jeffrey Steinbrink, Tom Tenney, Harry Wonham, Judith Yarros-Lee, and Jim Zwick generously gave me their advice, support, and friendship.

I owe special thanks to Jervis Langdon Jr. for making the Elmira College Center for Mark Twain Studies and Quarry Farm a hospitable and valuable site for scholars. I am honored that the center allowed me to serve as a scholar-in-residence during the summer of 1997. Karen Ernhout, Michael Kiskis, Gretchen Sharlow, and Mark Woodhouse made my stay in lovely Elmira fruitful and fun. It's no wonder Mark Twain did his best work there—although I suspect he would have been less productive had he had cable television.

I am deeply indebted to both Robert Hirst and Victor Doyno for their help and advice in reading, transcribing, examining, and discussing "The Great Republic's Peanut Stand." I must thank Margalit Fox of the *New York Times* for helping bring Mark Twain's "The Great Republic's Peanut Stand" to the attention of the world, and helping to put copyright discussions on the national agenda.

I have had the pleasure of discussing copyright issues with some outstanding legal scholars in the process of composing this project: Yochai Benkler, June Besek, Michael Birnhack, Andrew Chin, Julie Cohen, William Forbath, Jane Ginsburg, Mike Godwin, Peter Jaszi,

David Lange, Mark Lemley, Lawrence Lessig, Neil Netanel, Beth Simone Noveck, and Jonathan Zittrain. The work of James Boyle, Rosemary Coombe, Margaret Radin, and Pamela Samuelson has inspired me to voice the case for the public interest in copyright policy.

For feedback and intellectual inspiration, I owe Chuck D., John Perry Barlow, and Richard Stallman a great deal. Discussions with Jello Biafra and John Flansburgh about copyright and the music industry have influenced this book as well.

The faculty and staff at the Berkman Center for Internet and Society at Harvard Law School included me in its programs and kept me informed of evolving issues. The Open Law experiment, in particular, was a great help.

Authors don't thank librarians and teachers enough. This project could not have been written without the help of librarians at Wesleyan University, the State University of New York at Buffalo, Elmira College, the Library of Congress, the University of California at Berkeley, Cornell University, the Buffalo and Erie County Public Library, Yale University, the University of Illinois at Urbana-Champaign, the University of Texas at Austin, and New York University. Librarians in the Williamsville Central School District, especially Joyce Zobel, taught me how to read. Williamsville teachers such as Mildred Blaisdell, Regina Derrico, and Sue Holt taught me how to write.

I particularly need to thank New York University librarian Nancy Kranich and the staff of the American Library Association. Being the custodians of our information and cultural commons, librarians took an early interest in my work. I look forward to many years of working with them. Also, the staff and officers of the Electronic Frontier Foundation have been helpful in allowing me to participate in public discussions about copyright issues and the electronic information environment.

I have presented portions of this work before sessions of the American Literature Association, the American Studies Association, the Modern Language Association, the New York State Communication Association, and the American Studies Association of Texas. At my side through many of those sessions were Melissa Homestead and David Sanjek. Their input was invaluable to the intellectual journey this subject has taken me on. I also presented portions of this project before faculty and students at the University of Texas, Wesleyan University, New York University, Harvard University, the New School University, and

Brown University. The feedback I received at these institutions was invaluable.

At the University of Texas, I owe particular thanks to the following people, some of whom have moved on to other institutions: Robert Berdahl, Walter Dean Burnham, Sheldon Ekland-Olson, Peter Flawn, Neil Foley, Ron Gibson, Lewis Gould, Robert Hardgrave, Robert King, Richard Lariviere, Gail Minault, David Montejano, Adam Newton, Patrick Olivelle, and Kamala Visweswaran.

The American Studies Department at the University of Texas supported me in every way possible. My time in the graduate program extended across terms of two excellent chairs, Robert Abzug and Jeff Meikle. They both handled departmental business with warmth, humor, skill, and patience. Bill Stott first suggested I pursue an academic career, and I will always be grateful for his early and constant friendship and support. Thanks also to Janice Bradley, Patricia Burnham, Al Crosby, Janet Davis, Desley Deacon, Cynthia Frese, Lydia Griffith, Melanie Livingston, and Mark Smith for their wonderful advice and support. My peers through graduate school taught me as much as anyone did. My dissertation committee read an early version of this work and gave trenchant advice that helped make it a real book. The committee included Kevin Gaines, William Forbath, Neil Netanel, Jeff Meikle, Robert M. Crunden, and Shelley Fisher Fishkin. A special acknowledgment goes to the memory of Professor Crunden, who passed away soon after the dissertation defense. During my time in the graduate program, he challenged me at every turn. He never let me get away with merely passable work.

I wrote much of this book during a wonderful year at Wesleyan University. The following people were responsible for making that year highly productive: Jonathan Cutler, Jeff Kerr-Ritchie, Donna Martin, Jim McGuire, Eliza Petrow, Claire Potter, Renee Romano, Ashraf Rushdy, Kate Rushin, Peter Rutland, and Jennifer Tucker. Donna Martin retired as my year at Wesleyan ended. She will go down in history as one of those rare and legendary administrators who can slash through the thickest bureaucracy with a single phone call.

At New York University, this book has benefited from encouragement and feedback from Trish Anderson, Amy Bentley, Deborah Borisoff, Lane Browning, Jonathan Burston, Robin Means Coleman, Todd Gitlin, Dan Hahn, John Lang, Ted Magder, Elizabeth McHenry, Mark

Crispin Miller, Christine Nystrom, Neil Postman, Arvind Rajagopal, Jay Rosen, Mitchell Stephens, Aurora Wallace, Ellen Willis, and Marion Wrenn. Neil Postman was a particularly important figure in the composition of this book. His leadership of the Department of Culture and Communication ensured I had the time and resources to research and write this book. But more than that, Neil's friendship has been a great boon to my life in the Big City. Neil is a combination of Obi-Wan Kenobi and Casey Stengal. His wit, charm, and brilliance have made my time at NYU a pleasure.

I have tried to follow the examples of other scholarly and experimental works intended to enrich democracy: James Fishkin's deliberative polls; James Carey's essays that explain how communication creates culture; and Jay Rosen's efforts to instill a sense of public duty among journalists. In the spirit of John Dewey, Fishkin, Carey, Rosen, and others have argued for and described ways to make the American public sphere richer and more meaningful. I hope this book can contribute to that effort.

My students at Concordia University at Austin, the University of Texas, Wesleyan University, and New York University have taught me more than I could ever have taught them.

My former life as a journalist gave me many friends and role models, especially Molly Ivins. Katrina vanden Heuvel and Art Winslow at the *Nation* allowed me to present my views of the Napster controversy in a timely manner. Rick Karr at National Public Radio has been a valuable sounding board for my thoughts on technology and music. Rob Walker at *Slate* kept me honest.

Many friends offered encouragement and support through the execution of this book. They include Karen Adams, Leah Archibald, Josh Brewster, Diane Burch Beckham, Joe Belk, Catherine Collins, John Council, John Fitzpatrick, Catherine Haddad, David McBride, Mark McCulloch, Joe Mendelson, Sue Murray, David Nather, Dan O'Neill, Karl and Lisa Pallmeyer, Bob Randall, Catherine Simmons, Greg Speller, Paula Stout, Karine Walther, and Michelle Valek. Among these friends, Sue Krenek deserves special notice for suggesting I write about the intersections of copyright and culture in the first place. Blame her for fueling my hubris.

In the American Studies community, Gena Caponi-Tabery, Joel Dinerstein, Kim Hewitt, Charlie Keil, Brett Gary, John Gennari, David Roediger, and Carlo Rotella encouraged me at every turn.

At New York University Press, Niko Pfund sought out this book with his characteristic energy and passion. After Niko left NYU Press for a higher station, Eric Zinner took this book through editing and production without missing a step. Composing a first book is a frightening process. I am glad I had their guidance and confidence at every step.

The phrase "a gentleman and a scholar" must have been invented to describe my patient and generous father, Vishnampet Sivaramakrishnan Vaidhyanathan. I have surrounded myself with the brilliant and talented, yet he still counts as the smartest person I have ever known. My mother, Virginia Vaidhyanathan, showed me the world and taught me not to fear it. The love of my sisters, Mehala and Vedana, kept me working during the hardest moments. Although my dear grandparents, Vedambal and V. M. Sivaramakrishnan, could not stay around long enough to read this book, I know they can feel it. They also can sense my love and appreciation for their children, grandchildren, and great-grandchildren. And to my dear remaining grandparent, Helen Evans: thanks for making everything possible, even when things seemed impossible. Your love means more than you could ever know.

Introduction

Vanity of vanities, saith the preacher; all is vanity.

And moreover, because the preacher was wise, he still taught the people knowledge; yea, he gave good heed, and sought out, and set in order many proverbs.

The preacher sought to find out acceptable words: and that which was written was upright, even words of truth.

The words of the wise are as goads, and as nails fastened by the masters of assemblies, which are given from one shepherd.

And further, by these, my son be admonished: of making many books there is no end; and much study is a weariness of the flesh.

—Ecclesiastes, 12:8–12

IN 1946, GROUCHO Marx received a letter from the legal department of Warner Brothers studios. The letter warned Marx that his next film project, *A Night in Casablanca*, might encroach on the Warners' rights to their 1942 film *Casablanca*. The letter prompted a reply from Marx that ridiculed many of the operational principles of rights protection in the film industry. First, Marx expressed surprise that the Warner Brothers could own something called "Casablanca" when the name had for centuries been firmly attached to the Moroccan city. Marx declared that he had recently discovered that in 1471 Ferdinand Balboa Warner, the great-grandfather of the Warners, had stumbled upon the North African city while searching for a shortcut to Burbank. Then Marx pondered how the filmgoing audience could possibly confuse the Marx Brothers project with the widely successful Warner Brothers production. American filmgoers, Marx argued, could probably distinguish between *Casablanca* star Ingrid Bergman and his blond brother Harpo Marx. "I don't know whether I could [tell the difference]," Marx added, "but I certainly would like to try."[1]

Then Marx turned the issue of name ownership on the Warners. He conceded that they could claim control of "Warner," but certainly not "brothers." Marx claimed, "Professionally, we were brothers long before you were." Marx pointed out that even before the Marx Brothers, there were the Smith Brothers, the Brothers Karamazov, Detroit Tigers outfielder Dan Brothers, and "Brother, Can You Spare a Dime?" which Marx asserted was originally plural, "but this was spreading a dime pretty thin, so they threw out one brother." Marx asked Jack Warner if he was the first "Jack," citing Jack the Ripper as a possible precursor. Marx told Harry Warner that he had known several Harrys in his life, so Harry Warner might have to relinquish his title as well. Marx concluded his letter with a call for solidarity among "brothers" in the face of attacks from ambitious young lawyers who might seek to curb their creative activities. "We are all brothers under the skin and we'll remain friends till the last reel of 'A Night in Casablanca' goes tumbling over the spool."[2]

The Warner Brothers legal department wrote back to Marx several times, asking for a summary of the plot of A Night in Casablanca so the lawyers could search for any similarities that might be actionable. Marx replied with a ridiculous plot summary about brother Chico Marx living in a small Grecian urn on the outskirts of the city. The legal department again wrote for more detail. Marx answered by saying he had substantially changed the plot of the film. The new story involved Groucho Marx playing a character named Bordello, the sweetheart of Humphrey Bogart, and Chico running an ostrich farm. Marx received no more letters of inquiry from the Warner Brothers legal department.[3]

In his responses to the Warner Brothers legal department, Marx made several points about mid-century trends in "intellectual property." These trends have grown more acute in the last decade and presently threaten creativity and access to information. American copyright law at the beginning of the century tilted in favor of consumers at the expense of producers. In an attempt to redress that antiproducer imbalance, courts, the U.S. Congress, and international organizations have succeeded in tilting the body of law dangerously the other way. Groucho Marx is gone, but Time Warner, Inc., is more powerful than ever.

Since the release of A Night in Casablanca, information, entertainment, and computer software have emerged as among the United States' most valuable resources and most profitable exports. Yet the legal system that supports and guides those resources, "intellectual property law," remains the murkiest and least understood aspect of American life and commerce. The rules seem to change every few years, yet remain a step behind the latest cultural or technological advances. Ignorance of the laws and fear of stepping over gray lines intimidate many artists, musicians, authors, and publishers. Meanwhile, copyright libertarians flaunt the difficulty of enforcement over the nation's computer networks, and rap musicians lift samples of other people's music to weave new montages of sound that have found a vibrant market. In recent years, the following phenomena have complicated the discussion over what sorts of "borrowing" and "copying" are allowed or forbidden under intellectual property standards:

- Rap stars 2 Live Crew parodied Roy Orbison's song "Oh, Pretty Woman." Orbison's licensing company, Acuff-Rose, sued the rap group, alleging that the new recording was not a true parody and thus was not protected by the "fair use" provision of the copyright law.
- In an airport, artist Jeff Koons spotted a picture postcard of a suburban couple hugging a litter of puppies. He instructed his understudies to build a sculpture of the couple and paint them ridiculous colors. Koons sold the sculpture to a museum, but the photographer sued him for copyright infringement and won. The photographer now has possession of the sculpture as part of the settlement.
- The U.S. government has pressured the Chinese government to crack down on publishers and vendors who issue unauthorized versions of American music, literature, and computer software.
- Motion picture companies in the 1970s urged the U.S. Congress to restrict the sale of video cassette recorders in the United States, fearing that duplication of films would limit first-run movie profits. After losing the antivideo battle in Congress and in the courts, the industry embraced the technology and opened up a whole new sector for redistributing its products. Then, in 2000, the industry again lowered heavy legislative and legal hammers to stifle a technology that allows unauthorized private, noncommercial access to and copying of digital video discs.
- Record companies in the 1980s stalled the introduction of digital audio taping equipment into the consumer market, fearing high-quality home musical copying would limit compact disc sales.

Then, in the spring of 2000, the recording industry initiated a slew of legal actions to restrict the proliferation of file-sharing services such as Napster, through which fans can share compressed music files.

- Apple Computer Corporation unsuccessfully sued Microsoft Corporation for copyright infringement. Apple accused the software giant of illegally basing its Windows format on Apple's Macintosh graphical user interface design.

All of these issues go deeper than the tangle of statutes and court decisions that weave the mesh of copyright law. They expose and depend on American ethical assumptions and cultural habits, including the notions of rewarding hard work, recognizing genius and creativity, ensuring wide and easy access to information, and encouraging experimentation in both art and commerce. More deeply, these issues raise questions about whether American culture, with its African American and American oral traditions and anti-authoritarian predispositions, can broadly deploy a legal framework drawn up by British noblemen three centuries ago. As American expressive culture becomes more technologically democratic, more overtly African American, more global and commercial, the archaic legal system it inherited has been remarkably able to accommodate all these changes, however imperfectly. The story of copyright law in the twentieth century has been the process of expanding, lengthening, and strengthening the ill-fitting law to accommodate these changes. Gradually the law has lost sight of its original charge: to encourage creativity, science, and democracy. Instead, the law now protects the producers and taxes consumers. It rewards works already created and limits works yet to be created. The law has lost its mission, and the American people have lost control of it.[4]

WHO IS COPYRIGHT FOR?

As a result of these and other cases, digital reproduction, international commerce, and digital music sampling have exposed gaps in the law's ability to deal with new forms of production and new technologies. Powerful interests have argued for stronger restrictions that intimidate artists, musicians, and computer hobbyists into respecting "property rights" at the expense of creative liberty. Others have abandoned all hope of legally constraining piracy and sampling, and have instead advocated a system of electronic locks and gates that would restrict access to only those who agree to follow certain strict guidelines.

This book argues against both those positions. Through a series of case studies in different media through the twentieth century, it argues for "thin" copyright protection: just strong enough to encourage and reward aspiring artists, writers, musicians, and entrepreneurs, yet porous enough to allow full and rich democratic speech and the free flow of information. The book opens with an examination of Mark Twain's role in defining the terms of debate for literary copyright in the first decade of the century. It will then show how some key Supreme Court decisions brought the new media of film and recorded music under the copyright umbrella, poking a hole in the wall that separated the protection of specific expression and the freedom to use others' ideas. The experiences of jazz and blues composers flesh out the complexities of how the law handles "works made for hire" and the ethnic politics at work in issues of ownership and control of American popular music. The book will then use rap music to explore how postmodern sensibilities and new technologies have exposed deep flaws in the law. Finally, it will examine some disturbing trends in international "intellectual property" law that may fundamentally change how American literature, music, film, software, and information will be produced, bought, sold, and used in the twenty-first century.

The chief goal of this work is to explain how essential the original foundations of American copyright law are to our educational, political, artistic, and literary culture. Lately, as a result of schools of legal thought that aim to protect "property" at all costs and see nothing good about "public goods," copyright has developed as a way to reward the haves: the successful composer, the widely read author, the multinational film company. Copyright should not be meant for Rupert Murdoch, Michael Eisner, and Bill Gates at the expense of the rest of us. Copyright should be for students, teachers, readers, library patrons, researchers, freelance writers, emerging musicians, and experimental artists. Because the body of law has grown so opaque and unpredictable in recent years, copyright policy discussion has resided in the domain of experts who have the time and money to devote to understanding and manipulating the law. Copyright myths have had as much power as copyright laws. The interests of the general public have been ignored by the movements to expand copyright in the 1990s. Organizations of librarians and scientists have taken stands against odious policy proposals, but they are matched against lawyers for Microsoft and Disney. It is not a fair fight. My prescription for this problem is to bring the discussion of copyright issues into the public sphere, where it once was.[5]

As literary historian Michael Warner explains in his book *The Letters of the Republic,* the idea of a public sphere was central to early American republican ideology, the same ideology that produced and justified American copyright law. The emergence of an independent press culture enabled the development of a public sphere and allowed those who were sanctioned to participate in it (literate white males) to simultaneously criticize the state and commercial culture. Not coincidentally, Warner argues, late-eighteenth-century American print culture was the site of shifting and emerging definitions of terms such as "individual," "print," "public," and "reason." All of these terms lend themselves to the foundations of American copyright law. So this project builds upon Warner's: the eighteenth-century public sphere was essential to the establishment of copyright law, and copyright's subsequent transformations coincide with the general structural transformation of the public sphere. A cycle has developed. The corruptions of copyright have enforced, and been enforced by, the erosions of the public sphere.[6]

Five decades before Jürgen Habermas described the structural transformation of the public sphere in the twentieth century, Walter Lippmann and John Dewey sensed these changes as well. They each prescribed different and opposing treatments for what ailed—and still ails—American society. In *Public Opinion* (1922), Lippmann described the failure of the liberal republican model of communication. He argued that the world in the twentieth century had grown so complex and diffuse, and questions of public concern required so much specialized knowledge, that the general public was unable to deal with issues intelligently or efficiently. Mass communications by the 1920s had ceased operating as the site of dependable or substantial information about the world. Instead, Lippmann asserted, all that most readers could discern from the mass media was a series of confusing "stereotypes," fuzzy and distorted "pictures in our heads." Lippmann believed that "true," dependable, and useful information was fixable and usable, but only if a class of experts could filter, edit, and certify the information first. This priestly class of educated experts, Lippmann argued, should have a central role in all discussions and decisions of public policy. It should guide, if not determine, public opinion. In other words, Lippmann sensed that the republican public sphere had eroded. He argued that an elite state council could replace it. Lippmann wanted to shift the duties of the public sphere to the state itself.[7]

John Dewey reviewed Lippmann's *Public Opinion* in the *New Republic* in 1922. Five years later, Dewey assembled a broad indictment of Lippmann's ideas in the book *The Public and Its Problems* (1927). Recognizing that such a council of Brahmin experts would threaten real democracy, Dewey instead called for a reinvigoration of local public spheres. The public should be better educated to be able to distinguish between solid description and mere stereotypes, Dewey argued, and a broader cross-section of the public must be included in the public sphere. "We lie, as Emerson said, in the lap of an immense intelligence," Dewey wrote. "But that intelligence is dormant and its communications are broken, inarticulate and faint until it possesses the local community as its medium."[8]

Alas, Dewey lost the battle. American political culture since Lippmann's *Public Opinion* has been marked by steady centralization and corporatization of information and access. Experts have simultaneously assumed control of the information necessary for decision making and increased their influence over the means of exercising power. While the electorate has structurally expanded through civil rights legislation, potential voters protest their disconnection from the process of decision making by recusing themselves. Occasionally, technological innovations such as the Internet threaten to democratize access to and use of information. However, governments and corporations—often through the expansion of copyright law—have quickly worked to correct such trends. Therefore, considering copyright issues as a function of the failure of the public sphere simultaneously reveals the poverty of the public sphere and the ways in which a healthy public sphere would depend on "thin" copyright policy.

Copyright policy is set through complex interactions among a variety of institutions. International organizations, federal agencies, Congress, state legislatures, law journals, private sector contracts, and the habits of writers, artists, and musicians all influence the operation of the copyright system. Often these forums operate without sufficient understanding of the "big picture" of the copyright system: its role, purpose, and scope. Seldom are copyright issues adequately examined through the instruments that might contribute to a healthy public sphere—magazines, newspapers, and popular books.

There is no "left" or "right" in debates over copyright. There are those who favor "thick" protection and those who prefer "thin." At the extreme margins there are property fundamentalists and there are libertarians. Some believe that copyright is an artificial and harmful monopoly that should be destroyed or at least ignored. There are those who consider copyright a natural right, one that morally derives from the very act of imagining and creating. Others believe copyright should adhere to a "labor" theory of value: investing effort and adding value to a previous work or set of data should generate legal protection. And some others adhere to the position argued in this book: copyright is the result of a wise utilitarian bargain, and it exists to encourage the investment of time and money in works that might not otherwise find adequate reward in a completely free market. There are costs and benefits, winners and losers in every policy act. Examining these costs and benefits, and publicly debating them, can yield a more just and efficient copyright system, and possibly a more dynamic culture and democracy.

SHIFTING THE FOCUS

This book has another mission: to shift the terms of discussion about copyright in scholarly circles from the theoretical to the empirical. In other words, I want to move the debate away from such metaphysical concepts as whether an autonomous "author" exists, whether such a being could produce a stable "text" or "work," and whether that text could be in any measurable way "original." These are all interesting questions, but they are questions that can fade from significance if we consider actual incidents of human beings creating, labeling, and selling books, songs, or sculptures. As we can see from examining the products we associate with Mark Twain, Willie Dixon, and Bill Gates, "authorship" is theoretically suspect, texts are unstable and determined in large part by their readers, and originality is more often a pose or pretense than a definable aspect of a work. Scholars such as Cathy Davidson, Martha Woodmansee, Mark Rose, Peter Jaszi, and David Sanjek have shown us that the questions Roland Barthes and Michel Foucault raised about our western notions of authorship are powerful and important. Yet raising these questions is not sufficient. There is much more work to be done.[9]

For most people and in most usages, an "author" is an obvious concept. An author is a person who writes something. If prompted, many people will elaborate on the notion by differentiating a "creative" author from a mere transcriber. This distinction carries with it a sense of cultural hierarchy, with the creator on the north side of the equation. As we will discover later in this work, the distinction yields legal and commercial differences as well. But these common definitions and distinctions have come under severe scrutiny by philosophers and literary theorists.

French literary theorist Roland Barthes, in a 1968 essay called "The Death of the Author," opened a line of exploration that means to understand how European and American literary culture has arrived at its common definitions and system of rewards for an author. Barthes wrote his essay to urge a shift in critical attention away from the human being who readers imagine stands above the action of a work, tugging on narrative marionette strings. Barthes defined this imagined "author" as the sum of the assumptions of psychological consistency, meaning, and unity that readers and critics had traditionally imposed on a text. Counter to the traditional understanding of authorship, Barthes called for a different way of understanding the process of reading: as a game played entirely by the reader. The reader or critic, not the author, produces the meaning of the text, Barthes argued. By taking the historical or biographical author out of the search for meaning in a text—by killing the author—Barthes empowered the reader within the environment of textuality.[10]

In response to Barthes, philosopher Michel Foucault redefined—and thus revived—the author as a relevant, if not imperative, function of reading, criticism, and literary analysis. To do this, Foucault imagined a culture in which the idea of an "author" would be dead. Foucault noted that without a legal definition of an "author," the language of critical discourse would lack its operational vocabulary and habits of analysis. Without a name to attach to a work, no one could be held accountable for the content and ramifications of the work. Foucault's author, one who could be held accountable, is a legally prescribed and described entity, not necessarily a flesh-and-blood human being, and certainly not exclusively a brooding romantic "genius," toiling in darkness and channeling a muse. An author is not just a "writer" for Foucault. Graffiti on a bathroom wall has a writer, Foucault noted, but not an author. The law and thus the culture use the idea of an "author," even if it is merely a proper name, as a locus for a complex network of activities and judgments that deal with ownership, power, knowledge, expertise, constraints, obligations, penalties, and retribution. Foucault defined the author as a legal and cultural function, but one that matters deeply to how a culture understands, uses, and is manipulated by texts. So for Foucault, the author matters. But it matters for what it does in a culture, not necessarily whom it represents. This depersonalized "author-function" has four traits. It is linked to the legal system that regulates discourse within a culture. It operates differently in different cultures. An "author" does not precede a "work" (much as for Jean-Paul Sartre's human being, essence does not precede existence), but comes into being only as it functions in a legal and cultural environment. Lastly, it represents not simply an actual identifiable human being but perhaps several independent, contradictory, or conflicting identities.[11]

What do we do about "authorship" once we have labeled it "constructed"? How does such a label help us build a more democratic system for the exchange of cultural production? How does it help us encourage new and emerging artists and musicians against the overwhelming force of companies like Microsoft, Time Warner, and Walt Disney? We can deconstruct the author for six more decades and still fail to prevent the impending concentration of the content, ownership, control, and delivery of literature, music, and data. As law professor Mark Lemley has argued, attacking the bogeyman of "romantic authorship" is misguided because romantic authorship neither explains many of the most important changes in copyright law over the past two hundred years nor prescribes a way to improve the ways copyright law works.[12]

A seventeen-year-old mixing rap music in her garage does not care whether the romantic author is dead or alive. She cares whether she is going to get sued if she borrows a three-second string of a long-forgotten disco song. We must get beyond such esoteric discussions about the rise of the romantic author. Instead, we should define an "author" broadly, as a cultural entity: a "producer." Since 1909, the copyright statute has recognized this broad sense of authorship, the "unromantic" author. The unromantic author might be a young rapper with a $2,000 MIDI sampling machine or a corporation like Disney, through a team of writers working on the cartoon version of *Don Quixote*. American copyright law itself undermines any romantic sense of individual genius. It recognizes both Microsoft and Miles Davis as authors in a legal sense. The law has changed over the course of the century to create that special legal entity that in fact has little or nothing to do with a personified "author" as we traditionally imagine. Still, we must deal with the "producer" in some form, in court if nowhere else.

THE CASE AGAINST "INTELLECTUAL PROPERTY" TALK

From the middle of the nineteenth century, those who have pushed to enlarge and deepen copyright protection have invoked the need to protect authors from "theft." As we shall see in the chapters to come, some of those claims were warranted, and the U.S. Congress adjusted the laws to deal with these problems. However, since 1909, courts and corporations have exploited public concern for rewarding established authors by steadily limiting the rights of readers, consumers, and emerging artists. All along, the author was deployed as a straw man in the debate. The unrewarded authorial genius was used as a rhetorical distraction that appealed to American romantic individualism. As copyright historian Lyman Ray Patterson has articulated, copyright has in the twentieth century really been about the rights of publishers first, authors second, and the public a distant third. If we continue to skewer this "straw man" of authorship with our dull scholarly bayonets, we will miss the important issues: ownership, control, access, and use.

It is essential to understand that copyright in the American tradition was not meant to be a "property right" as the public generally understands property. It was originally a narrow federal policy that granted a limited trade monopoly in exchange for universal use and access. Lately, however, American courts, periodicals, and public rhetoric seem to have engaged almost exclusively in "property talk" when discussing copyright. The use of "property" as a metaphor when considering copyright questions is not new. The earliest landmark cases in British copyright discuss "the great question of literary property."[13] And as we will see, Mark Twain invoked property talk to shift the debate away from what was good for America at large to what would benefit successful authors. However, throughout the eighteenth and nineteenth centuries in both England and the United States, property talk was balanced and neutralized by policy talk—a discussion of what is best for society.

The phrase "intellectual property" is fairly young. Mark Lemley writes that the earliest use of the phrase he can find occurs in the title of the United Nations' World Intellectual Property Organization, first assembled in 1967. Soon after that, the American Patent Law Association and the American Bar Association Section on Patent, Trademark, and Copyright Law changed their names to incorporate "intellectual property." Over the past thirty years, the phrase "intellectual property" has entered common usage with some dangerous consequences.[14]

What happens when all questions of authorship, originality, use, and access to ideas and expressions become framed in the terms of "property rights"? The discussion ends. There is no powerful property argument that can persuade a people concerned about rewarding "starving artists" not to grant the maximum possible protection. How can one argue for "theft"?

Therefore, we must change the terms of the debate once again. If this book can persuade readers that copyright issues are now more about large corporations limiting access to and use of their products, and less about lonely songwriters snapping their pencil tips under the glare of bare bulbs, maybe it can revive the discussion. Instead of trying to prevent "theft," we should try to generate a copyright policy that would encourage creative expression without limiting the prospects for future creators. We must seek a balance. Historically and philosophically, "intellectual property" accomplishes neither. The idea and the phrase have been counterproductive. Instead of bolstering "intellectual property," we should be forging "intellectual policy."

FROM TWAIN TO 2 LIVE CREW

When and how did "property talk" start dominating American copyright discourse? Public and congressional debates over copyright reform from 1870 through 1909 set the tone for the rest of the twentieth century. Because of the work of Mark Twain and others, "property talk" gained a place in the public imagination. Its power grew steadily after that. Twain lived and wrote at the moment when copyright issues leaped off the printed page and into the atmosphere of sight and sound. At the moment when Twain found reason to applaud the 1909 revision of the copyright law, American culture and technology rendered it outdated once again. The first two decades of the twentieth century saw the invention of phonographs and recording machines. Ragtime composers, who mastered their art through communal creativity and an emphasis on style, suddenly had to come to terms with the fear that an unprotected work would leave the author without financial reward. These changes made popular expression profitable. From the first two decades of the twentieth century, we see the beginning of the practice that would haunt black musicians for decades: white composers filing for copyright protection on works created out of the commons of African American aesthetic traditions.

During this time, the most influential legal mind of the twentieth century, Justice Oliver Wendell Holmes, almost single-handedly re-wrote American copyright law and allowed it to creep into areas for which it was never intended. The habits and structures of these new in-dustries, music and film, almost immediately undermined the integrity and simplicity of the idea/expression dichotomy. As this book shows, these decisions were somewhat out of character for Holmes.

Since the 1830s, copyright law has worked well while it only had to deal with the written word, and when few firms could afford the ex-pense of producing and marketing books. Not coincidentally, the Amer-ican architects and original interpreters of the law at the time held a strong sense of obligation to a rich public sphere. To understand the ways that copyright law can conflict with and inhibit American cultural expression, we must consider the centrality of orality to American cul-ture, as performed through country and blues-based music and the tall tale. A hundred different people can sing about Stagger Lee or John Henry, but the person who sings it best gets rewarded most. Style mat-ters more than substance in oral cultures. No one raises objections that "Stagger Lee is my song." Oral traditions that sprout written traditions handle questions of authorship and originality differently than long-time written traditions do. The American oral-written tradition revels in common tradition and chains of influence, and uses them with wit and style. This aesthetic is clearest within African American oral, liter-ary, and musical traditions.[15]

Zora Neale Hurston, in an anthropological essay on African Amer-ican expression, explained how a fixation on European notions of authorship and originality allowed a misreading of black aesthetics: "The Negro, the world over, is famous as a mimic. But this in no way damages his standing as an original. Mimicry is an art in itself. If it is not, then all art must fall by the same blow that strikes it down." Hurston explained that what white commentators derided as "mim-icry" was actually skillful rendering and repetition. The practice has its own internal aesthetic sense, its own "originality." As Hurston wrote, "Moreover, the contention that the Negro imitates from a feeling of inferiority is incorrect. He mimics for the love of it. . . . He does it as the mocking-bird does it, for the love of it, and not because he wishes to be like the one imitated."[16]

Orally based literatures are likely to be heavily informed by immediate audience response, and the storyteller must react to what has been told before and to what is going on around him. The storyteller has an important role, one of demystified authorship. Yet there is no overriding concern for authorial "originality" as copyright law defines it. As American popular music grew steadily Africanized, authorship grew fuzzier and authorial creativity became more of a legal concept than a cultural one. If the United States adhered strongly to the principle of authorial reward as the sole function of copyright law, every rock-and-roll musician would owe money to Mississippi Delta blues musicians. Instead, we consider the twelve-bar blues to be community property, a valuable commons for all Americans to enjoy.

Concurrent with the triumphs of black expression in the last half of the twentieth century, a technological boom fostered a true democratization of expression. Photocopy machines, cheap cameras, film, video tape, and digital and computer technology have allowed almost any person to distribute a facsimile of almost anything to almost anywhere. This convergence of cultural change and technological liberation has created what cultural theorists have dubbed "the postmodern condition." Against this background, rap music has grown to dominate American popular culture in the last two decades. It has also rendered copyright law incapable of arbitrating under the old definitions of "author," "work," or "originality." Any person with a series of recorded tracks from old songs can fuse them together with a $2,000 electronic mixer and rap over the bed of other people's music, creating a new "work" composed by dozens of "authors." As a result of this ill fit between art and law, no one knew what the guidelines for digital sampling were for the first decade of recorded rap music. Artists, growing fearful of suits from large record companies, tended to sample obscure songs. Licensing fees fluctuated irregularly, and no one could safely predict the penalty for unauthorized sampling. On any given day, a rap artist might have gotten ripped off by an overpriced licensing fee, or a publishing company might have been burned by charging too little for a sample that helped produce a top hit. After a landmark sampling case in 1991, the practices solidified, but not for the better. The practice of sampling without permission has all but ended. However, this move to protect established songwriters at the expense of emerging ones runs counter to both the intent of copyright law and the best interest of society.

REDISCOVERING INTELLECTUAL POLICY

Copyright should be about policy, not property. Many recent trends and changes in copyright laws—including proposals that would protect the content of databases both domestically and internationally—are bad policy. These changes threaten democratic discourse, scholarly research, and the free flow of information. The goal of the entire copyright system should be to recognize the pernicious repercussions of restricting information, yet to reward stylistic innovation. To envision the best possible copyright system—one that would encourage creativity and democracy—we must revise our notion of intellectual "theft." You cannot "steal" an idea, a style, a "look and feel." These things are the raw material of the next move in literature, art, politics, or music. And using someone's idea does not diminish its power. There is no natural scarcity of ideas and information. To enrich democratic speech and foster fertile creativity, we should avoid the rhetorical traps that spring up when we regard copyright as "property" instead of policy. We must also rediscover, reinvent, and strengthen the idea-expression dichotomy. And we will be able to have a more informed public discussion about the purpose and scope of copyright.

This book has three goals. The first is to trace the development of American copyright law through the twentieth century. After examining the principles and history of British and American copyright law, it will proceed to a series of accounts of how copyright law has affected American literature, film, television, and music. The second goal is to succinctly and clearly outline the principles of copyright while describing the alarming erosion of the notion that copyright should protect specific expressions but not the ideas that lie beneath the expressions. The third and most important purpose of this book is to argue that American culture and politics would function better under a system that guarantees "thin" copyright protection—just enough protection to encourage creativity, yet limited so that emerging artists, scholars, writers, and students can enjoy a rich public domain and broad "fair use" of copyrighted material. While "thick" copyright has had a chilling effect on creativity, thin copyright would enrich American literature, music, art, and democratic culture.

This book is the result of six years of unsystematic intellectual grazing. The questions I ended up answering diverged greatly from the questions I asked six years ago. I started with too many assumptions and too little knowledge. Now I have too many assumptions and too much knowledge. That's some progress at least.

This is not a legal history. It's a cultural history of a legal phenomenon. I've spent many hours in law libraries, but I'm not a lawyer. My lack of legal training is both a strength and a weakness. I have been free to survey the literature and material without the strictures of legal theory guiding me. I have also been able to view the copyright system as a producer and consumer might, rather than as an arbitrator or advocate would. I did not fear that unconventional views might hinder my legal career, because I have none. However, ignorance is not a very effective tool in scholarship. I would not recommend it. So I made sure to seek guidance from some of the finest legal minds I could find to help me out. An exciting community of legal scholars have argued the public's case in these debates. Using their work, I have tried to describe a process by which a well-balanced copyright system can encourage new cultural expression and help democracy work better. Or, more precisely, I have criticized an emerging copyright system that increasingly works against those goals. Literature, music, and art are essential elements of our public forums. They are all forms of democratic speech and should be encouraged and rewarded, not chilled with threats of legal action.

1

Copyright and American Culture

Ideas, Expressions, and Democracy

AT SOME POINT late in every televised baseball game, an announcer sounds the familiar warning: "No pictures, descriptions, or accounts of this game may be rebroadcast or retransmitted without the expressed, written consent of the office of the Commissioner of Major League Baseball." Baseball fans rarely question whether this statement is true. It turns out that this declaration is a far stronger warning than copyright law justifies. If one baseball fan is watching the seventh game of the World Series on television, and another is out of the country, say, in Argentina, there is no legal authority that could or would stop the first fan from writing a detailed description or account of the game and sending it via e-mail to the other. The office of the commissioner may claim to protect the specific pictures that emanate from the television broadcast because the network and Major League Baseball have agreed to share control of those rights. They have an interest in preventing sports bars from charging admission to view a televised game that might be available only on satellite or pay-per-view, for instance. But if a newspaper photographer captures a photo of a great over-the-shoulder catch in centerfield, she controls the copyright to that image. Her job will require her to "retransmit" the image over a modem and phone wires to her newspaper, and the newspaper will probably retransmit it to the Associated Press for other papers to use. In addition, all the sports reporters covering the World Series retransmit descriptions and accounts of the game to all their readers. They never ask for or receive written consent to do so. Besides, who was the "author" of Don Larson's perfect game in the World Series? The Office of the Commissioner? Whenever Americans encounter legal language, there is the distinct possibility they will believe whatever it commands. Major League Baseball is taking liberties, and therefore we are losing them. This is but one example of how the mythology of copyright interferes with the public's access to information. The public generally has more rights under the law than networks, publishers, and record companies want to concede. However, the widespread public perception that copyright law protects ideas, information, and data has a chilling effect on journalism, scholarship, analysis, criticism, and debate.

PATENTS, TRADEMARKS, AND COPYRIGHTS

There are three main branches of "intellectual property" law in the United States: patent, trademark, and copyright law. In recent years, a fourth area, trade secret law, has grown in importance as a way of rewarding commercial innovations outside the public licensing schemes that patent and copyright law employ. In addition, most industries that deal in "intellectual property" contractually constrain their participants such that contract law becomes de facto "intellectual property" law. Lately, there have been some efforts to create new types of "intellectual property" law to handle new practices and technologies such as architecture, semiconductor design, and database production. Each of these branches of what has become known as "intellectual property law" has distinct forms and functions, but many people blend their terms and purposes when discussing "intellectual property." To fully examine the development of copyright law in the twentieth century, we must clearly understand its distinct place within "intellectual property" in general.

Patent law encourages invention. It grants a temporary monopoly to an inventor of a tangible, useful, and "nonobvious" device or process. Patents cover inventions and processes, not words, texts, or phrases. A patent monopoly lasts a much shorter time than copyright does—twenty years compared with life of the author plus seventy years—but protects more broadly. A patent protects the ideas, as well as the specific invention itself, so that a similar invention that operates along the same lines as the protected invention would be considered an infringement. Patents come in three types. Utility patents protect new processes, machines, or compositions of matter (and improvements on previously invented processes, machines, or compositions). Design patents protect new ways of planning or constructing articles of manufacture. Plant patents protect new varieties of vegetation created through breeding or genetic engineering. Plant patents are especially valuable for both agribusiness and pharmaceutical development. A product must meet three standards to qualify for patent protection: usefulness, novelty, and nonobviousness. These used to be high standards to meet. But occasionally cases arise—as in the attempt to patent the human genome—that weaken, evade, or complicate these standards. Once a product is covered by a patent, the patent holder is required to place the details of the design in the public record, so that others might benefit from new or newly applied knowledge. In exchange for the public service of disclosure, the patent holder temporarily receives exclusive rights to make, sell, and authorize others to make or sell the patented product.[1]

Trademark law lets a company protect and enjoy its "goodwill" in the marketplace. A trademark is some specific signifier such as a logo, design, color scheme, smell, sound, or container shape that points to the product's origin. It allows and provides an incentive for a company to offer a consistent product or some predictable quality. For instance, whenever you buy a beverage labeled "Coca-Cola," you assume from the name on the can that it will taste a certain way, and that it will taste just like the last Coke you drank. Although, as legal scholar Rosemary Coombe notes, trademarks do nothing to guarantee a product's quality or consistency. The social value of trademarks is minimal. Their commercial and proprietary value is enormous.[2]

Trade secret law, which is extralegislative in origin and nature, is a powerful part of "intellectual property." It has few limitations. An idea's perceived value is the only basis for a trade secret. The secret maker declares something a secret, so it is. Examples of subjects of trade secrets include chemicals, complex (and not necessarily "new" or "nonobvious") manufacturing processes, lists of customers or potential clients, "source code" for computer programs, and corporate policies. There are two "standards" for trade secret legal protection: "secrecy" and "competitive advantage." In other words, a trade secret ceases to be a trade secret once the secret gets out by legal means or was easy to ascertain in the first place. And, if the company fails to realize any real benefit from protecting a trade secret, then distributing the information in question would not make the distributor legally liable. Trade secrets theoretically can last forever. They are essentially the payoff for not patenting or copyrighting expressions, information, or processes. Once patented, a process or formula would be highly protected, but only for twenty years. Trade secrets, if properly enforced, can be powerful and valuable commercial tools. The best example of a successfully protected trade secret is the recipe for Coca-Cola. If the company had patented it, the formula long ago would have lapsed into the public domain. By keeping the information unprotected, Coca-Cola retains complete control for as long as it wants. Trade secrets are violated through larceny, spying, or bribery. Unlike federal patent and copyright laws, trade secret laws are extended and enforced through the common law.[3]

Copyright, on the other hand, was intended to protect literary, artistic, musical, and computer-generated works for a limited period of time. This grant of a limited monopoly against republication is supposed to provide enough of a reward to encourage creativity. *Black's Law Dictionary* defines copyright as "the right of literary property as recognized and sanctioned by positive law."[4] The law, in the British and American traditions, is based on the concept that an "author" can create a distinct "work" by instilling his or her effort and skill to render it "original." Originality is a fundamental principle of copyright. It implies that the author or artist created the work through his or her own skill, labor, and judgment.[5]

COPYRIGHT DEFINED

American copyright emanates from the U.S. Constitution, which directs Congress to create a federal law that provides an incentive to create and distribute new works. The law grants an exclusive right to copy, sell, and perform a work of original authorship that has been fixed in a tangible medium. The monopoly lasts for a limited time and is restricted by several provisions that allow for good faith use by private citizens, journalists, students, and scholars. Copyright was created as a policy that balanced the interests of authors, publishers, and readers. It was not intended to be a restrictive property right. But it has evolved over recent decades into one part of a matrix of commercial legal protections now called "intellectual property." Although they have different philosophical foundations and histories, copyright has become bound in practice to such areas of the law as trademark regulation, patent law, unfair competition law, and trade secrets.

Copyright is more than one right. It is a "bundle" of rights that includes the exclusive right to make copies, authorize others to make copies, create derivative works such as translations and displays in other media, sell the work, perform the work publicly, and petition a court for relief in case others infringe on any of these rights. Control of these rights can be transferred—or "licensed"—via contract with another party. For instance, a novelist owns the copyright for an unpublished manuscript, but must sign a contract that transfers some elements of that bundle of rights to a book publisher before the book can reach stores. The novelist might retain the "derivative works" portion of that bundle and later negotiate a contract to transfer that right to a motion picture studio. Part of the problem with understanding the nature of copyright is that the word *right* is embedded in it. When Americans read the word *right*, the adjective *inalienable* tends to jump in front of it. However, copyrights would be more accurately described as "copyprivileges." According to American habits of political thought, rights preceded the state; privileges emanate from the state. Copyright is a "deal" that the American people, through its Congress, made with the writers and publishers of books. Authors and publishers would get a limited monopoly for a short period of time, and the public would get access to those protected works and free use of the facts, data, and ideas within them.

THE ROLE OF COPYRIGHT

The framers of the U.S. Constitution instructed Congress to develop a statute that would grant an incentive for authors and scientists to create and explore. Without a legal guarantee that they would profit from their labors and creations, the framers feared too few would embark on creative endeavors. If there were no copyright laws, unscrupulous publishers would simply copy popular works and sell them at a low price, paying no royalties to the author. But just as importantly, the framers and later jurists concluded that creativity depends on the use, criticism, supplementation, and consideration of previous works. Therefore, they argued, authors should enjoy this monopoly just long enough to provide an incentive to create more, but the work should live afterward in the "public domain," as common property of the reading public. A monopoly price on books was considered a "tax" on the public. It was in the best interest of the early republic to limit this tax to the amount that would be sufficient to provide an incentive, but no more and for no longer than that. This principle of copyright as an incentive to create has been challenged in recent decades by the idea of copyright as a "property right." Therefore, many recent statutes, treaties, and copyright cases have seemed to favor the interests of established authors and producers over those of readers, researchers, and future creators. These recent trends run counter to the original purpose of American copyright.

James Madison, who introduced the copyright and patent clause to the Constitutional Convention, argued in *The Federalist* that copyright was one of those few acts of government in which the "public good fully coincides with the claims of individuals." Madison did not engage in "property talk" about copyright. Instead, Madison argued for copyright in terms of "progress," "learning," and other such classic republican virtues as literacy and an informed citizenry. Copyright fulfilled its role for Madison because it looked forward as an encouragement, not backward as a reward. This fit with the overall Madisonian project for the Constitution. If the federal government were to operate as the nexus of competing interests, each interest would need to approach the public sphere with reliable information. Information could be deemed reliable only if it were subject to public debate. Ideas could be judged beneficial only if they had stood the tests of discourse and experience.[6]

When President George Washington declared his support for the Copyright Act of 1790, he proclaimed that copyright would stabilize and enrich American political culture by "convincing those who are entrusted with public administration that every valuable end of government is best answered by the enlightened confidence of the public; and by teaching the people themselves to know and value their own rights; to discern and provide against invasions of them; to distinguish between oppression and the necessary exercise of lawful authority." In other words, Washington believed that only through free and easy access to information could the public educate itself to be strong enough to resist tyranny and maintain a state that did not exceed its charges. Copyright encouraged learning, so it would benefit the republic, Washington reasoned.[7]

Thomas Jefferson—author, architect, slave owner, landowner, and the most important American interpreter of John Locke—had no problems with the laws of the land protecting private property. Yet he expressed some serious misgivings about copyrights. These concerns were based on Jefferson's suspicion of concentrations of power and artificial monopolies. While in Paris in 1788, Jefferson wrote to Madison that he rejoiced at the news that nine states had ratified the new Constitution. "It is a good canvass," Jefferson wrote of Madison's work, "on which some strokes only want retouching." Primarily, Jefferson wanted a Bill of Rights attached to the document. But he also desired an explicit prohibition against monopolies, including those limited and granted by the Constitution: patents and copyright. While Jefferson acknowledged that a limited copyright could potentially encourage creativity, it had not been demonstrated. Therefore, Jefferson wrote, "the benefit of even limited monopolies is too doubtful, to be opposed to that of their general suppression."[8]

The following summer, as Congress was sifting through the proposals that would form the Bill of Rights, Jefferson again wrote to Madison from Paris. This time Jefferson proposed specific language for an amendment that would have allowed copyrights and patents, despite his doubts, but forbidden any other type of commercial monopoly. "For instance," Jefferson wrote, "the following alterations and additions would have pleased me: Article 9. Monopolies may be allowed to persons for their own productions in literature, and their own inventions in the arts, for a term not exceeding —— years, but for no longer term, and no other purpose." Jefferson lost this battle, as he did many battles before 1800.[9]

Significantly, the founders, whether enamored of the virtuous potential of copyright as Washington was, enchanted by the machinery of incentive as Madison was, or alarmed by the threat of concentrated power as Jefferson was, did not argue for copyrights or patents as "property." Copyright was a matter of policy, of a bargain among the state, its authors, and its citizens. Jefferson even explicitly dismissed a property model for copyright, and maintained his skepticism about the costs and benefits of copyright for many years. Fearing, justifiably, that copyright might eventually expand to encompass idea protection, not just expression protection, Jefferson wrote in 1813,

> If nature has made any one thing less susceptible than all others of exclusive property, it is the action of the thinking power called an idea, which an individual may exclusively possess as long as he keeps it to himself; but the moment it is divulged, it forces itself into the possession of everyone, and the receiver cannot dispose himself of it.

Jefferson then elucidated the flaw in the political economy of copyright as property. Unlike tangible property, ideas and expressions are not susceptible to natural scarcity. As Jefferson wrote of copyright, "Its peculiar character, too, is that no one possesses the less, because every other possesses the whole of it. He who receives an idea from me, receives instruction himself without lessening mine; as he who lights his taper at mine, receives light without darkening me." Therefore, Jefferson feared, the monopolists could use their state-granted power to strengthen their control over the flow of ideas and the use of expressions. Monopolies have the power to enrich themselves by evading the limitations of the competitive marketplace. Prices need not fall when demand slackens, and demand need not slacken if the monopoly makes itself essential to the economy (like petroleum or computer operating systems). But to accomplish the task of bolstering the value of these monopolies, those who control copyrights would have to create artificial scarcity by limiting access, fixing prices, restricting licensing, litigating, and intimidating potential competitors, misrepresenting the principles of the law and claiming a measure of authenticity or romantic originality. But when Jefferson warned of these potential negative externalities, they were more than a century away. Even in the early twentieth century, jurists considered Jefferson's warnings, and skepticism about idea protection kept monopolists at bay. As Justice Louis Brandeis wrote in a dissenting opinion in 1918, "The general rule of law is, that noblest of human productions—knowledge, truths ascertained, conceptions and ideas—become, after voluntary communication to others, free as the air to common use." Both Jefferson and Brandeis dissented from the conventional wisdom of their times, but nevertheless influenced the philosophy of copyright. So in the early republic and the first century of American legal history, copyright was a Madisonian compromise, a necessary evil, a limited, artificial monopoly, not to be granted or expanded lightly.[10]

THE SCOPE OF COPYRIGHT

An author can claim a copyright on many categories of creative expression, including literary works, audiovisual productions, computer software, graphic designs, musical arrangements, architectural plans, and sound recordings. According to the Copyright Act of 1976, a work is protected in all media and for all possible derivative uses as soon as it is fixed in a tangible medium of expression. This means that as soon as a writer types a story on a computer or typewriter, the work carries the protection of copyright law. Authors need not register the work with the Copyright Office of the Library of Congress unless they plan to pursue legal action against someone for violating the copyright.

The law specifically protects the "expression," but not the facts or ideas that underlie the expression. If one person writes a song that expresses the idea that world peace is desirable, that songwriter cannot prevent others from writing later songs, plays, or novels that use, criticize, or champion the same idea. However, subsequent songwriters should choose different lyrics, chord structures, and arrangements to ensure they do not trample on the original songwriter's copyright. In another example—one that corresponds to a case that reached the U.S. Supreme Court in 1991—it is clear that copyright does not protect "information." One company produced a telephone directory for an area. A second company used that list of names, addresses, and phone numbers, alphabetized by surname, to produce a second and competing directory. The first company sued, claiming copyright infringement. However, the Supreme Court ruled that the 1976 statute and a century of case law clearly stated that copyright protects only original works of authorship, not data. Alphabetization did not count as an "original" method of arrangement. There is a strong philosophical and policy argument for leaving facts, data, and ideas unprotected. The framers of the Constitution realized that for a democracy to function properly, citizens should have easy access to information and should be able to debate and criticize without fear of lawsuits.[11]

For the same reason, the framers insisted that Congress be able to grant copyrights for a limited time only. They asserted that after authors had profited for a reasonable amount of time, their works should belong to the public and contribute to the richness of the culture and politics of the nation. For more than 120 years, American authors could enjoy copyright protection for mere 14-year terms, or, after 1831, 28-year terms which were renewable for another 14 years. From 1909 through 1978, the term was extended to 28 years, renewable for another 28 years. All works created since 1978 fell under the 1976 revision, which set the term as the life of the author plus 50 years, to benefit the author's kin. Most European nations in 2001 grant copyrights for 70 years past the death of the author, and the U.S. Congress in 1998 extended U.S. copyright to match the European term by passing the "Sonny Bono Copyright Term Extension Act."

Since 1891, the United States has signed a series of treaties that grant reciprocal copyright protection throughout the world, with few exceptions. The 1891 treaty with the United Kingdom protected American authors throughout the English-reading world, and protected British authors within the United States as well. Before this reciprocal treaty, British books sold at a much lower price in the United States than American-written books did, but British authors saw no return from the pirated editions. British authors felt stiffed, and American books could not compete with cheaper British works. Leveling the playing field benefited both groups.[12]

But recent efforts to standardize copyright protection around the globe have been more complicated. Developing nations with weak currencies have spawned thriving black markets for pirated American films, compact discs, and computer programs. In an economy in which a popular American music compact disc might cost a consumer a week's wages, pirated versions offer an affordable choice at a fraction of the price. The U.S. government—on behalf of its software, music, and film industries—has been pressuring developing nations to enforce international treaties that protect copyrights. Meanwhile, European nations and media companies have been urging the U.S. government to abandon many of its copyright principles in favor of maximum protection for authors and producers. European nations have consistently granted a higher level of protection to authors and artists than American laws have. Most European copyright traditions lack the notion that copyright embodies a balance of interests that include the public as well as creators.

FAIR USE AND PRIVATE USE

How can a writer make fun of a television show without borrowing elements of its creative expression? If the writer had to ask permission from the producers of the show, the parody would never occur. No one would grant permission to be ridiculed. Yet parody is an important part of our culture. Without criticism and comment, even ridicule, democracy cannot operate optimally. Without referring to or freely quoting from original works, newspaper editorials, book reviews, and satirical television shows could not do their work. If students had to ask permission from publishing companies for every quotation they used in term papers, education would grind to a halt.

This limited freedom to quote—"fair use"—is an exemption to the blanket monopoly protection that artists and authors enjoy. Fair use evolved within American case law throughout the nineteenth and twentieth centuries, and was finally codified in the Copyright Act of 1976. The law specifically allows users to make copies of, quote from, and refer to copyrighted works for the following purposes: in connection with criticism or comment on the work; in the course of news reporting; for teaching or classroom use; or as part of scholarship or research.

If a court is charged with deciding whether a use of a copyrighted work is "fair" or not, the court must consider the following issues: the purpose or character of the use, such as whether it was meant for commercial or educational use; the nature of the original, copyrighted work; the amount of the copyrighted work that was taken or used in the subsequent work; and the effect on the market value of the original work. So, for example, if a teacher copies three pages from a 200-page book and passes them out to students, the teacher is covered by fair use. But if that teacher photocopies the entire book and sells it to students at a lower cost than the original book, that teacher has probably infringed on the original copyright. More often than not, however, fair use is a gray and sloppy concept. Commercially produced parodies are frequently challenged examples of fair use. The U.S. Supreme Court has recently granted wide berth for parody, however, as a way of encouraging creative, free, and rich speech.[13]

In addition to fair use, Congress and the federal courts have been unwilling to enforce copyrights in regard to private, noncommercial uses. Generally, courts have ruled that consumers are allowed to make copies of compact discs for use in their own tape players, and may record television broadcasts for later home viewing, as long as they do not sell the copies or display them in a public setting that might dilute the market value of the original broadcast. So despite the warnings that accompany all broadcasted sporting events, most private, noncommercial, or educational copying of copyrighted works falls under either the fair use or private use exemptions to the law.[14]

The Clinton administration has agreed to several multinational treaties that would radically alter American copyright law. One provision would establish a new type of intellectual property law to protect data, trumping the Supreme Court ruling that copyright specifically excludes data protection. Another would introduce to U.S. law the concept of an author's "moral rights," which would give authors veto power over proposed parodies of their work. A third provision would result in a prohibition on attempts to circumvent software that controls access to copyrighted material. Along with the proposal to extend the duration of copyright protection to seventy years past the life of the author, American copyright in the twenty-first century will work very differently than it has for the past two centuries.

THE IDEA/EXPRESSION DICHOTOMY

The thematic spine of this work is the alarming and steady erosion of a very valuable—yet theoretically suspect—legal construction: the idea/expression dichotomy. American copyright law has clearly protected only specific expressions of ideas, yet allowed free rein for ideas themselves. During Constitutional Convention discussions over federal copyright protection, republican leaders recognized that complete control over books by the British Crown and the Stationers' Company had limited public discourse and stifled criticism of royal and parliamentary policy. James Madison and others insisted that American copyright clearly protect distinct expressions of ideas for a limited time, while allowing others to freely use, criticize, and refer to the ideas that lay beneath the text. Copyright was to be a balance between the interests of the producer and the interests of the society of consumers, voters, and readers. The idea/expression dichotomy was to be at the crux of this balance. As Melville Nimmer, the author of the definitive copyright textbook, wrote, "[T]he arena of public debate would be quiet, indeed, if a politician could copyright his speeches or a philosopher his treatises and thus obtain a monopoly on the ideas they contained."[15]

The dichotomy is not merely a given. It has many complications and flaws. But it is best explained through textual examples. Consider the specific string of text: "And he said, Take now thy son, thine only son Isaac, whom thou lovest, and get thee into the land of Moriah; and offer him there for a burnt offering upon one of the mountains which I will tell thee of."[16] The same underlying idea could be expressed as: "Oh, God said to Abraham kill me a son. Abe said, 'man, you must be putting me on.'"[17] While the first expression is unprotectable under American copyright law because the King James Version of the Old Testament is in the public domain, the second expression is quite protected.

The second expression, written by Bob Dylan in 1965, is considered an "original" expression of a very old idea. Quoting the lyric in another work might require permission and perhaps payment of a fee. Nonetheless, a future songwriter should be fairly sure she may legally refer to the Abraham story in other words without fear of a lawsuit from Bob Dylan or his licensing organization, the American Society of Composers, Authors, and Publishers (ASCAP).

Every copyright textbook and authors' guide mentions the idea/expression dichotomy, but few fully explore it as a complicated and troublesome concept. In the widely used *Kirsch's Handbook of Publishing Law for Authors, Publishers, Editors, and Agents,* copyright attorney and author Jonathan Kirsch declares in the second paragraph of his first chapter that ideas are commodities worth trying to protect, but the law does not go far enough to protect them. He explains that traditional copyright law specifically excludes idea protection, but advises prospective authors that they may use contract law to protect their submitted ideas.[18]

Since the 1976 copyright revisions, the idea/expression dichotomy has been part of the federal statute. The text of section 102 (b) of the copyright law reads: "In no case does copyright protection for an original work of authorship extend to any idea, procedure, process, system, method of operation, concept, principle, or discovery, regardless of the form in which it is described, explained, illustrated, or embodied in such work." The House Report from the 1976 bill states: "Copyright does not preclude others from using the ideas or information revealed by the author's work. . . . Section 102 (b) in no way enlarges or contracts the scope of copyright protection under the present law. Its purpose is to restate, in the context of the new single Federal system of copyright, that the basic dichotomy between expression and idea remains unchanged."[19]

In other words, the 1976 revision codified a principle that had developed through the case law over the course of more than a century. For instance, in 1879, a federal court ruled in the case of *Baker v. Selden* that just because an 1859 book entitled *Selden's Condensed Ledger, or Bookkeeping Simplified* described a new and detailed method of bookkeeping, Selden could exert no control over a later publication of a book that summarized the double-entry system and provided examples of columned forms one could use with the system. In denying that Baker had violated Selden's copyright, Justice Bradley ruled that "there is a clear distinction between the book, as such, and the art which it is intended to illustrate. . . . To give to the author of the book an exclusive property in the art described therein, when no examination of its novelty has ever been officially made, would be a surprise and a fraud upon the public."[20]

Although the dichotomy has eroded in practice through the course of the twentieth century, some recent legal rulings still invoke it, and thus preserve it. For example, in a 1991 decision in *Feist Publications, Inc. v. Rural Telephone Service,* the U.S. Supreme Court ruled that the information in a telephone directory was not in itself protectable under copyright, because the names, addresses, and phone numbers represent the purest expression of facts or ideas, and mere collection and alphabetization do not meet the standards of "originality" that the law requires to deserve protection. Justice Sandra Day O'Connor wrote: "This case concerns the interaction of two well-established propositions. The first is that facts are not copyrightable; the other, that compilations of facts generally are. That there can be no valid copyright in facts is universally understood. The most fundamental axiom of copyright law is that 'no author may copyright his ideas or the facts he narrates.'"[21]

COMPLICATING THE DICHOTOMY

Alas, in both theory and practice, the idea/expression dichotomy is not as simple as that. Once again, consider an Old Testament passage: "And Cain talked with Abel his brother: and it came to pass, when they were in the field, that Cain rose up against Abel his brother, and slew him."[22] The last part of this passage can be expressed in the grammatically simpler version: "Cain killed Abel." It can also take the passive form: "Abel was killed by Cain." The verb could be more specific: "Cain choked Abel until he died." Do these four sentences "mean" the same thing? Most of the time, certainly. But the fourth sentence could be misread as meaning that Cain continued to choke Abel until Cain himself died. The writer of this sentence might have meant the fourth sentence to mean the same thing as "Cain killed Abel," but an audience unequipped with biblical or cultural context might miss the intended meaning if it incorrectly guessed the antecedent to the pronoun *he.*

The gap between what was originally intended and what is read or perceived—the slipperiness of meaning—has for centuries consumed the interest of linguistic and literary thinkers. Where does "meaning" come from? It might come from its source, the writer, speaker, drummer, dancer, or singer. It might be generated entirely within the audience, either individually or collectively. These questions are painfully relevant to an examination of the idea/expression dichotomy. If there is a clear distinction between the expression and the ideas that undergird that expression, then the dichotomy makes sense under all circumstances, and we can proceed with confidence. However, much recent theoretical work has complicated this commonsense notion. For some, the space between what we might consider ideas (or "objects" in general) and their linguistic expressions has collapsed. Maybe we live in a universe of language and images, and nothing else. Perhaps we as audience members have such complete control over the construction of meaning that the text itself is everything and the intent of the author means nothing. The very underlying idea of an independent "underlying idea" might be a myth or an illusion.[23]

In the sentence "Cain killed Abel," we find several signs that we can assume carry meaning. Before we go about interpreting the sentence as a whole, we understand "Cain" as a sign that signifies a man, perhaps the son of Adam and Eve. We understand "Abel" as a sign representing a man, another son of Adam and Eve. We impart (or extract) meaning to the sign "killed" as the preterit tense of the verb to *kill*. We assume that our audiences share a set of definitions, systems of grammar, an understanding of the habit of naming human beings and of the various actions associated with killing and dying. Therefore, we assume our audiences can agree on basic meanings. Still, we can imagine contextual complications. What if the reader assumed that Cain was instead a stand-up comic, not the son of Adam? Then the verb "killed" takes on a whole different, and benign, meaning. Abel would be the object of entertainment, not violence. But under most circumstances, to most readers, the sentence "Cain killed Abel" carries a fairly stable meaning.

One of the reasons we can understand the specific expression "Cain killed Abel" as just one of several ways to express the idea of a human being named Cain killing a human being named Abel is that we can form pictures in our heads of people doing things. But not all signs have referential "signifieds," or sources, in the real world. Consider this sentence from the U.S. Declaration of Independence, "We hold these truths to be self-evident, that all men are created equal."[24] We can't literally "hold truths" in our hands. While we can picture "men" in our heads, we cannot picture "equal," except within another set of symbols (signs), such as a blindfolded woman holding a scale. Of the list of signs in this sentence, the two most troubling for our analysis are "truths" and "equal." Can we understand either of these terms as anything but the terms themselves? We could define them as "not their opposites," but that does not get us any farther, just around a circle. That's not to say that we cannot create working definitions of either "truth" or "equal." We can and do all the time. However, in all of those definitions, the operative nouns and verbs are always just as nebulous. "Truth" is an idea, and only an idea. It is not an object or an action. "Equal" is the adjectival form of the noun *equality* and the verb *equate*. It is just as absent from our experience when it is used as a human trait, as opposed to a mathematical concept or an act associated with measurement and commerce.

Is there an underlying idea to the expression "We hold these truths to be self evident, that all men are created equal," when that expression is merely a collection of ideas itself? How can there be an idea/expression dichotomy if we are considering only ideas in the first place? Is an idea anything more than its expression? If there is no distinction between that specific expression and the ideas it expresses, then the distinction becomes meaningless. When we realize that the ideas that inspired Jefferson's expression had very different meanings in 1776 than in 1998—Jefferson did not intend his statement to include women or nonwhites, for example—we threaten to have our confidence in meaning erode from under us. Have we stumbled upon a fault that renders the dichotomy irrelevant to discussions of the role of copyright in democratic speech?

No, we have just stumbled upon another example of the imprecision of language and the slipperiness of meaning, which is very different from asserting the irrelevance or impossibility of meaning. It is nothing profound, just interesting. In fact, we can and do understand both "truth" and "equal" long before we get to the Declaration of Independence. Both terms are in common usage on *Sesame Street*, for instance. We as a community of readers carry around with us some idea of the meaning of these two terms. We can select different terms to describe both Jefferson's original meaning and our recent reinterpretations of the statement. While every sentence can have several meanings extracted by different communities of readers, every underlying idea can be expressed in several distinct ways. Because of this, we can empirically show that there are a priori ideas that undergird this specific

expression by choosing a different sentence structure or a set of syn-
onyms to do the same work. For example: "Every human being is considered to be worth the same as every other human being." It may lack
the poetic cadence, the rhetorical power, and the economy of Thomas
Jefferson's version, but it expresses the same idea to a certain community of interpreters. We can even render the ideas that underlie the expression "all men are created equal" in digital form, a series of ones and
zeros that constitute the simplest possible grammar. Therefore, in practice and under most circumstances, the idea/expression dichotomy that
is so essential to protecting specific texts while allowing free and rich
speech can often work, even if it doesn't always work.

This distinction between specific expressions and underlying ideas
is the most widely misunderstood aspect of copyright law. Journalists, consumers, writers, and artists often feel constrained in what they
may express or create if another has already tilled that intellectual soil.
Headlines frequently claim that "plagiarism suits" have been filed
when they are in fact copyright infringement claims. Plagiarism is not
in itself a crime or an actionable civil offense under the principles of
copyright law. Plagiarism is an ethical and professional issue, not a
legal one. The general public is often confused about this distinction because the concept is so muddled or ignored within both the popular and
legal discourses of intellectual property. For instance, a 1998 cover story
in The *Atlantic Monthly* that described some current debates over copyright protection carried the unfortunate title "Who Will Own Your Next
Good Idea?" In fact, according to traditional tenets of the law, we all
would. But, as subsequent chapters will show, the distinction has been
steadily collapsing for a century, so perhaps the article was not so mis-
leading after all.[25]

There is, in fact, a growing body of law called "idea protection," but
much of it lies outside copyright cases and statutes. It is a complex web
of trade secret laws, unfair competition laws, contractual obligations,
and industry traditions. Idea protection evolved because copyright law
explicitly denies protection for ideas and reserves it for expressions. But
habits of the literary, film, music, and computer industries, as well as
the pernicious influence of European "moral rights" thought and the
pervasive use of "property" discourse, have created the possibility of
using copyright law to limit the use and distribution of ideas, instead
of just expressions of those ideas. So when Art Buchwald got offended
that Paramount released a hit motion picture that slightly resembled a

treatment he had submitted to the same studio, he sued and won—but not based on copyright principles. Buchwald argued that the studio had violated a contract with him. Buchwald's victory in his suit on behalf of the idea he submitted for an Eddie Murphy film that ultimately became *Coming to America* (1989) has thrust idea protection into the public consciousness, but with little subtle analysis. The Buchwald case received substantial media coverage, but was almost always referred to as a "plagiarism suit." Besides the fact that "plagiarism" is not a legal cause of action, most press accounts ignored the fact that Buchwald's attorneys knew that a copyright infringement suit would be hard to win on idea protection grounds. So instead, they sued in a California state court charging a violation of contract, and won. The Buchwald trial has had a wider legacy than his effort to clean up Hollywood business and accounting practices. The coverage of that case has injured the cause of "thin" copyright protection. When very different words and phrases such as "idea theft," "copyright violation," "appropriation," and "plagiarism" are used interchangeably in the public discourse surrounding the commerce of creativity, the idea-expression dichotomy becomes harder to define, harder to identify, and therefore harder to defend.[26]

2

Mark Twain and the History of Literary Copyright

ON FRIDAY, DECEMBER 7, 1906, Senator Alfred Kittredge of South Dakota called Mr. Samuel Langhorne Clemens to the dark oak witness table in the Congressional Reading Room of the Library of Congress. A crowd had gathered, larger than those to which the joint Committee on Patents was accustomed. People came to hear America's favorite author and humorist assume his public character of Mark Twain and give his thoughts on the latest copyright revision bill. Distinguished and popular figures such as Thomas Nelson Page and Rev. Edward Everett Hale had warmed up the crowd for Twain. As the seventy-one-year-old writer approached his chair to face the committee, he removed his overcoat. The crowd gasped. In the middle of a Victorian winter, the iconoclast had donned a cream-colored flannel suit. As William Dean Howells described the incident, "Nothing could have been more dramatic than the gesture with which he flung off his long loose overcoat, and stood forth in white from his feet to the crown of his silvery head."[1]

"This is a uniform," Twain told reporters before testifying. "It is the uniform of the American Association of Purity and Perfection, of which I am president, secretary and treasurer, and the only man in the United States eligible to membership."[2] The suit, which he introduced at the hearing, became part of his public persona over the last four years of his life. Twain was so strongly identified with a white suit that a rare Twain impersonator in 2001 would dare perform without wearing one.

The world remembers the white suit better than what Twain said in the hearing. But his arguments and his way of assuming the imperial voice of American authorship have had a much deeper effect on the laws and customs of communications industries across the globe. His testimony was prescient and influential. Congress did not pass the copyright bill that session but did pass a more moderate version three years later that became the law under which publishers, record companies, and even early computer programmers operated through the next seventy years. When Congress revised the law again in 1976, it adopted many of Twain's views and gave him what he had asked for seventy years before: protection that lasts fifty years after the death of the author. Since 1976, United States courts and international negotiators have moved American copyright law even closer to Twain's wishes.

Twain's 1906 public pronouncements on copyright were carefully crafted to persuade an American public and a Congress that did not share his views on authorship and literary "property." Through his public writings and testimony, he subverted, upended, and twisted the dominant American discourses of policy making: empiricism, pragmatism, and utilitarianism. Twain publicly wrote and spoke with a strong American accent in terms that pragmatists and utilitarians could grasp. Yet he was quite European on issues of literary property and political philosophy. He had immersed himself in a Continental value system of authorship, yet Americans thought he was one of their own. Almost a century after he took his public stand, American copyright law has finally started to reflect Mark Twain's vision of what it should be. But Americans are not necessarily better off for it.

Twain's opinions about copyright evolved over the course of his professional lifetime. Early in his career, Twain enjoyed that he could purchase high-quality volumes of British literature and essays at a much lower price than in England. The United States, by virtue of not signing a reciprocal copyright treaty with the United Kingdom, was one massive public domain for British works. Cheap books encouraged literacy, according to the conventional wisdom, and Twain for the most part adhered to that wisdom. Later in his career, after seeing his books ruthlessly pirated by both British and Canadian publishers, and after considering the deleterious effects of the dominance of British works in American homes, schools, libraries, and literary circles, Twain decided he was not so enamored of cheap books, whether they were written by him or by Charles Dickens. Still, at the apex of his writing career, the 1880s, he was a copyright realist, concerned with balance and fairness, but keenly aware of the freedom the idea/expression dichotomy afforded authors. After the United States agreed to an international copyright treaty in 1891, Twain concentrated his legal studies on the differences in authors' rights and status between Europe and the United States. So from about 1898 until the end of his life in 1910, Twain endorsed maximum protection for authors, the thickest possible copyright, at the expense of both readers and publishers.

As Mark Twain went, so went the nation. From before the Revolution, American copyright law expressed tensions between republican and populist political visions. But by early in the United States' second century, political and literary leaders had moved away from populist literary ideals when it came to copyright policy. Copyright by the end of Mark Twain's life at the dawn of the twentieth century was the site of tensions between republican ideals and proprietary interests. This dynamic tension reinforced a delicate and powerfully successful balance in copyright and the culture industries right through most of the twentieth century. But at the beginning of the twentieth-first century, the republican roots of copyright are almost forgotten in public discussions of copyright and virtually absent from the concerns of policy makers. So to rehistoricize and reinvigorate the debate, we must examine the birth of copyright in the British Isle.

COPYRIGHT AS CENSORSHIP

The earliest British copyright laws were instruments of censorship.[3] In 1557, the Catholic Queen Mary Tudor capped off a 120-year monarchal struggle to censor printing presses in England by issuing a charter to the Stationers' Company, a guild of printers. Only members of the company could legally produce books. The only books they would print were approved by the Crown. The company was authorized to confiscate unsanctioned books. It was a sweet deal for the publishers. They got exclusivity—monopoly power to print and distribute specific works—the functional foundation to copyright. The only price they paid was relinquishing the freedom to print disagreeable or dissenting texts. While professional authors had no declared standing before the law according to the practices of the Stationers' Company, authors certainly played an economic role in the bookmaking process. The printers paid authors for their manuscripts and in return received exclusive rights to them. The authors not only received professional compensation and standing through the bookmaking process; they could be assured that their works would not be pirated or misrepresented in the market. To earn the exclusive copyright protection afforded by the Stationers' Company charter, a publisher had to receive written permission from the author. Therefore, the British professional author did have de facto standing and recognition in the process as early as the sixteenth century.[4]

The operation of the Stationers' Company demonstrates two fundamental principles of original English copyright law. First, it emanated from a governmentally decreed statute, not some revealed natural right of authors. Second, it granted a monopoly, which meant a publisher could set a price for a book without considering market pressures. Several succeeding monarchs, two Lord Protectors, and many Parliaments continued the system with some minor revisions for the following 137 years.[5]

The Crown extended its authority over printers through the restrictive licensing system to the American colonies as well. While only one American printer clashed directly with the British monarch, colonial governors chilled colonial presses by selectively issuing monopoly licenses. The General Court of Massachusetts issued an order in 1662 forbidding any printer from publishing anything without a license. The order sprang directly from fears that religious dissenters might incur royal displeasure by using colonial presses to spread unrest.[6]

In 1673, Massachusetts passed the first colonial copyright statute. While American publishers could have claimed protection for their monopolies through British law, enforcement was easier with local authority. As with all copyright efforts before 1709, the 1673 Massachusetts act did not mention the legal standing of authors, only publishers. No other colonies took up the copyright effort. Basically, piracy was not a problem in the colonies. Publishers colluded out of a sense of mutual obligation, or—more likely—out of a desire to keep prices artificially high through an informal cartel. Most significantly, since no colonial publisher could afford to anger the governor or king, few publishers were willing to publish anything without the guarantee of a monopoly through licensing.[7]

One seventeenth-century colonial publisher did stand up to the licensing system. In 1680, a printer named William Nuthead, sponsored by a gentleman named John Buckner, established a print shop in Jamestown, Virginia. It did not last long. The colonial government had voiced strong opposition to the practice of unlicenced printing. The records of the laws of colonial Virginia report this item: "February 21, 1682, John Buckner called before Lord Culpepper and his council for printing the laws of 1680, without his excellency's license, and he and the printer ordered to enter into bond in £100 not to print anything thereafter, until his majesty's pleasure should be known." Nuthead soon moved his press to St. Mary's City, Maryland.[8]

American colonial governors were reacting to the political turmoil of seventeenth-century England. They did not want the infection of dissent to spread across the Atlantic. The methods and targets of censorship in England had changed from the time of Mary to Charles II. Parliament had grown stronger during the 137-year term of the Stationers' Company monopoly and had come to realize that censorship was possible without granting monopolies to favored publishers. Oliver Cromwell's rise and fall had opened many questions to debate, such as the extent of tolerable censorship and the dangers of monopolies. Eventually, Charles II insisted on keeping the power to censor close to his court, in the office of a royally appointed Surveyor of the Press. The Surveyor raided some printers' houses to burn antimonarchal tracts that lay around from previous years, so the Stationers were not held in high esteem after the Restoration. But through all that turmoil, English law recognized the power of a publisher to exclusively print and distribute particular works. Stability was essential to control. But the publishers were steadily losing political power. Despite constant lobbying by the Stationers' Company to keep their monopoly powers intact, the final renewal of the Licensing Act expired in 1694.[9]

Was there a way to buffer the pernicious effects of a monopoly, avoid the perils of censorship, and stabilize the book market such that authors would be able to produce works with the confidence that they would reap some financial reward? The Stationers conceded that they had to compromise—limit their monopoly—if they were to restore stability to the marketplace. As Lord Camden later described the Stationers' lobbying efforts: "(Publishers) came up to Parliament in the form of petitioners, with tears in their eyes, hopeless and forlorn; they brought with them their wives and children to excite compassion, and induce Parliament to grant them statutory security." They failed to excite compassion, so they sought out allies who might induce some action.[10]

THE STRAW MAN: RECOGNITION OF AUTHORSHIP

The Stationers' Charter and the licensing acts that followed it were clearly publishers' laws. They regulated printing, yet had no dimension of property to them. Although authors had status and a place in the commercial process of bookmaking, they were not mentioned as parties to the legal calculus. That changed in 1709, when publishers appealed to the interests of authors to renew their monopoly protection. To secure what would become known as the Statute of Anne, printers argued that the interests of both authors and the public were harmed by the lack of price stability in the marketplace. The title of the legislation read: "An Act for the Encouragement of Learning, by Vesting the Copies of printed Books in the Authors, or Purchasers, of such Copies, during the Times therein mentioned."[11]

The Statute of Anne, often erroneously dubbed "the first copyright law," established two levels of copyright. The first level was issued in the name of the author for all books that would be published after the act took effect. The term of protection was for fourteen years, renewable for another fourteen years. In other words, this reward for authorship was an "encouragement of learning," an incentive to produce more books. The second level reinforced the Stationers' exclusive rights to previously published works for a nonrenewable twenty-one-year term. The addition of these term limits created the first codified notion of a "public domain," a collection of works old enough to be considered outside the scope of the law and thus under the control of the public and the culture at large. Although the author was mentioned as the beneficiary of the statute, the act was really another regulation of the practice of printing and selling books, not writing them, and a recognition of the public's interest in the process. The codification of authorship was merely an appeal to a straw man. A manuscript is worth nothing on the market until an author assigns the rights to a publisher. At that point, the publisher is the real player in the legal and commercial game. Mainly, the Statute of Anne was an elaborate attempt to regulate publishers, a way to balance the interests of the bookprinting industry with the concerns that monopolies were growing too powerful in England.[12]

Once Parliament forged the compromise in 1709 in the Statute of Anne, the duration of the copyright monopoly became the most divisive issue. It pitted publishers, who wanted to be able to control the prices of their works after copyrights expired, against the book-buying public, which wanted access to inexpensive material. It also pitted a new breed of publishers—the pirates—against the established members of the Stationers' Company. Once the twenty-one-year grandfather clause that covered previously published works expired in 1732, a conflict was destined to be resolved by the courts.

THE STATUTE OR THE COMMON LAW?

Soon after the Statute of Anne's twenty-one-year term on exclusive rights to "the classics" expired, a court was called upon to answer the fundamental questions of copyright. Does copyright flow from the pen of the person who wrote a work or from the state? Was copyright a product of a statute, and therefore limited to the statutory term, or a right secured by that ill-behaved and ill-defined beast, the common law, and therefore perpetual? In other words, who is copyright for? Is it for the author? Should it serve the publisher? Should it benefit the public? What about the Crown? In the eighteenth century, British courts ruled on two relevant cases, each with different outcomes.

After being disappointed in Parliament by the compromise embodied in the Statute of Anne, printers moved their attention to the courts. In English law, there is a constant tension between the principles that slowly bubble up out of the cauldron of individual court decisions and Parliament's grand, sweeping policies. Petitioners often ask courts to decide whether there is a deeper principle "at common law" that precedes and perhaps supersedes a statute. Many jurists, such as William Blackstone, considered common law, which by nature changes slowly, a necessary buffer on the unpredictable and radical potential of legislation. The English common law system invites conflict and uncertainty, which are its strengths and weaknesses, its sources of both flexibility and stability. From Blackstone on, the mainstream of British legal thought remained defiantly proud that its common law supplied a measure of predictability while European nations, with their clean and clear codes of law, were relatively chaotic. While the rest of Renaissance Europe was busy adopting the rediscovered Roman legal code, England declined. With ethnocentric fervor, British jurists resisted codification. The principles of English law would always exist in and emanate from the cases and decisions that courts heard.[13]

So the Stationers decided they needed to force a court case in which they could argue that an author (their favorite weapon) had a right at common law to control the printing of a work forever. After all, they argued, writers created new works by mixing their labor with the raw materials of existing ideas and stories. This "mixing metaphor" is the operative principle behind John Locke's theory of property. If the Stationers could get the courts to certify that the principles of common law, which gave landholders perpetual rights to their land and all its uses, apply to works of literature, then the onerous antimonopolistic parts of the Statute of Anne would no longer apply, and only the exclusivity would remain.[14]

The Stationers planned to have a sympathetic court rule on a bogus claim, a collusive suit, in which one member would intentionally republish another's work, and the plaintiff would claim perpetual copyright at common law. One bookseller named Tonson agreed to sue another, Collins, who had agreed in advance to lose and decline to appeal. An appeal would have been potentially disastrous to the Stationers, because the final court of appeal would have been the House of Lords, which had already expressed its copyright philosophy through the Statute of Anne. The booksellers funded legal representation for both sides, and happily argued the common law side more forcefully and skillfully before a sympathetic judge, Lord Mansfield. However, just after Lord Mansfield heard the initial arguments, he ordered the case to be heard by the full court of the Chancery. Somehow, the judges learned that the suit was collusive, so they dismissed the case of *Tonson v. Collins*.[15]

A real case came to light in 1769. The poet James Thomson sold the rights to his poem "The Seasons" to a publisher named Andrew Millar. Millar printed the poem in 1729 and enjoyed the exclusivity afforded by the Statute of Anne for the entire twenty-eight-year term. After the poem had entered the public domain, another printer, Robert Taylor, printed "The Seasons." Millar sued and won. The judges who heard the case ruled that the act of creation instills a property right in the work, and that Thomson had assigned that right forever to Millar. Lord Mansfield again heard this case, and wrote an opinion that reflected this new theory of "literary property" and the natural law justification for common law copyright: "Because it is just, that an author should reap the pecuniary profits of his own ingenuity and labour. It is just, that another should not use his name, without his consent. It is fit that he [the author] should judge when to publish, or whether he ever will publish. It is fit, he should not only choose the time, but the manner of publication; how many; what volume; what print."[16]

But the legal saga of "The Seasons" continued and turned back on itself five years later, in the 1774 case of *Donaldson v. Beckett*. After Millar won his case in 1769, he died. Millar's estate sold the rights to "The Seasons" to a syndicate of fifteen printers that included Thomas Becket. Sensing an opportunity to exploit a flaw in the new common law copyright, appeal it, and once and for all establish a public domain of available works, a Scottish publishing company run by John and Alexander Donaldson issued an unauthorized edition of "The Seasons." Becket sued and obtained an injunction against the Donaldson edition. The Donaldsons appealed, and the case went all the way to the House of Lords. The Lords clearly ruled that there had never been any such thing as copyright at common law. Before *Millar v. Taylor*, no judge had reached such an opinion, so common law copyright's standing in the body of law was very weak and directly contradicted the letter and spirit of the Statute of Anne. The idea that authors had a natural property right to their work as a principle of common law lasted only five years. However, the arguments and the rhetoric, the "property talk" that informed the decision in *Millar v. Taylor*, have lasted more than two hundred years. Nonetheless, the decision in *Donaldson v. Becket* stated unequivocally that copyright was a state-granted privilege that should last for a limited time, not a perpetual natural right that flows magically from an author's pen.[17]

THE AMERICAN WAY

The story of American copyright begins even before the Constitution of the United States, which guarantees some form of federal copyright protection. Freed from the restraints of the Crown and colonial governors, American printers had more incentive to pirate others' works, while American authors had less incentive to produce original works. In reaction, many states enacted copyright statutes after the Revolution divorced American courts from British statutory law. In an effort to standardize copyright law, the Constitutional Convention adopted a provision allowing Congress to write laws "to promote the progress of science and useful arts." Congress delivered protection to authors and publishers in the Copyright Act of 1790.

The road to the Act of 1790 began with Noah Webster's efforts to get each state to pass a copyright act that would protect his work as both an author and a publisher. Early proponents of a national copyright standard included Jeremy Belknap, the founder of the Massachusetts Historical Society (and author of *The Foresters,* the first American novel to receive federal copyright protection in 1792), and Thomas Paine, the revolutionary pamphleteer whose hatred of censorship was a driving force in his life and work. But Webster, the assembler of the most popular volume published in America, his blue-backed speller, was the most effective lobbyist. Because the Articles of Confederation did not specifically grant Congress the power to write laws that would regulate copyrights, Webster worked on individual state legislatures beginning in 1782. After failing in New York and New Jersey, Webster succeeded in convincing the Connecticut legislature to pass the first American copyright statute in January 1783. The law was entitled "Act for the encouragement of Literature and Genius." It granted any author who was a resident of the United States control over the printing, publishing, and selling of a work for a term of fourteen years, renewable for another fourteen years. The law also required that the author "furnish the Public with sufficient Editions," such that an author could not benefit from the protection of the law while restricting access to his work. Such a balance, a tradeoff, between public good and private reward served as the germinal idea of American copyright, and in many ways the Connecticut law served as a model for the first national statute in 1790. Soon after his success in Connecticut, Webster convinced the legislatures of Massachusetts, New York (despite his previous failure), New Jersey, New Hampshire, Rhode Island, Virginia, and Delaware. Pennsylvania and Maryland joined in, but with much weaker laws that would not go into effect until all the other states concurred. Therefore, both the terms of the laws and the level of enforcement and dates of enactment differed among the states. It became clear to Webster, Madison, and others that copyright was one of the areas of law that would be best dealt with on a federal level.[18]

The introduction of the author into the legal matrix of copyright, as we have seen, occurred in the first decade of the eighteenth century, and culminated in the Statute of Anne in 1709. Mindful of the principles of that debate, and of the dangerous power that monopoly licensing gave both the state and the favored publishers, James Madison and Noah Webster set about establishing the working principles of American copyright just after the Revolution.

The phrase that emerged from the Constitutional Convention became article 1, section 8 of the Constitution: Congress shall have the power to "promote the Progress of Science and useful Arts, by securing for limited Times to Authors and Inventors the exclusive Right to their respective Writings and Discoveries." This phrase makes it clear that copyright and patent laws are meant to benefit the public first and foremost, so the public can enjoy the fruits of "Science and the useful Arts." The clause also embodies the incentive principle, that copyright law should allow enough exclusivity to "promote" further creation, but only "for limited Times."[19]

While campaigning for constitutional ratification in New York State, James Madison wrote about the copyright clause in Federalist 43: "The public good fully coincides in both cases [copyright and patent] with the claims of individuals," thus reiterating the principle that incentive, not property or natural law, is the foundational justification for American copyright.[20]

Soon after Congress passed the first federal copyright statute in 1790, Noah Webster set about trying to extend it. He succeeded in amending the act in 1802 to include the protection of the design, engraving, and etching of prints. By 1831, Webster had garnered enough support to extend the term of copyright protection from fourteen years (renewable for another fourteen years), to twenty-eight years (renewable for fourteen more). The 1831 law also allowed the author's widow and children to file for a renewal. Webster had fought for perpetual copyright protection, despite the constitutional provision forbidding it. Most of the American cultural production of the nineteenth century operated under the provisions of the copyright law of 1831, and the term of copyright protection would not be extended until 1909, and again in 1976 and 1998.[21]

As the American population grew in the first half of the nineteenth century, readership grew and therefore publishing grew. The first fifty years of the century saw every major eastern city at least double its number of bookselling firms. New York City went from fewer than 60 in 1800 to more than 340 by 1850. The expansion was not only demand-driven, but also facilitated by technological advances such as the Isaac Adams steam press and various new typesetting methods.[22] The future looked bright for American publishers. The only problem for American authors was that the public seemed to want only novels that resembled the works of Sir Walter Scott. By 1830, ten publishing firms in Philadelphia alone printed editions of Scott's works.[23]

In the early republic, American professional authorship was struggling to establish itself but found itself handicapped by legal and cultural barriers. That a legislature would grant legal standing to an author and encourage creativity by granting a limited monopoly to distribute creative works was central to the efforts to codify American copyright between 1776 and 1790. Yet some published histories of American authorship ignore the legislative evidence and assume that because there was no identifiable "author class" in America, there was no sense of "authorship" in the public and legislative discourse. Several historians have traced the dissemination of copyright laws throughout the United Kingdom and its subsequent colonization of other parts of the world. Many of these historians attribute the rise of authorship and the need to protect authorial originality to England of the eighteenth and nineteenth centuries. There is little historical foundation for that assumption. In fact, Harry Ransom, former chancellor of the University of Texas and a pioneering copyright historian, noted that authorial pretensions occupied even ancient Greek and Roman writers. For example, the Roman poet Martial complained against writers issuing false claims to others' work, what he called *plagium*, or kidnaping. In addition, anthropologist Ruth Finnegan has attacked as simplistic and ethnocentric the assumption that oral cultures fail to recognize authorship. "Authorship" is too often defined in ahistorical European terms.[24]

So the historical origins of originality and authorship are as murky as the concepts themselves. What is clear, however, is that during the eighteenth and nineteenth centuries, British authors organized to protect their financial interests and place in society. They called for a valorization of their profession. They recognized that they controlled a valuable financial and cultural commodity in a thriving empire that based its imperialistic motivations on the superiority of its culture. They lobbied for copyright laws to protect their financial interests.[25]

In 1834, the U.S. Supreme Court dealt a blow to the natural law mystification of the author by ruling that a copyright is a privileged monopoly, and that it should be limited to allow competitive printing to disseminate knowledge cheaply. The case arose from a dispute between two reporters for the United States Supreme Court. Henry Wheaton had for many years compiled the reports of the Court. His successor, Richard Peters, decided to supplement the continuing reports with a series of "condensed reports" that included decisions that had been published by Wheaton years earlier. Wheaton argued that Peters had infringed on his copyrights both through the copyright statute and through common law. The circuit court tossed out the statutory claim because Wheaton had not complied with all of its requirements. It declined to rule on the common law question, so Wheaton appealed to the Supreme Court. Writing for the majority, Justice McLean declared that the United States recognized no common law notion of copyright, and argued that a perpetual monopoly would not be in the interest of the public.[26]

THE BRITISH ROMANTICS

Meanwhile, over in England, the long battle between authors and publishers had changed by the 1830s. As the British author rose in status, British publishers noticed that they benefited as well from the emerging "star system." Authors and publishers ceased fighting as they realized that they both benefited from a strong copyright system and the rising cultural value of literacy and learning. As the nineteenth century rolled in, more people realized they could make a living as writers for an expanding readership. Both sides soon recognized the political power of the claim that authorial genius "deserved" not just an incentive, but an ample reward for work done on behalf of the Empire and culture.[27]

In 1837, William Wordsworth's friend Thomas Noon Talfourd, an author and a member of Parliament, opened a campaign for revision of the Copyright Act on behalf of the authors. The term Talfourd proposed—the author's lifetime plus sixty years—drew opposition from the book trade, most notably from Thomas Tegg, who specialized in cheap reprints. This opposition roused Wordsworth to action. He organized a petition drive among British authors in support of the extension. In 1839, Wordsworth, Robert Southey, Thomas Carlyle, and other literary figures submitted petitions to Parliament. Finally, under the stewardship of Lord Mahon, Parliament passed the Copyright Act of 1842, which lasted until the twentieth century. This provided a term of the author's lifetime plus seven years, or forty-two years from publication—whichever was longer. The authors were fairly happy with their efforts.[28]

American authors and publishers fought a similar battle fifty years later than the British romantics did, and it lasted a decade into the twentieth century. First, authors struggled against American publishers for a copyright treaty that would protect their works throughout the English-reading world; second, they worked to extend the duration of copyright protection. This heightened the struggle between American authors and publishers, and established the struggle between authors and readers.[29]

AMERICAN REALISTS

In the last three decades of the nineteenth century, the proliferation of literary periodicals such as the *Atlantic Monthly* and *Scribner's,* the expansion of literacy, the success of subscription book sales across the continent, and the influence of the writing class in Boston and San Francisco further complicated the battle between producers and consumers. In the wake of two landmark copyright cases, *Wheaton v. Peters* and *Stowe v. Thomas,* American authors by the 1880s had organized themselves as authors had in England. In Wordsworth's place at the head of the political charge against publishers was a publisher, Samuel Clemens. To achieve his ends he donned his literary mask as the champion of American expression, Mark Twain. Twain and other American authors were inspired not only by their British counterparts fighting to better their position, but by the fate of one of their own in American courts.

In 1853, a U.S. circuit court heard a case that Harriet Beecher Stowe and her husband filed against F. W. Thomas, the publisher of a Philadelphia German-language newspaper, *Die Freie Presse*. Thomas had translated *Uncle Tom's Cabin* into German without permission or payment and sold the book in the United States. There was no statutory guideline for how translations would affect an author's rights, so the U.S. Third Circuit Court of Appeals ruled that the 1831 Copyright Act protected only the precise words Stowe used, and not her ideas, which were really the subjects of translation.

As Judge Robert Grier wrote in his decision: "An author may be said to be the creator or inventor, both of the ideas contained in his book, and the combination of works to represent them. Before publication he has the exclusive possession of his invention. His dominion is perfect. But when he has published his book and given his thoughts, sentiments, knowledge or discoveries to the world, he can have no longer an exclusive possession of them." Grier echoed the sentiments that Jefferson had expressed forty years earlier. "Such an appropriation [the claim to property in ideas themselves] becomes impossible, and is inconsistent with the object of publication," Grier wrote.

> The author's conceptions have become the common property of his readers, who cannot be deprived of the use of them, or their right to communicate them to others clothed in their own language, by lecture or by treatise. The claim of literary property, therefore, after publication, cannot be in the ideas, sentiments or the creations of the imagination of the poet or novelist, as disserved from the language, idiom, style, or the outward semblance and exhibition of them.

Then Grier employed the metaphor of clothing to describe the difference between idea and expression.

> A "copy" of a book must, therefore, be a transcript of the language in which the conceptions of the author are clothed; of something printed and embodied in a tangible shape. The same conceptions clothed in another language cannot constitute the same composition; nor can it be called a transcript or "copy" of the same "book." I have seen a literal translation of Burns' poems into French prose; but to call it a copy of the original, would be as ridiculous as the translation itself.

Here Grier invoked—perhaps invented—a very strict definition of the idea/expression dichotomy, twenty-seven years before the case of *Baker v. Selden,* when the Supreme Court outlined the concept. "Hence, in questions of infringement of copyright, the inquiry is not, whether the defendant has used the thoughts, conceptions, information or discoveries promulgated by the original," Grier wrote, "but whether his composition may be considered a new work requiring invention, learning and judgment, or only a mere transcript of the whole or parts of the original, with merely colorable variations."[30]

As Melissa Homestead has shown in her article "The Author/ Mother in the Marketplace and in Court: Harriet Beecher Stowe and the Copyright in *Uncle Tom's Cabin,*" the case of *Stowe v. Thomas*, while understudied by other Stowe scholars, literary historians, and copyright historians, was central to Stowe's standing as an author and legal agent, and to the dominant copyright philosophy in the mid-nineteenth century. Congress, at the behest of authors and publishers, included translations and dramatic adaptations among authors' rights in a copyright revision law of 1870, opening the first fault in the idea/expression dichotomy. For American authors, though, the 1853 case would serve for decades as an example of how courts were unlikely to reward them for their work. The antiproperty rhetoric of Grier's decision pushed authors into a fervent defense of copyright as property, a strategy they felt appealed to the public's affection for frontier individualism and justice.[31]

TOWARD AN ANGLO-AMERICAN COPYRIGHT TREATY

Duration and level of protection for American authors were not the only issues on the table during the nineteenth century. The Stowe case revealed a far more serious problem: American works were subject to piracy in both English and translation, and European authors could reap no profit from their works being printed for the burgeoning American reading public. By 1890, only one European nation, Russia, had joined the United States in resisting international copyright agreements. For decades, American authors voiced frustration over getting underpriced in the American marketplace by pirated versions of the works of Charles Dickens and Walter Scott. Likewise, from the 1830s through the 1880s, British authors and political leaders pushed the U.S. Congress to adopt a reciprocal copyright agreement to limit piracy.[32]

American readers were hooked on inexpensive books. And British works not only carried heavier social and intellectual value—they were cheaper. A London reader who wanted a copy of Charles Dickens's *A Christmas Carol* would have to pay the equivalent of $2.50 in 1843. An American Dickens fan would have to pay only six cents per copy.[33]

Throughout the nineteenth century, those who favored international copyright relied on two arguments. Neither of the arguments was ultimately very persuasive. The first was that the lack of protection for British authors was blatantly unfair to them, and that a basic sense of justice should prevail; the second was that international copyright would be in the interest of developing a national body of literature in the United States, so that American literature might be something more than a vulgar offshoot of the British tradition. The four arguments against international copyright were much more effective: Expanding

American literacy, especially on the frontier, demanded cheap yet excellent books; there was no inherent "property right" in literature (courts on both sides of the Atlantic had upheld this principle); extending copyright protection to foreigners meant granting a monopoly to them at the expense of the American reading public; and American publishing houses and the labor they employed needed the de facto protectionism that piracy afforded.

Undeterred by the cultural, political, and economic forces arrayed against them, a corps of fifty-five British writers and poets petitioned the U.S. Congress in January 1837 to approve a bilateral copyright treaty. They included Carlyle, Southey, and Maria Edgeworth. Senator Henry Clay backed the British authors, but few others did. Clay submitted a bill five times between 1837 and 1842. All five attempts failed. Booksellers and typesetters opposed the bills. Several prominent American authors and political leaders, including Washington Irving, Edward Everett, and John Quincy Adams, supported the bills. Only two major publishing houses, Appleton and Putnam, supported Clay's bills.[34]

Frustrated by the Americans' unwillingness to agree to a level literary playing field, British prime minister Palmerston in 1842 made high-level contacts with the executive branch to get them to agree to a copyright treaty, which, unlike Clay's bills, would have to be approved only by the Senate. Palmerston's efforts made no difference. That year, however, one Englishman who had the ear of many Americans, Charles Dickens, toured the United States. At many stops, Dickens pleaded for international copyright. Yet his audiences were filled with fans who had happily paid very low prices for American-printed leather-bound copies of his work, from which Dickens earned nothing. Dickens was asking his readers to pay more money for his product, and they were in no mood to do so. Dickens returned to England bitter and frustrated, more over witnessing slavery in the United States than over the copyright situation. When Dickens's account of his tour, *American Notes,* came out in 1843, fifty thousand pirated copies sold in the United States in three days.[35]

After the Civil War, the British government made several more attempts to convince the U.S. government to agree to a treaty, and authors strengthened their organization. Nothing changed in the law, however, until the large American publishers made it clear to congressional leaders that the publishing and piracy climate had changed radically because of a "cheap books" movement among younger up-start publishers.

Starting well before the Civil War, large American publishers—usually based in New York City or Boston—colluded to keep the prices of their pirated European works artificially high. They did this through a system known as the "courtesy principle." Under the principle, a major publishing house announced its intention to bring out a foreign book either through a trade journal or through letters to other publishers. The venerable publisher Henry Holt championed the courtesy principle and testified about its value and demise before the Senate when it was considering an international copyright bill. Holt wanted not only to be able to sell the foreign works he brought out at a premium without six other editions to compete against it, but also to push American publishing toward gentlemanliness. Holt considered price-fixing "gentlemanly."

Among the authors whose work Holt tried to control, Thomas Hardy serves as the best example of how the courtesy principle worked. Holt had for years prided himself on introducing American readers to Hardy's work, and on more than one occasion he berated other publishers, such as the unpredictable Harper Brothers, for trying to bring out competing editions of Hardy's work. More often than not, the other major publishers deferred to Holt and let his house retain its list of Hardy works. "We of course claim Hardy as our man as we have introduced him to the American public and when we add that we have published all his works by direct arrangement with the author, we trust that you will withdraw in our favor," Holt wrote to Lippincott in June of 1875. Lippincott allowed Holt to publish *The Hand of Ethelbert* without competition. Part of the reason efforts toward international copyright failed for most of the nineteenth century was that the courtesy principle worked just well enough to keep American publishers happy. Holt paid Hardy, but he did not have to. Hardy was in no position to negotiate or demand a better royalty rate than the one Holt offered him. But soon after Holt published Hardy's *Far from the Madding Crowd* (1874) and *The Hand of Ethelbert* (1875), the courtesy system collapsed.[36]

In 1874, the Chicago publishing firm of Donnelly, Gassette and Lloyd recognized that every respectable middle-class American household would seem all the more respectable with a sizable library of major works of British literature lining the walls of its parlor. The firm started the Lakeside Library, which sold books at the startlingly low price of ten, fifteen, or twenty cents per volume. Within five years, the Lakeside Library carried 270 titles. Soon after the Lakeside Library announced its intentions, Erastus Beadle, the baron of the Civil War-era dime novels, introduced a competing list, the Fireside Library. George P. Munro, a former Beadle employee, started the Seaside Library, which would grow to be the most successful of the cheap books lines. Frank Leslie started a list he called "The Home Library of Standard Works by the Most Celebrated Authors." By 1877, American readers had their choice of fourteen "cheap books" libraries. The paper was uniformly cheap and flimsy, the typesetting sloppy, and the format hard to read. Some of the earlier editions lacked covers to keep their costs low. But soon the cheap publishers realized that the spine was in many cases the most attractive—and most visible—part of a book. So by the 1880s, most of the cheap books libraries appeared in cloth bindings at a slightly higher price, but with the same cheap paper inside. Needless to say, none of these publishers were part of the eastern seaboard elite club of publishers who were led by Henry Holt. So none of them conformed to the courtesy principle.

Of the established houses, Harper and Brothers leapt on the cheap books movement first, and with the biggest splash. In 1877, Harper slashed the price of its Library of Select Novels. It then launched a paperback discount line, the Franklin Square Library, which cost ten cents per volume. Urban bookstores, which had mainly ignored the mail order and magazine rack sales of cheap book libraries, began stocking the Harper and Brothers libraries and soon began ordering the other libraries, such as Seaside.

Prices dipped, orders increased, and the courtesy principle withered. American readers had their choice of dozens of editions of their favorite British authors in a wide variety of prices and quality. There was chaos in the American publishing industry by the early 1880s. Soon, stores and mail order companies returned boxes of volumes. Munro cut a deal with a soap company to give out a volume with each bar of soap sold. Cheap libraries started bringing out works by authors who had no public reputation in the United States. As American works from early in the century entered the public domain, some of the cheap books publishers issued libraries of American authors.[37]

By the late 1880s, major American publishers and authors united to champion international copyright so that they could bring some stability to the publishing market. The Authors' Club, the major vehicle for

American authors to express their desire for international copyright, changed itself in 1882 into the American Copyright League under the stewardship of journalist and novelist Edward Eggleston, *Century Magazine* editor Richard Watson Gilder, and lawyer and critic Brander Matthews. Mark Twain and James Russell Lowell were two of the more notable writers who were active in the league, which claimed to represent as many as 700 authors. Gilder was also close friends with Richard Rogers Bowker, who ran both *Publisher's Weekly* and the Publishers' Copyright League. As a result, both leagues worked in concert when testifying or lobbying Congress and when pleading in print for international copyright. The rhetoric of the American Copyright League, predictably, rang with themes of "civilizations" and "property rights." Congress still balked at the league's proposals throughout the 1880s. The league's best effort during the 1880s came in January 1886, when the Senate Committee on Patents held hearings on an international copyright bill. Witnesses in favor of the bill included Henry Holt, Bowker, George Putnam, Lowell, and Twain. Bowker presented a petition signed by 145 of the most noted American authors, including Louisa May Alcott, Henry Ward Beecher, Twain, Henry George, Walt Whitman, Joel Chandler Harris, Bret Harte, Oliver Wendell Holmes Sr., Francis Parkman, and John Greenleaf Whittier. Twain managed to get himself invited onto the floor of the Senate to twist arms in favor of the effort, but his official statement was brief and lukewarm.[38]

Testifying against the bill, Philadelphia pirate Henry Carey Baird made a succinct attack. He had five major points: Only unexpressed thought is property, but expressed thought belongs to the public; property laws are domestic concerns, and should not be the subject of treaties; British authors are welcome to naturalize in the United States if they want protection equal to American authors; the United States should not trade away its public interest to protect the rights of foreigners; foreign authors should not have the power to influence or fix the price of American books.[39]

Baird's testimony did not kill the bill by itself, of course. He was neither more persuasive nor more powerful than the forces of major American writers and publishers. However, Baird and his fellow pirates still had organized labor and the spirit of protectionism on their side. Between January and March of 1886, unions and trade groups deluged Congress with petitions opposing the measure. It died soon after.[40]

The last part of the political machine that would eventually convince Congress to agree to international copyright was the printers' unions in the major eastern cities. As book prices spiraled downward, squeezing profits from the established firms, the newer "cheap books" publishers had to cut costs as well. Many operated in cities where the printers' unions were weak, and most quickly abandoned unionized white men who were unwilling to print and bind books for pennies per day. Instead, many of the cheap publishers employed nonunion women and shared and reused printing plates to set type. The printers' unions realized that while the lack of international copyright was protecting the jobs of more American printers, the workers who filled those jobs were the wrong kind—women instead of men. By the late 1880s, the unions flipped sides and joined the major publishers and authors in support of some measure of international copyright. In 1888, the Typographical Union passed a resolution in favor of the bill then pending in Congress. Local chapters soon sent messages to their representatives in favor of passage. The debate lasted through the winter of 1890–91, but the bill was finally passed by both houses in March of 1891 and promptly was signed by President Benjamin Harrison.[41]

By the end of the nineteenth century, publishers and authors had taken great strides in fighting the republican principles that had informed early American copyright laws and cases. And as the United States stepped forward to assert itself as an imperial power in the world, Mark Twain prepared to assume the position once held by Noah Webster, the champion of private publishing interests cloaked in the rhetoric of noble public service.

THE MAN IN THE WHITE SUIT

Mark Twain was a master of the intricacies of copyright law and of the power of "property talk" from early in his career as a public figure. In 1875, William Dean Howells asked Twain to publish his views on the need for international copyright protection in the *Atlantic Monthly*. Twain wrote back to offer much more than a simple article. He proposed an elaborate lobbying plan: "My plan is this—You are to get Mr. Lowell and Mr. Longfellow to be the first signers of my copyright petition; you must sign it yourself and get Mr. Whittier to do likewise." Twain would then hire a person to travel the country to gather the remaining signatures from authors, make a thousand copies, and deliver them personally to the president and members of Congress. He would get the president to mention the petition in a major speech, line up a powerful sponsor in each house, and solidify the votes before he proceeded. "You see," he wrote to Howells, "what I want to drive into the congressional mind is the simple fact that the moral law is 'Thou shalt not steal'—no matter what Europe may do."[42]

Opponents of standardized copyright protection had argued that American readers could get cheaper foreign works if they were not protected by international copyright, and that even if the United States offered protection to foreign authors, European leaders were unlikely to reciprocate. When lawyer and critic Brander Matthews wrote an article attacking other countries for allowing piracy of American authors, Twain wrote a response that pinned the problem on the U.S. government.[43] When a congressional committee considered the bill, Twain testified and said he hoped "a day would come when, in the eyes of the law, literary property will be as sacred as whiskey, or any other of the necessaries of life."[44]

Twain started studying copyright laws during the 1870s when he lost substantial money to Canadian pirates who had recopied his work without offering him compensation. Throughout the 1870s and 1880s, Twain would spend a weekend in Canada to celebrate the publication of another book. He would apply for and receive a Canadian copyright that would simultaneously protect him throughout the British Empire and its commonwealths, essentially the English-speaking world. Twain was sensitive to all aspects of copyright protection because he was a popular and successful author who suffered major setbacks as a less than successful publisher. He even tried to have "Mark Twain" issued as a trademark so that when his copyrights expired, the new publishers could not use the pen name to sell his books.[45] Whether testifying before Congress or criticizing Christian Science founder Mary Baker Eddy, Twain frequently argued that the author deserved full protection for the work he did and often invoked the concept of "originality." But Twain the storyteller, on several occasions, boasted of lifting stories and ideas from others. As he wrote in an article about international copyright in 1888: "But then, we are all thieves."[46]

Twain was able to recognize the flaws in the concept of the autonomous author and all its pretensions. Twain was a publisher and author, but he also was a storyteller. Twain as author and Twain's works are foundational to all the conflicts that complicate American copyright law: originality and genius; piracy and plagiarism; European professional authorship and African American storytelling. And Mark Twain was one of the most successful promoters of "property talk" in American copyright discourse.

Samuel Clemens, in his dual role as Clemens the businessman and Mark Twain the writer, relentlessly pushed for more than thirty years to reform American copyright laws. He wrote magazine articles and testified before Congress. He also corresponded with several congressional leaders about the status of legislation. As one of the leading authors in the United States, he raised the strongest and often best-informed voice in the fight to protect authors' legal status and financial potential.

But Twain had another role that seemingly contrasted with his public stance as the champion of the authorial class: He was a borrower. The ways Mark Twain constructed his journalism, fiction, and speaking careers demystify the notion of authorial originality. Many of the devices, characters, and events that he used in his fiction were unapologetically lifted from others. Twain was not hung up on originality. In his work, he frequently alluded to other authors and works, and even to his own previous works, to signify on what had come before and to satirize flaws in literature and society. Mark Twain was firmly embedded in storytelling tradition that lay outside the romantic assumptions of authorial distinction that informed the philosophical tenets of copyright law. It would be too easy to divide Mark Twain the author-thief and Sam Clemens the protective businessman, publisher, and father along the familiar "twins" model. Many Twain scholars have settled on this personal and professional dichotomy to explain complexities and contradictions in Twain's life and work. However, employing the "twins" idea, while literary and convenient, is not always the best way to explain complexity. Clemens was a busy, contradictory, living human being who traveled, read, and changed his views several times in his lifetime. Growth, contradiction, and complexity were the norms for Twain, as they are for all active minds. They are not enigmas that should be reduced to simplistic binaries.[47]

At first glance, Twain's two authorial preoccupations—telling others' stories and ensuring he was adequately compensated for them— seem contradictory and hypocritical. But if we examine his career closely, and view copyright with a level of sophistication that approaches his, we will see that his authorial habits did not conflict with business interests. For Twain, his ordeals with copyright were not internal struggles between theft and originality, between art and commerce. He just changed over time and, like Walt Whitman, did not fear contradicting himself.

MINING AND WRITING

Early in Mark Twain's literary career, he showed a deep interest in the philosophical underpinnings of property law. In *Roughing It* (1870), Twain wrote of an educated Easterner who was serving as U.S. Attorney for the Nevada Territory, General Buncombe. The locals sought a way to snub the lawyer, so they played a practical joke on him. A fellow named Dick Hyde had a ranch in Washoe district. One day he rode up to Buncombe's office to ask for representation in a suit against Tom Morgan, who owned the ranch immediately above Hyde's on a steep hill. Twain wrote,

> And now the trouble was that one of those hated and dreaded landslides had come and slid Morgan's ranch, fences, cabins, cattle, barns and everything down on top of *his* ranch and exactly covered up every single vestige of his property, to a depth of about thirty-eight feet. Morgan was in possession and refused to vacate the premises—and said he was occupying his own cabin and not interfering with anyone else's—and said the cabin was standing on the same dirt and same ranch it had always stood on, and he would like to see anybody make him vacate.

Morgan argued that since he had stayed on his ranch as it slid down the hill, and Hyde had moved to avoid the landslide, Morgan retained the property rights over it. Buncombe took the case, argued before the court, and lost. The judge ruled that Hyde certainly had both the evidence and the law on his side, yet "it ill becomes us, worms as we are, to meddle with the decrees of Heaven. It pains me that Heaven, in its inscrutable wisdom, has seen fit to move this defendant's ranch for a purpose. . . . Heaven created the ranches and it is Heaven's prerogative to rearrange them, to experiment with them, to shift them around at its pleasure." It took two months for Buncombe to figure out he had been had by the townspeople.[48]

Although Twain presented this story as a tall tale executed at the expense of an educated jurist, it raises some important questions that resonate in both real property and copyright theory: Is ownership a matter of location or substance? Does Dick Hyde own the land because he owned the area within those lines on a map, or does Morgan own it because he owns the actual dirt and house that make up the property? Similarly, does an author forever "own" the string of words he or she produces, or does it enter the public domain as "commons"—to use political science terminology—once it reaches the eyes, minds, and bookshelves of the reading public? Copyright, like land in Nevada, is slippery. Property rights in America are traditionally a matter of convention and agreement, and not, as the judge in the landslide case asserted, a matter of divine decree or "natural" law. While Twain employed an appeal to divinity as a target of ridicule in the landslide case, he actually grew to hold by the end of his life opinions about copyright law that were remarkably similar to the judge's "natural law" ruling about real property.

But in the 1870s and 1880s, Twain concentrated on the literary trade imbalance between England and the United States. Therefore, his thoughts on copyright were less concerned with philosophy and more grounded in economic reality. While he was concentrating on establishing and expanding his reputation, it became clear to him that the absence of a reciprocal copyright treaty among Canada, the United Kingdom, and the United States had two very deleterious effects: Popular American authors, such as himself, would lose money from cheap editions of their works pirated by British and Canadian publishers; and emerging American authors would have a difficult time achieving the market demand, reputation, and "shelf space" needed for success because American pirates showered the reading public with cheap editions of British works.

As Victor Doyno shows in *Writing Huck Finn: Mark Twain's Creative Process,* many pirated British works enjoyed an exponential price advantage over comparable American works. While the first American edition of *The Adventures of Tom Sawyer* sold by subscription for $2.75 in 1876, the Canadian pirated editions sold for 50 cents to $1 per copy. Meanwhile, readers had to choose between buying an emerging American author's new work for at least 50 cents per copy, or Sir Walter Scott's *Ivanhoe* for 10 to 15 cents. Among the books young Tom Sawyer berates Huckleberry Finn for failing to read at the end of *Adventures of*

Huckleberry Finn are stories by Baron von Trenck (10 cents per volume), and Cellini's *Casanova* (50 cents). Twain himself owned a $1.50 anthology of European literature of the type Tom Sawyer worshiped.[49]

This market discrepancy—or "inefficiency," as an economist might call it—worked to the disadvantage of both the American author, whose books were too expensive to compete, and the British author, who saw no return for his or her efforts from consumers in the United States. Yet U.S. copyright policy intentionally enforced the discrepancy because the winners of this game were two constituencies more powerful than authors on either side of the Atlantic: American readers and the American publishers who pirated British works. Even Twain benefited from this system as a reader, and expressed his mixed feelings in a letter to Howells in 1880. "My notions have mightily changed, lately. Under this recent & brand-new system of piracy in New York, this country is being flooded with the best of English literature at prices which make a package of water closet paper seem an 'edition de luxe' in comparison," Twain wrote. "I can buy Macaulay's History, 3 vols., bound, for $1.25. Chambers's Cyclopedia, 15 vols., cloth, for $7.25. (we paid $60), and other English copyrights in proportion; I can buy a lot of the great copyright classics, in paper, at from 3 cents to 30 cents apiece. These things must find their way into the very kitchens and hovels of the country. A generation of this sort of thing ought to make this the most intelligent and the best-read nation in the world." Twain closed the letter with a declaration that he was against a copyright treaty with England, despite his opportunity to profit from such a contract.

> Morally, this is all wrong—governmentally it is all right; for it is the *duty* of governments—and families—to be selfish and look out simply for their own. International copyright would benefit a few authors, and a lot of American publishers, and be a profound detriment to 20,000,000 Americans; it would benefit a dozen American authors a few dollars a year, & there an end.[50]

Over the next three years, as he finished *Adventures of Huckleberry Finn*, Twain grew to realize that Americans were not buying the works of Lord Macaulay in anything approaching the numbers in which they were consuming the sugary novels of Sir Walter Scott. Twain's frustration with the choices of the American reading public, so well articulated in both *Life on the Mississippi* and *Adventures of Huckleberry Finn*, moved him in full support of a level playing field for writers and publishers throughout the English-reading world. As he founded his publishing house and studied the intricacies of the law further, Twain pushed himself to the forefront of the movement for international copyright during the 1880s.

Twain's arguments for an international copyright treaty were motivated by his desire to see American literature taken seriously by—if no one else—American readers. As Twain wrote in an article in *Century Magazine* in 1886:

> The statistics of any public library will show that of every hundred books read by our people, about seventy are novels—and nine-tenths of them foreign ones. They fill the imagination with an unhealthy fascination with foreign life, with its dukes and earls and kings, its fuss and feathers, its graceful immoralities, its sugar-coated injustices and oppressions; and this fascination breeds a more or less pronounced dissatisfaction with our country and form of government, and contempt for our republican commonplaces and simplicities; it also breeds a longing for something "better" which presently crops out in the diseased shams and imitations of the ideal foreign spectacle: Hence the "dude."

Twain's open letter issued a blunt enough warning that Congress was not in fact serving the interests of its people by keeping foreign works cheap: "Thus we have this curious spectacle: American statesmen glorifying American nationality, teaching it, preaching it, urging it, building it up—with their mouths; and undermining it and pulling it down with their acts."[51]

When Twain testified before a Senate committee later in 1886, he balked at endorsing the particular international copyright bill in question because he thought it harshly treated British publishers, many of whom had treated him well, and unjustly absolved the American system. By this time, he had grown tired of political finger-pointing between the two nations, when both were responsible for the massive price differences. In addition, Twain had grown somewhat pleased with British copyright law because it afforded longer protection for works and allowed Americans to gain protection by traveling to England during the publication. Twain's biggest problem with the 1886 copyright proposal, known as the Hawley Bill, was that it would punish publishers who had been reprinting British works cheaply, and probably close them down, laying off many printers. He urged a protectionist amendment that would require a foreign work to be printed in an American plant to receive American copyright. His objections were complex and technical, but he did not waver in his call for reciprocal protection among England, Canada, and the United States.[52]

Congress agreed to international copyright provisions in 1891, with a bill that Twain endorsed wholeheartedly. "If we can ever get this thing through Congress, we can try making copyright perpetual, some day," Clemens wrote to Howells. Lengthening the duration of copyright protection became his political passion.[53] Over the next nineteen years, Twain would rely on knowledge, experience, and self-interest derived from his multiple roles as author, publisher, and political commentator. As a partner in the Charles L. Webster and Company publishing house, Twain had made money issuing the memoirs of former President Ulysses S. Grant. He promptly lost money investing in the Paige typesetting machine.[54] Even if he didn't earn much on the final balance sheet through those experiences, Twain claimed he learned much. He wrote in 1906: "A man must be both author and publisher, and experienced in the scorching griefs and trials of both industries, before he is competent to go before a copyright committee of Parliament or Congress and afford it information of any considerable value."[55]

BORROWER, THIEF, OR TRANSLATOR?

Twain was clearly willing to appeal to the aesthetic values of originality and authorship when it suited him, as it did with his support of stronger copyright laws. Twain's real attitudes toward authorship and originality were—as with most of his thought—complex and sometimes contradictory. His public stance seems to validate the romantic and imperial sense of authorship. His critical voice fluctuates between a defense and a dismissal of romantic authorship. Yet in his own work, he shows no qualms about borrowing both style and substance from other storytellers.

In his 1907 edition of *Christian Science*, Twain ridiculed the authorship of Mary Baker Eddy for her book *Science and Health*. "It many be that there is evidence somewhere—as it has been claimed—that Mrs. Eddy has charged upon the Deity the verbal authorship of *Science and*

Health. But if she ever made that charge, she has withdrawn it (as it seems to me), and in the most formal and unqualified ways," Twain wrote. Eddy had written in her autobiography that she had sued to protect her copyright on the book.

> Thus it is plain that she did not plead that the Deity was the (verbal) author; for if she had done that, she would have lost her case, and with rude promptness. It was in the old days before the Berne Convention and before passage of our amended law of 1891, and the court would have quoted the following stern clause from the existing statute and frowned her out of the place: "No foreigner can acquire a copyright in the United States."[56]

Twain quoted another book about Christian Science in which Eddy claimed she was merely a "scribe" for God's words. "A scribe is merely a person who writes. He may be a copyist, he may be an amanuensis, he may be a writer of originals, and furnish both the language and the ideas." Twain again appealed to Eddy's own words to see which of these forms of scribe she claimed to be.

> If we allow that this present scribe was setting down the "harmonies of Heaven"—and certainly that seems to be the case—then there was only one way to do that I can think of: listen to the music and put down the notes one after another as they fell. In that case Mrs. Eddy did not invent the tune, she only entered it on paper. Therefore—dropping the metaphor—she was merely an amanuensis, and furnished neither the language of *Science and Health* nor the ideas.

Twain concluded, "the Deity was the author of the whole book, and Mrs. Eddy merely His telephone and stenographer."[57]

So for Twain, in the Mary Baker Eddy case at least, the author is the one who furnishes ideas. The author is the originator who deserves the protection for which he fought. Twain accused Eddy of playing someone else's part and appealing to the legal codification of authorship for financial reward. But he could just as easily have argued the other side. As he wrote in an article about international copyright in 1888, "But then, we are all thieves."[58]

Throughout her life, Twain's good friend Helen Keller was plagued by accusations of plagiarism. Twain was quick to comfort and defend her. In a 1903 letter to Keller, Twain revealed the other side of his notions of originality and authorship when he discussed the nature of plagiarism:

> Oh, dear me, how unspeakably funny and owlishly idiotic and grotesque was that "plagiarism" farce! As if there was much of anything in any human utterance, oral or written except plagiarism. The kernel, the soul—let us go further and say the substance, the bulk, the actual and valuable material of all human utterances—is plagiarism. For substantially all ideas are second-hand, consciously and unconsciously drawn from a million outside sources, and daily used by the garnerer with a pride and satisfaction born of the superstition that he originated them; whereas there is not a rag of originality about them anywhere except the little discoloration they get from his mental and moral calibre and his temperament, and which is revealed in characteristics of phrasing.[59]

In this letter to Keller, Twain is demystifying the very ideal of authorship that he would applaud before Congress three years later. A major difference, of course, is that no money is at stake when he is merely musing about the nature of originality. Another difference might be that the work in question in this letter is not Twain's, so he is less judgmental about accusations of plagiarism and "theft." But later in the same letter, Twain cited a humorous example about *The Innocents Abroad* in which he confessed to excessive influence, if not outright plagiarism:

> In 1866 I read Dr. Holmes' poems, in the Sandwich Islands. A year and a half later I stole his dictation, without knowing it, and used it to dedicate my *Innocents Abroad* with. Then years afterwards I was talking with Dr. Holmes about it. He was not an ignorant ass—no, not he: he was not a collection of decayed human turnips, like your "plagiarism court;" and so when I said, "I know now where I stole it, but whom did you steal it from," he said, "I don't remember, I only know I stole it from somebody, because I have never originated altogether myself, nor met anybody who had."[60]

In this letter to Keller, Twain explored some ideas that seem remarkably postmodern: He ascribed a mosaic quality to creativity and described the multiple voices that inform a text. "No doubt we are constantly littering our literature with disconnected sentences borrowed from books at some unremembered time, and now imagined to be our own," he wrote. This could just as easily describe a mosaic of samples in rap music from the 1990s. Twain also wrote to Keller about perhaps the strongest theoretical claim for the demystification of the autonomous author:

> When a great orator makes a great speech you are listening to ten centuries and ten thousand men—but we call it his speech, and really some exceedingly small portion of it is his. But not enough to signify. It is merely a Waterloo. It is Wellington's battle, in some degree, and we call it his; but there are others that contributed. It takes a thousand men to invent a telegraph, or a steam engine, or a phonograph, or a photograph, or a telephone, or any other important thing—and the last man gets the credit and we forget the others.[61]

Twain's own explanation for the concern over originality and influence was that those who write and claim creative superiority are merely vain. "These object lessons should teach us that ninety-nine parts of all things that proceed from the intellect are plagiarisms, pure and simple," Twain wrote to Keller. "And the lesson ought to make us modest. But nothing can do that."[62]

While testifying or writing on copyright, Twain seemed to stand firmly in the romantic stream of authorship, with all its trappings of originality and ownership and creativity. But Mark Twain the writer swam in a different river: one that swirled around and churned everything that fell in so it came out in a different and amazing order. Mark Twain at work was basically an American storyteller. And, in the tradition of American storytelling, Twain was informed by both black and white, oral and written, southern and northern aesthetics. Originality and authorship play a much different role in oral traditions, and therefore played a complex role in Twain's creative process.

In the *Atlantic Monthly* in November of 1874, Twain published an account he entitled "A True Story, Repeated Word for Word as I Heard It." In the piece, Twain asks a question of "Aunt Rachel," a servant in the summer house his family enjoyed in Elmira, New York: "Aunt Rachel, how is it that you've lived sixty years and never had any trouble?" Aunt Rachel was really Mary Ann Cord, the cook at Quarry Farm and a former slave. Her response, rendered in dialect, forms most of the rest of the text of the piece. It is a harrowing story of tragedy and dignity. "Aunt Rachel" lost all seven of her children as they were sold away from her. In the end, one of her sons returned to her after running away. She concludes, "Oh, no, Misto C——, I hain't had no trouble. An' no joy!" In the entire piece, only a smattering of the text is in Mark Twain's voice. The rest might well have been transcribed precisely by Twain, as he claims in the title. Who is the author of the piece? Copyright law affected only expressions fixed in print. So legally, Cord had no legal claim to authorship. But it was her experience, her story, her ideas, and her expression that made the piece possible and interesting. Twain was merely a scribe, as Mary Baker Eddy was for God. Yet by the time Twain published the piece in the *Atlantic,* he had it copyrighted in his own name. *Atlantic* editor William Dean Howells praised Twain for his accurate portrayal of African American speech, and paid Twain the highest rate the magazine had ever offered. Twain republished "A True Story" in *Sketches, New and Old* in 1875. Twain's experience putting Mary Ann Cord's voice on paper, along with a similar piece in which he introduced a young boy he called "sociable Jimmy," helped him train himself for his longest and most significant dialect work, *Adventures of Huckleberry Finn.*[63]

In many ways, Twain serves as a revolving door in the exchange of ideas between oral and written traditions. Brought up listening to black storytellers, he spent years trying to master their rhetorical skills. In his essay "How to Tell a Story," Twain claimed, "I only know how a story ought to be told, for I have been almost daily in the company of the most expert storytellers for many years." Twain then explained the differences between British wit and American humor, and how American humor requires a much defter sense of delivery. He also championed the American storyteller as an "artist." The paradigm of his story-telling lesson is one he heard as a boy from an old black man, Uncle Dan'l, called "The Golden Arm." He would frequently tell this story on his moneymaking lecture circuits, getting paid as a performer, not an author. Twain did write out "The Golden Arm" in "How to Tell a Story," and, of course, copyrighted and made money from it.[64] Twain's fascination with orality and storytelling expressed itself in his efforts to record the oral methods in two dimensions. Twain wrote a fan letter to fellow recorder Joel Chandler Harris in which he dubbed Harris the master translator. Twain also complained about the futility of recording a well-told story in print.[65]

Early in his career, in Nevada and California, Mark Twain mastered telling both his own and other people's stories in a better way—usually funnier. As he joined haughty literary circles in Hartford and New York City, Twain moved from being a "mere" storyteller to being a major author. He was doing, writing, and investing in "new things." Simultaneously, the United States was becoming more literate and more literary. As the twentieth century dawned, Twain's changes would become America's changes.

Like Elvis, Twain is open to accusations of blatant theft of African American modes of expression, an idea wonderfully ironic in the context of his time, when many thought of blacks as merely artistic mockingbirds. But, again like Elvis, Twain played a more complex role. Twain is a transmission figure. He brought the richness of storytelling to an increasingly fragmented reading public. He brought the South north and the West east. Most important, his style enriched both black and white literary traditions. Ralph Ellison credited Twain with presenting the most compelling portrait of how whites see blacks in *Adventures of Huckleberry Finn*.[66] The voices he gave to Huck and Jim would influence writers for a century. To double that complexity, his efforts to champion professional authorship and extend copyright protection would determine the nature of much of American creativity just as much as Huck Finn did.

PIRACY OR PLAGIARISM?

We are still stuck with a complication, if not a contradiction. Twain clearly and loudly protested the unauthorized copying of his works in England and Canada. The money he lost haunted him for years. Yet Twain seemed willing to overlook, forgive, or even wink at his and others' habits of borrowing stories from others. Was Twain a hypocrite? No, he was just aware of the distinction between piracy and plagiarism. For Twain, piracy was theft. Plagiarism was bad manners. In a case of piracy, a product is sold in its entirety (usually under false pretenses), and the producer of the original product receives no compensation for his or her work. Piracy is the violation of the entire body of a work, and thus obviously an appropriation of specific expression. Piracy is an offense created by the notion of copyright. It could not exist as a concept without the granted monopoly of copyright that it violates. Plagiarism is much older and more complex. It comes in many forms. A writer can use a small portion of another's work, yet fail to credit the source, and be accused of plagiarism. At its extreme, authors can use data that another compiled, research another did, and fraudulently portray the work as their own. Plagiarism is more often than not an unrequested and uncredited use of another's ideas. Because plagiarism is more generally understood as "idea theft," it is not necessarily—perhaps rarely—a violation of copyright law. If a film studio files suit against a person who has made and sold unauthorized videotapes of one of its films, it is fighting piracy. If the studio tries to stifle another studio's efforts to make a new version of a similar story, it is fighting something closer to plagiarism. The studio would be protecting ideas, and must rely on threats, public pressure, or legal intimidation to prevent the plagiarism. If a screenwriter pitches an idea to a studio, but is rejected, only to find a similar tale told on film, she can complain of idea theft, but not necessarily a copyright violation. Twain fought Canadian publishers who undersold his own publishing house's editions of his books, but could issue no claim that the stories behind *The Prince and the Pauper* or "The Celebrated Jumping Frog of Calaveras County" were his property. And as should be clear, Twain was a rampant plagiarist, as we commonly understand the term. Perhaps we can consider copyright infringement to be a specific, illegal subset of the wide array of ethical offenses called plagiarism.

That's not to argue that noninfringing forms of plagiarism are not objectionable. They are just not obviously actionable. Some bad manners are very bad. In science, medicine, and the humanities, plagiarism is a professional problem that can harm those who actually did the work. It can deny the originators credit, fame, professional advancement, and honor. It can be a sign of something worse than bad manners in the mind of the plagiarist. Plagiarism can be so habitual that it resembles a pathology. But it's usually not. Stealing a joke and retelling a story are hardly violations of gravity equal to signing one's name to another's cancer research. American society in the late twentieth century grew so sensitive to accusations of plagiarism that companies developed computer programs to scan documents for similar sentence constructions and vocabulary. Citation and originality have become such an absurd preoccupation that hardly a major political campaign goes by without one candidate accusing another of "stealing my ideas." Accusations of plagiarism have become the favorite weapon of those who wish to attack political columnists, and humorous columnists are the easiest targets. Obviously, accusations of plagiarism are rare—almost unimaginable—within cultural expressions that are oral in nature, such as storytelling, blues, and jazz. This may be why Twain dismissed such talk in his own day. How could Twain keep track of all the stories he heard as a child? How could he stop himself from writing down and selling the best stories he heard from Mary Ann Cord and Uncle Dan'l? How could Helen Keller be expected to create a string of footnotes, or even remember her sources, for her own writing? As we have adopted the concerns of professionalized writing to the common commerce of ideas and expressions, we have lost sight of the crucial distinctions on which Twain rested his creative habits and career.[67]

MARK TWAIN'S DIALOGUE ON COPYRIGHT

A recently reexamined Twain manuscript shows the author experimenting with several arguments in favor of extending the term of copyright protection for authors in the United States. This manuscript, written in Kaltenleutgeben, Austria, in 1898, lay largely ignored in the Mark Twain Papers at the University of California at Berkeley until March 1997. The manuscript is written in the form of a Socratic dialogue. In it, Twain rehearsed his copyright "act" and arrived at his most persuasive—and tricky—script for his public pronouncements on copyright. In a larger sense, this manuscript represents a major move within Twain's intellectual journeys: from storyteller to political essayist; from western tenderfoot to international man of letters; from poet to philosopher. In 1884, Twain finished his version of the *Odyssey,* in the guise of *Adventures of Huckleberry Finn.* Through Huck Finn, Twain assumed the role of the American Homer, rendering the repetition and revision of the American oral tradition into print, trying his best to retain the freshness, richness, irony, and flavor of the speakerly text. But as he thrust himself into the often frustrating copyright debates through the late 1880s and 1890s, Twain recognized the difficulties a humorist or storyteller might encounter while trying to make serious points. After all, Plato had excluded the followers of Homer from his Republic. So in 1898, Twain put aside his Homeric pretentions and instead generated an imitation of a stilted

Platonic narrative to outline his public philosophies. Twain employed a Socratic dialogue to petition for naturalization in Plato's Republic.[68]

Twain called the piece "The Great Republic's Peanut Stand." It contains almost seven thousand words and fills fifty-nine handwritten pages. Although Twain was active and vocal throughout his professional career on copyright issues, "The Great Republic's Peanut Stand" is his only extended dissertation on copyright theory. His frequent letters to friends and congressmen and his brief ejaculations about what he considered to be the inherent unfairness of American copyright law form an interesting but ultimately uncohesive picture of Twain's evolving thoughts on the issue. This 1898 dialogue fills many gaps in Twain's copyright discourse and answers some questions about how Twain arrived at his conclusions and chose his tactics.

Although he composed this dialogue in his study in the Austrian Alps just as the British Parliament took up the issue of extending the duration of copyright protection, he chose not to publish it in its entire form during his lifetime. He scribbled "Never Published—SLC [Samuel L. Clemens]" at the top of the first page.*[69] Twain did publish another dialogue on copyright reform in the *North American Review* in 1905, and it loosely borrowed some of the arguments explored in "The Great Republic's Peanut Stand." However, it also contained many other passages that Twain researched and wrote specifically for that article.[70] Ultimately, Twain used "The Great Republic's Peanut Stand" as an exercise that would yield his most noted and significant statements on copyright, his testimony before the Congressional Joint Committees on Patents in December of 1906.[71]

Through "The Great Republic's Peanut Stand," Twain articulated a way to push his rather "un-American" ideas about copyright in distinctly "American" language by trying to answer these questions for himself: By what right does the public claim ownership of the products of an author's work after a certain period of time? How is American culture served by limiting the author's claim? Could anyone think up a better system that would serve the public interest and reward authors at the same time? These are issues that preoccupied Mark Twain throughout his adult life. Twain was more than fascinated by the theory and practice of copyright; he was financially interested as well. He was a successful writer and lecturer, but a failed publisher. He had been cheated by Canadian and British "pirates" who had published unauthorized versions of his work and undersold his publishers' prices.[72]

As we have seen, Twain had played an integral part in organizing authors and publishers to successfully fight for an Anglo-American copyright agreement in 1891 that protected authors throughout the English-reading world. Pleased with the victory authors had achieved internationally, Twain looked to alter the domestic policy toward his advantage. For the last two decades of his life he set about trying to lengthen the duration of copyright protection. In Twain's day, an author controlled the rights to his or her work for twenty-eight years, and could apply to renew the copyright for another fourteen years. However, survivors could not apply for the fourteen-year extension. This concerned Twain because he feared his daughters would not be able to live as comfortably as they had in their youth without his royalties. Twain testified before a 1906 congressional committee in support of a bill that would have extended the duration of protection to the lifetime of the author plus fifty years. However, as "The Great Republic's Peanut Stand" shows, Twain actually favored perpetual copyright protection that would reward his heirs or estate forever.

"The Great Republic's Peanut Stand" is a dialogue between a senator and a "Wisdom Seeker," who is Twain himself. The senator holds the classic American republican opinion that a book should enter the public domain after the law has granted its author a reasonable monopoly on its sale and distribution. The theory behind that policy, as expressed in the U.S. Constitution and every major copyright law enacted by Congress until 1998, is that the public will benefit from cheap editions of the best books, yet authors will still have an incentive to produce new books. This economic argument, as expressed by political philosophers and policy makers from Adam Smith to James Madison to most of Twain's contemporaries, irked Twain.[73]

Through his "Wisdom Seeker" voice, Twain picks at the premises of the argument and demands empirical evidence that limiting copyright does in fact produce cheap books and benefit a reading public. Twain appeals to the European *droit moral, droit d'auteur,* or "moral rights," theory of copyright. Twain concurs with such natural law theorists as William Blackstone and William Wordsworth, and pits himself against realists like James Madison, Thomas Jefferson, Lord Macaulay, and Adam Smith. Copyright in Europe evolved as a way to reward artistic and authorial contributions to culture, not as the result of a utilitarian bargain among authors, publishers, and the public, as it did in the United States. Nations that have a tradition of protecting "moral rights" tend to limit the uses to which copyrighted expression can be put. These nations tend to limit fair use, revisions, and parody. The penumbra of moral rights is viewed as part of the author's powers by virtue of creating something. They flow from the author's pen, regardless of whether they enrich the public.[74]

By 1898, at the age of sixty-three, Twain was much more of a "wisdom giver" than a "seeker," and in the dialogue itself the wisdom seeker almost immediately abandons any Socratic distance and jumps in with his conclusions ready, to bludgeon the senator with his experience and knowledge of both the writing and publishing professions. By page 4 of the manuscript, the wisdom seeker has tired of his teasing questions and the senator's stock answers. He simply declares that having an expiration date on a book's copyright destroys any chance for it to be republished in a cheap and accessible form.

> SENATOR: There is a reason for limiting copyright, and a sound one. Justice to the author demands that he shall have a fair return for his labor; justice to the public demands that the book shall be their property afterward.
>
> WISDOM SEEKER: They have perpetual ownership, then—the thing denied to the author as being against public policy?
>
> S: Yes.
>
> WS: Have they earned this?
>
> S: It is not a question of earning; they have a right to take what they will.
>
> WS: I understood you to say that justice demanded that the property be delivered to them. Have you shifted your ground?
>
> S: This is quibbling.
>
> WS: Call it so. I am satisfied if you are. There is a reason for turning the property over to the public? What is it?
>
> S: The public advantage.
>
> WS: They get an advantage, do they?
>
> S: Certainly.
>
> WS: How?
>
> S: They get the book cheaper.
>
> WS: What makes you think that?
>
> S: It isn't a matter of thinking; I know it.
>
> WS: How do you know it?

> s: It stands to reason that a book which is not saddled with a royalty can be issued at a cheaper rate than when it is so saddled.
>
> ws: So it is theory you are going upon, not fact?
>
> s: Facts are not needed in such a plain case; they would be superfluous.*75

In this passage the senator is expressing the classic republican argument that cheap books can spread literacy and encourage public discussion. But Twain then turns that argument on its head. In the next passage of the dialogue, Twain relies on an empirical line of questioning to deflate the senator's republican theory. He also introduces the rather weak argument that the lack of copyright protection is the cause of the failure of so many books to find a willing publisher.

> s: Absence of copyright resurrects many a dead book and restores it to life and circulation—to the advantage of the public.
>
> ws: And the publisher.
>
> s: Wm. T. Stead has restored two or three hundred dead books to life in England, and has sold millions of copies at a trifling price.
>
> ws: Why did the books die?
>
> s: I do not know.
>
> ws: Expiration of copyright killed them. When a selling book's copyright dies, a number of publishers take it up and issue a single edition of it; they skim the cream, then drop it, running no further risks with it. It ceases from being advertised. It drops out of the public notice and is forgotten. All in five years—possibly in two. The book is lost to the public; whereas in some cases it might have lived fifty years longer under copyright protection. In seizing the property, the public robbed both itself and the author's children, and gained an advantage for nobody. In Europe, Tauchnitz, whose cheap and beautiful paper editions you are acquainted with, still goes on steadily selling, to this day, a number of foreign books which died in their own countries years ago when copyright protection failed them.*76

Twain argues here that with extended copyright protection, an author or his or her family might have an incentive to seek out a willing publisher. Without such an interested agent, Twain asserts, the publisher will simply assume there is no market interest in most books. Twain pushes the senator to consider those authors who have been able to keep their books in print, despite having no financial reward for them once they enter the public domain.

In this dialogue Twain makes an overt appeal to a sense of American cultural inferiority prevalent at the very dawn of what was to be its imperial age. Within two years, of course, Twain would lose faith in any sense of "American Civilization" as a fact or goal. Still, as he showed in his congressional testimony in 1906, he was not above exploiting the imperialist and nationalist rhetoric to foster public support for the extension of copyright protection.[77]

The senator has one more weapon to use in support of a limited term of copyright. The senator appeals to the arguments that Lord Macaulay made in the British parliamentary debate over copyright in 1841. Thomas Babington Macaulay lived from 1800 to 1859. He is best known as an essayist and historian, but he also became a minister of Parliament in 1830, and established his powers as an orator in the Reform Bill debates. As a historian, he is remembered for writing *The History of England from the Accession of James II,* which was published between 1848 and 1862, although he left the fifth volume unfinished at his death. During debates over extending copyright protection for British authors, Macaulay fought a proposal to grant British authors copyright protection for the life of the author plus sixty years, as the French law did, and succeeded in retaining the twenty-eight-year term then in effect.

Macaulay skillfully shifted the issue from one of property rights and rewards to one of monopoly power and taxation. A copyright is functionally a temporary but necessary monopoly for an author, he asserted. Only one publisher may market a work. This monopoly necessarily increases the price of the book above the market value of older works already in the public domain. The difference between the sale price of the monopolistically published book and a similar public domain book (subject to downward price pressure if more than one publisher has issued it) is the "tax" the author demands from the reader. As with all taxes, the liberal Macaulay argued, it should be high enough to accomplish its incentive purpose, but not a penny higher. Nor should it last a day longer, he argued.[78]

S: Didn't Macaulay make one [an argument for limited copyright duration]?

WS: No. Very far from it. He left out the essential fact—and there is only one: that 999 out of every 1,000 books die long within the copyright limit; and he left out the argument that it is puerile in a nation to degrade itself to the meaning of a solemn law to steal the remaining book.

S: Macaulay convinced a Parliament that wanted to raise the limit to 60 years.

WS: A Parliament of what? Publishers? No, sir—a Parliament of statesmen. A Parliament of publishers would have laughed at him.

S: How do you come to know so much about this matter?

WS: I know the secrets of both sides. I bought my knowledge, and paid cash for it.

S: How?

WS: I financially backed a publishing house ten years.

S: Certainly you ought to know something about it.

WS: Speaking within the bounds of modesty—I hope—I claim to know as much about it as any man alive; and a good four times as much as Macaulay divulged. He may have divulged all he knew, for he was but a mere author, after all, but back of his data lay the *essential* thing, and that was not brought to light.

S: If Macaulay had kept still—

WS: England would have raised the limit to 60 years and we should have followed suit.

S: Would 60 years satisfy you?

WS: No. It would merely do what the present limit does— cover the life-time of 1 book in 1,000, and no more. And when that book has lived 60 years, the chances are very good that it will live 40 more. I detest the principle. A limit whose only possible function is to provide for the stealing of 1 book in 1,000 is a childish and dishonorable thing, and a paltry business for a great nation to be engaged in.*[79]

Here Twain, after disposing of Macaulay by questioning whether the public ever enjoys "tax relief" from a work entering the public domain, takes a firm stand in favor of perpetual copyright protection, a position he knew would never enjoy widespread support.

Twain also acknowledges that such a proposal could not pass constitutional scrutiny, because the U.S. Constitution specifically required patents and copyrights to be "for limited times." Small obstacles like constitutionality did not dissuade Twain from outlining for the senator an elaborate system of rewards and incentives that he believed would maximize the number of books in circulation, minimize their prices, and stabilize the earnings of authors and their families.

> WS: As a beginning, I would amend the law and make copyright perpetual.
>
> S: Go on.
>
> WS: Next, I would introduce a 20-year stage—to this effect. When a copyright had been in force 20 years, I would *require* the publisher to issue a cheap edition, and keep it always on sale.
>
> S: *How* cheap?
>
> WS: One-eighth of the retail price of the book's cheapest existing edition.*[80]

Since Twain has already evaded the restrictions of Article 1 of the Constitution, nothing stops him from advocating a proposal that would violate the First Amendment as well. Therefore, he declares he would have Congress force publishers to produce books regardless of content or market demand.

> WS: Very well. On New Year's Day, authors and publishers would all start fair, without partialities for anybody. The old lot of authors now long before the public, and the new lot, of recent fame, could issue books under perpetual copyright, and sit down and observe results. It will be like surface mining. Have you ever been a surface miner?
>
> S: No.
>
> WS: Well, it is like this. The boys lock to the new gold field, and each stakes off a claim for himself, under the conditions provided by the laws of the camp. A claim 20 feet square, let us

say. At the end of a couple of months it will turn out that Jones and Brown have struck it very rich, Robinson, Peters and Walker fairly rich, several others achieve "grub money," and nothing more. It has been a matter of luck, in all cases— no one knew what was under the ground. Now if those miners were stupid and unjust, their camp-law would limit claim-ownership to a specific term, and when the term was up the unlucky ones could rush in and dig gold in the fortunate claims of Jones, Brown, Robinson, Peters and Walker— but they don't do that; only stupid and unfair copyright laws do that. Would Jones, Brown and Co. like that kind of camp law? Necessarily not. Then why should a publisher who has stumbled upon a fortunate book like it?

S: I suppose he shouldn't.

WS: Of course he shouldn't. My proposed law starts at the publishers level. At the end of 20 years, all who have chanced to strike a rich book in the meantime are left in its undisturbed possession.

S: Summarized, your law—

WS: Would benefit the publisher, because it would protect his valuable books from raidings and destruction at the end of a term. It would benefit the author by giving him perpetual ownership in his property in place of a mere leasehold. It would benefit the public because it would compel cheap publication, and cut down the term for the delivery of it by 22 years. It would benefit the national literature, also, by enlarging its permanent volume; for it would enable some books to continue in life which would be hustled to death and flung away at the end of the term under the present evil system.*[81]

Twain's use of a mining analogy works for him on several levels. First, mining reflects Twain's second exposure to theories and practices of property and ownership (the first being slavery). Secondly, it is characteristically American. It generates images of daring entrepreneurs on the frontier. To achieve a provincially European goal, having the state and society appreciate and reward the author as a cultural and political hero, Twain uses American tools. By triggering images of adventurous, hardworking, and brave miners (an image he humorously exploded in

Roughing It) exploiting the seemingly limitless supply of land in the American West, he makes copyright seem like a case of simple distributive justice, rather than the complexly balanced policy it really is and was. Most significantly, though, Twain's use of the mining analogy solidly situates copyright theory as a matter of property rights, which in Twain's time was not always the locus of debate. For Twain, copyright was for benefit of the author, his ideal of a cultural entrepreneur, whereas for Madison, Macaulay, and the predominant body of American case law up until the end of the twentieth century, copyright was for the good of the public, a necessary evil to provide an incentive for creativity.

TWAIN'S LEGACY

In April of 1900, two years after working through his arguments in "The Great Republic's Peanut Stand," Twain appeared before a select committee of the House of Lords. Using tight summaries of the points he adumbrated in the 1898 dialogue, Twain made the case for perpetual copyright. But he took it one step further. Twain declared that there is no difference between the role of ideas in copyright and the role of ideas in real property. "The limited copyright makes a distinction between an author's property and real estate, pretending that both are not created, produced and acquired in the same way. The man who purchases a landed estate had to earn the money by the superiority of his intellect; a book is the result of an author's own brain in the same manner—a combination and exploitation of his ideas." This is an odd and specious argument. Certainly the person writing a check for a piece of land could have inherited the money. The person could have fraudulently presented a loan application to a bank. The person could have stolen the money. Of course, stealing is often an exercise of intellect as well, at least as much as recording a story told by Mary Ann Cord. The House of Lords was not swayed.[82]

Twain in 1900 collapsed the idea/expression dichotomy in a way no one before or since has tried to do: by attaching ideas to all forms of property, instead of claiming that there is a property right inherently attached to ideas themselves. The only explanation for this is that the ideal real property, to Twain, was still a mine. To be a successful miner, one had to have a clue, do some work, and get lucky. To

Twain, ideas, albeit shallow and dry, lay behind the silver mines of Nevada.

Twain testified before a U.S. congressional committee once more in 1906, this time in support of a complete revision of copyright law that would have stretched the duration of protection from twenty-eight years, renewable for another fourteen years, to the lifetime of the author plus fifty years.[83] "I think that would satisfy any reasonable author, because it would take care of his children. Let the grandchildren take care of themselves," Clemens said. He invoked a valorization of authorship, and noted that the legislatures of western nations have betrayed the noble class. "They always talk handsomely about the literature of the land, always what a fine, great, monumental thing great literature is, and in the midst of their enthusiasm they turn around and do what they can to discourage it."[84]

Congress failed to pass the bill Twain supported in 1906, which proposed that the duration of copyright extend through the life of the author and for fifty years more. Congress, largely because the Constitution forbids it, has never supported perpetual copyright in any form. The copyright bill of 1909 did get past Congress. President William Howard Taft signed it.[85] The "life plus 50 years" provision, however, did not survive committee scrutiny. Publishers had more political power, and they bested the authors. The two sides did forge a compromise of sorts that expanded protection. The 1909 law set the duration at twenty-eight years, with a renewal for twenty-eight more years. Clemens was not upset by the change, however. He wrote in a 1909 letter to Senator Champ Clark, one of the bill's sponsors, "Is the new copyright law acceptable to me? Emphatically, yes!" Clemens was satisfied with even a moderate extension of the duration. "At last—at last and for the first time in copyright history—we are ahead of England! Ahead of her in two ways: by length of time and by fairness to all interests concerned."[86]

Twain might have been pleased with the movement of copyright protection through the twentieth century, as well. The 1976 copyright law, to which the United States adhered until 1998, made the duration of protection life of the author plus fifty years. In 1998, Congress extended the duration to seventy years beyond the life of the author and granted all current copyrights twenty more years. While Twain's argument from an appeal to property rights and a sense of justice has persuaded Congress to extend the duration of the law, few of the expansions of copyright in the twentieth century would have pleased early republicans such as Madison.

By emphasizing the property rights of the author as the paramount purpose of copyright law, the United States has grown closer to Europe in copyright philosophy over the twentieth century. But by doing so it has jeopardized the idea/expression dichotomy, public domain, fair use, open access to information, and the ability to freely satirize, parody, or comment on an existing work. The United States was at the end of the twentieth century on the verge of completely rewriting its copyright framework and abandoning any sense of public good inherent in it. A century after Twain wrote "The Great Republic's Peanut Stand" in the Austrian mountains, his nation of birth was finally willing to grant him far more than he asked for, and far more than he or we need.[87]

But Twain could not have known in 1898 or 1906 or 1909 what such a rhetorical shift would mean a hundred years later. He could not have foreseen (although perhaps careful readers of *A Connecticut Yankee in King Arthur's Court* might argue) the globalization of markets for creative and information-based products and the reductions in the costs of duplication and transmission that the last half of the twentieth century has produced. We can speculate, however, that Twain was able to hold seemingly contradictory notions of creativity and copyright because through most of his professional writing career he maintained healthy distinctions between piracy and plagiarism and between ideas and expressions. Only near the end of life and career did self-interest win out and trump his concern for future authors and artists. Mark Twain's shifting thoughts on copyright parallel the disturbing trends in American copyright policy in the twentieth century.

3

Celluloid Copyright and Derivative Works

Or, How to Stop 12 Monkeys *with One Chair*

SOME PEOPLE CONSIDERED Groucho Marx and his brothers thieves. Many comedians who had their start on the vaudeville stage participated in the age-old habit of act appropriation and joke stealing. Everybody did it, but the Marx Brothers got caught a few times. They were more commercially successful in their transition to the film medium than most of their peers were. In many ways, they were bolder than just about any comics, then or since. Because of their audacity, or perhaps their carelessness, Groucho Marx, his brothers, their writers, and their studio were forced to defend at least three major copyright infringement suits in their careers. It's clear that the Marx Brothers, despite their creative comic genius, relied heavily on the works of others for their success.[1]

By the 1980s, the Marx Brothers' legacy, reputation, and body of work had solidified to such a degree that they became the plaintiffs behind lawsuits, instead of the targets of them. In 1979, one of the Marx Brothers' most successful films for Paramount, *Duck Soup* (1933), was among the pictures that movie studios cited in their unsuccessful suit against Sony Corporation to prevent the sale of Betamax machines for home video taping. Three years later, a federal court of appeals heard a complaint by Groucho Marx Productions Incorporated against a dramatic production company that had used likenesses of the Marx Brothers in a Broadway play called *A Day in Hollywood/A Night in Ukraine*. Claiming that the deceased Marx Brothers had assigned the rights to their likenesses to the company, Groucho Marx Productions tried to enforce a perpetual monopoly on the characteristics of its namesake: the painted mustache, elongated gait, slick hair, cigar, and glasses. The court ruled against Groucho Marx Productions, but the case remains an example of how valuable the Marx Brothers are as commodities long after they have ceased being creators—or borrowers.[2]

Between 1938 and 1979, Groucho Marx and the Marx Brothers went from being "copyright-poor," having to take or borrow material from others, to being "copyright-rich," even after death. During that same period, the motion picture industry as a whole exhibited this phenomenon as well. At its birth, the film industry had an interest in allowing free and easy adaptation of works from copyright-rich literary authors, such as Mark Twain and Jack London. As the industry grew more lucrative and screenwriters and directors more creative, studios found themselves on the plaintiff's side in copyright suits. But getting copyright-rich has not altered all of the behaviors of Hollywood executives. They still sometimes act as if they are copyright-poor as a way to get "copyright-richer," or just plain richer. Even in the late 1990s, the film industry was still trying to have it both ways, easily exploiting nonfiction works or stories from the public domain while lobbying for increased international and domestic copyright protection for their finished products. This chapter traces that shift: how the motion picture studios—like Mark Twain and other American authors before them—made themselves copyright-rich.

LEARNING FROM TWAIN, TAKING FROM TWAIN

Although Mark Twain made loud and frequent pronouncements about copyright law, he never seemed overly concerned with its effects on any industry except literary publishing. American copyright law had covered books, maps, and charts since 1790, engravings and printed musical compositions since 1831, photographs since 1865, dramatizations and translations since 1870. But in the last decade of the nineteenth century and the first decade of the twentieth century, the work of Thomas Alva Edison and others had opened up commercial possibilities for recorded music and moving pictures. Before the 1909 copyright revisions, the codified law did not deal with these new technologies, although occasionally courts saw fit to expand the law to new media. Even in the 1909 copyright law, motion pictures were left off the list of protected media. Although Twain was a great fan and friend of Edison and a bit of a technological maven, he did not seem to be interested in the storytelling potential of film in the last years of his life. Nor was Twain concerned with the effects of copyright on "derivative works,"

works in media such as stage and screen that were somewhat based on previously copyrighted works such as novels.[3]

Twain, however, was one of the earliest authors to have work used as the basis of a narrative film. In 1909, the penultimate year of Twain's life, his short story "The Death Disk" became the subject of one of the earliest one-reel dramas by the film pioneer D. W. Griffith. Between the years 1908 and 1913, Griffith produced, directed, and often wrote a series of one-reel films for the American Mutoscope and Biograph Company. During this time, Griffith built on the emerging art of narrative film and took it to new creative heights. Before he changed American filmmaking forever with his authorized 1915 production of Thomas Dixon's *The Clansman*, retitled *The Birth of a Nation*, Griffith retold stories written by other authors without permission.

"The Death Disk," published first in *Harper's Monthly* in 1901, is the tale of a little girl whose father is a colonel in Oliver Cromwell's army. Throughout the tale, the little girl is too innocent to realize that Cromwell is considering sentencing her dear father to death for disobeying orders in battle. In a strange twist, Cromwell meets the child and invites her into his court. He then offers the girl three wax disks, one red, two white. He instructs her to give one disk to each of the three colonels seated before him. She decides that the prettiest disk, the death disk, should go to her father. After Cromwell explains that she has sentenced her own father to death, the girl pleads with the Lord Protector and invokes a pledge he had made to obey her wishes. Cromwell spares the colonel's life.[4]

The story is simple and short. It occurs in two scenes: the home and the court. It has only four speaking parts: the parents, the child, and Cromwell. Griffith's film, of course, had no "speaking" parts as we know them. The dialogue was simply words framed on a black screen. The action was pure pantomime. But Griffith made several major changes to the story when he got hold of it. In his film, which was retitled *The Death Disc*, Griffith made the little girl's family Catholic victims of Cromwell's tyranny, not faithful members of Cromwell's radical Protestant movement as in Twain's story. Still, the family remains happily intact by the end of the one-reel picture.[5]

The degree to which we can claim Griffith "took" the story from Twain is unclear. Griffith spelled the title slightly differently. Nothing in the bulletin that advertised the film declared that the story was by Twain, while other Biograph bulletins often claimed that their stories were from well-known authors such as George Eliot, Charles Dickens, Leo Tolstoy, James Fenimore Cooper, and Alfred Lord Tennyson. And, as noted, Griffith made substantial changes to the circumstances of the family in the story. Still, Twain's short story seems to be the most likely source of the plot for the film.

Twain first came across the idea for a Cromwellian execution by lot in 1883 while reading Thomas Carlyle's five-volume *Oliver Cromwell's Letters and Speeches*. Carlyle gives a one-paragraph account of Cromwell facing two Welsh colonels and a drunken colonel from Pembroke. According to Carlyle, Cromwell ordered: "Death however shall be executed only upon one of them; let the other two be pardoned: let them draw lots which two." Two of the paper lots had the words "Life Given by God." The third lot was blank. After the prisoners refused to draw, Cromwell asked a child to make the choice. The drunken colonel from Pembroke was shot soon after he received the blank paper. In Carlyle's account, there was no plea from a cute child, no humane change of heart by a sentimental Lord Protector, and the death warrant was issued by paper, not wax disk or disc.[6]

Twain declared an interest in writing a Cromwellian tragedy in his notebook in 1883. He also wrote to William Dean Howells later that year suggesting that they collaborate on a story about such a fatal lottery. Twain finally got around to writing "The Death Disk" in 1899 while visiting London. *Harper's Monthly Magazine* published it in December 1901. Twain included the story in three collected volumes in his lifetime: *A Double-Barrelled Detective Story* (1902), *My Debut as a Literary Person* (1903), and *The $30,000 Bequest and Other Stories* (1906). Twain had the story dramatized at Carnegie Hall in 1902 as *The Death Wafer*. When Twain died in 1910, one published eulogy declared "The Death Disk" among his finest stories. So while the idea of execution by lot might have spread from Carlyle's history into the public consciousness by 1909, it is likely that the plot device of a darling child first giving the prettiest wax disk to her father and then pleading for his life probably came from Twain himself. If nothing else can be credited to Twain, the title of the story can.[7]

So we know that Griffith and Biograph decided to produce a film version of a story set in Cromwell's time, about a father who was sentenced to death by lottery. Let's assume that Griffith failed to seek or secure permission from either Twain or Harper Brothers. Perhaps to cover himself, Griffith changed some central elements of the story, changed the spelling of the title, and declined to mention Twain's name anywhere in the advertisements for the film. Had Griffith infringed on Twain's copyright? By the end—even the middle—of the twentieth century, certainly a court would have ruled that he had. But film rights and what have become known as "derivative work" rights were far from established in the first decade of the century. The idea/expression dichotomy was strong enough in 1909 to support such a bold move.

Examining the dynamic of "taking," or "borrowing," a story and shifting it across media and technologies reveals some troubling questions. What is so "derivative" about Griffith's borrowing a plotline, character types, and a handful of phrases from a well-known literary work? Presenting a short story in almost silent pantomime with limited dialogue cannot be an easy creative feat. At what point does Griffith's "value added" exceed that of the writer? How much of the short story derived from folk tales or stories orally related? How much of the original work derived from previously copyrighted work that had since lapsed into the public domain as copyrights expired? Isn't all creative work, when it comes right down to it, derivative? Is a plot an idea or an expression? How about a plot device? Is a character an idea or an expression? What sort of line should the law draw to maximize the amount and quality of creative expression that are available to the public? All of these questions, during Griffith's time, lacked answers. There was some conflicting case law that dealt with derivative works such as translations and dramatizations, but the lines were fuzzy and the new medium of film so radical that it was unclear how well those precedents would apply. Even today, there is more confusion than clarity about these questions.[8]

Did Twain infringe on Carlyle's work? The simple answer is no. Carlyle died in 1881, and so according to British law at the time, all his British copyrights still in effect at the end of his life entered the public domain by 1888, seven years after his death. The first edition of Cromwell's letters came out in 1845, so it would have entered the public domain in 1887, forty-two years after publication. Carlyle would not have enjoyed American copyright because he published before 1891. But even the long hypothetical answer—pretending that Carlyle's heirs did somehow retain rights to his work as late as 1901—is probably no. Twain recycled only the germ of the plot, the execution by lot. Carlyle might or might not have related a historical event in the text of his comments on Cromwell's letters. But Carlyle offered readers only 109 words in five sentences. Carlyle did not even reveal the sex of the child who drew the lots, or Cromwell's motivation for executing one of the colonels. Twain took the paragraph from Carlyle's comments (which he cited as his inspiration when he published "The Death Disk") and added characters, dialogue, setting, pathos, motivation, and tension to the story. Carlyle narrated an event. Twain wrote a story. Still, Griffith derived his film from Twain's work, and Twain derived his work from Carlyle. The only difference is the extent of change—the value added by each subsequent creator.[9]

Under a strict interpretation of the idea/expression dichotomy, Twain could control only the specific expressions of his story, such as character names, phrases, dialogue, and descriptions. The ideas, such as plot devices, events, motivations, and resolutions, would be free for any "second taker" to use to create new, albeit derivative, works. Therefore, the strictest reading of the idea/expression dichotomy would support the thinnest possible copyright protection.

But would we want the world's film industry (or any industry) to have that much license? Such a high, sturdy wall between idea and expression would reduce the financial incentive for authors to write books at all. For many authors, motion picture rights can be more lucrative than book rights. If film production companies could just tweak the details and alter the dialogue of a story like Mario Puzo's *The Godfather*, they would make movies that strongly resemble well-known stories without giving credit or compensation to the original author. Serious fiction (and nonfiction) writers would lose out. Many commercially successful authors, such as Puzo, would skip the book-writing process and just write screenplays. Occasional books would derive from films, but rarely the other way around. The world would have fewer books, poorer authors, and cheaper films. Such an incentive structure (or lack thereof) would be counterproductive and would fail to enforce the constitutional mandate "to promote the sciences and useful arts." Indeed, the film industry as we know it could not operate efficiently without some measure of "idea protection."

However, once the wall between idea and expression in the film industry crumbled to rubble, the transference of content from one medium to another justified absurd levels of copyright protection. This extremism—"thick" copyright protection and its general chilling effect on the use of previously expressed ideas—has impeded creativity as well. Many of the habits of the American motion picture industry derive from Griffith's improvised legal moves, and have ensured that the wall between ideas and expressions has eroded quickly. This erosion has generally, but not exclusively, worked in the motion picture industry's favor.

EDISON'S ADVENTURES WITH PATENTS
AND COPYRIGHTS

Occasionally, the distinct fields of intellectual property law intersect. It's a more common phenomenon at the end of the twentieth century, as companies struggle to defend market share through lawsuits over trademark and copyright, or computer companies try to protect their products through a combination of trade secrets, contracts, copyrights, and patents. But early in the twentieth century, such crossover rarely occurred. Books were books and printing presses were printing presses, and rarely did their controversies intersect. One exception was in the gestational film industry. It concerned the efforts by Thomas Edison to monopolize nearly every segment of it. Edison's experiences serve as a model for how later barons such as Bill Gates tried to create unnatural monopolies by manipulating copyrights, patents, contracts, and access to technology and works. Both patent and copyright law limit competition and therefore increase or at least stabilize prices for a product or service. Patents and copyrights are the only constitutionally mandated monopolies, created with the recognition that unfettered competition would drain creators of their financial incentive to create.

Thomas Edison knew the patent system well by the time he began capitalizing on the idea of mass-marketed motion pictures. One of Edison's assistants, William Kennedy Laurie Dickson, perfected a viewing machine in 1894 called the Kinetoscope. Edison licensed Kinetoscopes to a syndicate that placed them in departments stores, hotels, retail stores, and taverns around the country. They were a big hit, but their novel attractiveness soon wore off. Only one person at a time could view a Kinetoscope presentation, which was usually a simple array of photographs that would simulate basic motion. So while the Kinetoscope exhausted its appeal, inventors in Europe and the United States were busy making film projectors that could make motion pictures the equivalent of stage productions.[10]

Edison himself introduced a projector, dubbed the Vitascope, just two years after the Kinetoscope. Edison and his lab had not invented the Vitascope. A fellow named Thomas Armat had. Other inventors in France, England, and the United States were also producing early projectors in 1896. Edison simply purchased the marketing rights to Armat's machine so he could put his ample leverage in the marketplace behind it without fear of getting shut out. Soon theaters all over the world were enjoying the competition between Edison's Vitascope and a French-produced projector. Then a third force entered the projector market: American Mutoscope Company, which introduced a projector called the Biograph. Edison's former employee Dickson had developed the Biograph. Its success angered Edison and hastened the company to change its name to the American Mutoscope and Biograph Company, and later just the Biograph. The Biograph worked so well that it quickly displaced the projector competition from vaudeville theaters.[11]

Three companies—Edison, Biograph, and Vitagraph—produced almost all of the films released between 1895 and 1903. Not coincidentally, they also leased out the projection equipment needed to show their films. Filmmaking was still rather cheap, and most of the films were of actions such as trains approaching or people dancing. These companies made most of their money from exploiting their projector patents. Soon, the lure of filmmaking proved attractive to small entrepreneurs. To get around Edison's patents on cameras and production tools, they either imported cameras from Europe or hacked them. Some became so good at hacking equipment that they started selling it, undercutting Edison's prices. So Edison fought back with a barrage of patent suits. Soon Edison's lawyers were claiming that anyone who shot, produced, marketed, or projected motion pictures was infringing on his original patents, going back to the Kinetoscope. While the small film companies had generated the suits in the first place, Edison aimed for his larger competitors, Biograph and Vitagraph. Edison soon formed a brief and fragile alliance with Vitagraph, so Biograph remained his archrival for control of the motion picture industry.[12]

In a patent suit against Biograph, Edison found cold comfort. The court ruled that Edison could enjoy his patent for his camera, but Biograph could also defend a patent on its camera, which worked differently. The industry could have been stifled by this flurry of litigation, but the market was too lucrative for that to happen. Soon more minor players entered the film production and distribution practice, including such companies as Selig, Kalem, Essanay, and Lubin.

Edison's attacks on these newcomers generated the first motion picture copyright case, *Edison v. Lubin*, in 1903. Congress had not seen fit to insert the words "motion picture" into the text of the copyright code, and would not until 1912. But Edison wanted to protect his studio's work with the same tenacity he protected his inventions. Each time Edison released a film, he sent it to be registered as a photograph in the Library of Congress. After all, his lawyers figured, a motion picture was nothing but a series of photographs projected on a screen.

In one case, Edison's cinematographers had filmed the christening and launch of German Kaiser Wilhelm's yacht *Meteor*. Edison sent both the negative and positive print of the film to the Library of Congress. Somehow, a segment of the negative was separated from the reel, and Edison's competitor, Sigmund Lubin, acquired it. Lubin then made a positive print of the launch and released it for public view. Lubin's argument in defense of his actions was simple: copyright law did not protect motion pictures; and even if it did, nowhere on the frames of negatives did Edison leave the required copyright notice.

At the trial court level, Edison lost. Judge Dallas asked the definitive question on which this suit would rest: "Is a series of photographs, arranged for use in a machine for producing them in a panoramic effect, entitled to registry and protection as a photograph?" Then Dallas answered that question himself. Since 1865, when Congress extended copyright law to photographs, Congress had not considered the prospect of a completely novel form of expression. Dallas wrote,

> That section [of the U.S. copyright code] extended the copyright system to "any" photograph, but not to an aggregation of photographs; and I think that, to acquire the monopoly it confers, it is requisite that every photograph, no matter how or for what purpose it may be conjoined with others, shall be separately registered, and that the prescribed notice of copyright shall be inscribed upon each of them,

Dallas proclaimed that Congress must alter the text of the law before courts could extend copyright protection to this new medium, this series of photographs taken as a whole. This ruling served to "stiffen" the interpretation of copyright as applied to film and other new technologies. If Dallas's ruling had stood until Congress changed the law in 1912, the motion picture industry would have been even more chaotic than it was.[13]

Edison, however, did not want to wait for Congress to help him. Edison immediately appealed the case against Lubin to the Third Circuit Court of Appeals. There he found judges willing to consider that the protectable "expression" of a photograph is what viewers interpret from it, not the particular arrangement of the silver crystals on the celluloid substrate. In other words, what matters about a strip of film is not what it expresses frame by frame, because nobody pays to see it frame by frame. People pay to see the effect of running a series of frames through a lighted projector: the action on the screen. They pay for the effect of the technology, not the technology itself. In addition, the court ruled that by removing the ability of film producers to profit from the copyright monopoly, the lower court had not done all it could to apply copyright law to "promote the progress of science and useful arts." Therefore, the court ruled, Edison's projected moving image of the Kaiser's yacht leaving a harbor was protectable as one photograph under the copyright revision of 1865.[14]

One month before the Third Circuit Court of Appeals ruled on Edison's appeal of the lower court decision, another federal court ruled on a copyright suit that dealt directly with dramatizations, and obliquely with film representations and the idea/expression dichotomy. Hattie Delaro Barnes was a vaudeville performer of some infamy. She wrote and copyrighted her stage show, entitled *X-Rays of Society*, in 1897. In the show, Barnes impersonated famous actors and actresses. Between scenes, she would exit the stage to change costumes. During the changes, a projector showed scenes of her changing clothes in her dressing room and discussing the performance with her assistants.

By 1900, Barnes's act was well-known in New York City and elsewhere for its multimedia effects, humor, and bawdiness. That's when a theatrical manager named Edwin Miner decided to produce a show based on Barnes's style. Miner arranged for a thirty-six-inch-tall man, Adolf Zink, to perform similar scenes, pretending to be famous men and women. During the changes, Miner projected motion pictures of Zink changing in his dressing room. Zink performed different impersonations than Barnes, did not use her copyrighted script in any way, and used film of his own costume changes. Barnes sued Miner and Zink, hoping to convince the court that they had infringed on the copyrights of both her dramatic performance and the photographs that made up the costume changes. First, the court traced the similarities between the performances. The similarities were significant. But they were not necessarily infringements. The court decided, however, that the differences between the acts were great enough to rule in favor of the defendants, Zink and Miner. "It is apparent that the exhibition given by the defendants is unlike that given by the plaintiff, except that the general plan or plot of showing rapid changes of costume by means of photographic films and the Kinetoscope [probably a Vitascope—a Kinetoscope would not project] is substantially the same," wrote Judge Ray. "The main idea and purpose of each performance is to exhibit to the audience by means of moving pictures and the use of the Kinetoscope and a screen and darkened room a human being in nude or seminude conditions making quick changes of dress or costume." Ray also expressed concern that such nudity might render Barnes's copyright invalid anyway, because copyright law did not protect lewd or obscene expressions at that time. Ray did express reservations about whether enforcing Barnes's copyright would in fact "promote the progress of science or useful arts." But he put that issue aside. Ray decided to base the court's ruling on the fact that the defendants did not take anything "substantial or material" from Barnes's performance, "except the mere idea of representing rapid changes of clothing by a human being."[15]

Also in 1903, Edison released a film that would increase the creative potential of film and raise the ante in its relationship with copyright law. Edison's studio made the first American film to tell a story: *The Great Train Robbery*. An Edison employee named Edwin S. Porter directed the film, which was longer (1,100 feet) than any previous American production. Porter, unlike previous directors, did not just turn on a camera and ask his actors to mime actions and emotions. He edited. The final product captivated audiences with a silent story of a holdup, an exciting pursuit, and a thrilling capture. All subsequent films had to tell good stories just to make an impact on the public imagination. Edwin Porter, who would later hire a struggling writer and actor named David Wark Griffith to star in a film called *Rescued from an Eagles Nest* (1908), had raised the expectations of both moviemakers and their audiences.[16]

In 1905, the battle between Biograph and Edison spilled over from patent and distribution conflicts into copyright. That year, first Biograph, then Edison, made films that depicted the same slapstick comedy routine. In both films, a man places a personal ad in a daily New York newspaper. The man seeks an attractive woman, and the ad requests that such a woman appear at Grant's Tomb to meet the man, who hopes to marry the woman. First one woman approaches him, then another, then dozens more run toward him. The man runs. One of the women finally catches the man and forces him at gunpoint to come with her. The Biograph production was called *Personal*. Edison's company was not so economical with its use of words, and entitled its version *How a French Nobleman Got a Wife through the New York Herald Personal Columns*. The court examined both films and determined that while the story was almost exactly the same in both, the angles of certain shots around Grant's Tomb were different, and the subsequent chase scenes were shot in different locations: the Biograph scenes around New York; the Edison scenes in New Jersey.

Edison's cinematographer defended himself by telling the court,

> Each impression is a photograph of a pantomime arranged by me, and enacted for me at the expense of the owner of the film which I produced. My photograph is not a copy, but an original. It carries out my own idea or conception of how the characters, especially the French nobleman, should appear as to costume, expression, figure, bearing, posing, gestures, postures, and action.

Allowing that preliminary evidence indicated that Edison took only the idea for the film, not the specific expressions, from Biograph, Judge Lanning denied Biograph's request for an injunction against Edison. After Biograph failed to stop Edison from producing a film based on the same idea as one of its own films, it should be no surprise that Biograph was brave enough to release *The Death Disc* four years later.[17]

By 1908, all the major players in the motion picture industry were yearning for stability and relief from rampant litigation. The fiercest rivals in the industry—including Edison and Biograph—settled their differences that year by forging the Motion Picture Patents Company, a trust of ten companies that owned all the patents essential to moviemaking. The trust would license the use of its patents only to each other. Eastman Kodak colluded by allowing only trust members to buy its film. The companies would use only distributors who agreed to their set price schedule and excluded independent films. The theaters could show only Patents Company films on Patents Company projectors. But the most powerful weapon the Patents Company deployed was the lawsuit. It hired private investigators to weed out patent violators.

The company drove most of the independents away from the New York–New Jersey area, which was the center of the industry, to Southern California, where enforcement was looser and escape to Mexico possible. The survival of independents, and the establishment of Holly-wood, tempted some film distribution companies to defy the trust. Such an offense spurred the trust to create its own distribution company, which bought out or intimidated all but one of the smaller independent distributors. The sole survivor, William Fox of the Greater New York Film Rental Company, fought back with an antitrust suit against the Patents Company. Fox won, and the trust disintegrated, but the domi-nant forces of the motion picture industry struggled for the rest of the twentieth century to limit competition through such practices as "verti-cal integration" or "synergy."[18]

Despite its formidable power, the Patents Company set about starv-ing itself even before the courts killed it for good in 1918. By 1914, pro-liferating independent movie production companies released more and more interesting films than ever before. There was too much money at stake to play by the playground rules. Ignoring popular sentiments, the trust companies showed little interest in developing stables of stars, training talented directors, and pushing the creative limits of film. The trust strived to market a uniform commodity the public had to buy. By keeping the audiences' expectations low, the trust companies hoped to keep their salaries and marketing costs low as well. They knew excel-lence and creativity would be costly on the supply side, and free mar-ket competition would be expensive on the demand side. But the com-petition grew nonetheless, and so did creativity. In 1913, D. W. Griffith left a New York Patents company, Biograph, to form an independent company out in Hollywood. Griffith's break with Biograph symbolized more than ego and ambition. It emphatically showed that variety in a marketplace bolsters creativity, and thus promotes "science and the useful arts."[19]

THE STRANGE CAREER OF *BEN-HUR*

One case that might have altered Biograph's plans to exploit Mark Twain's work generated a ruling on appeal in March 1909, eight months before Biograph released *The Death Disc*. Ultimately, the case over a film version of the best-selling novel *Ben-Hur: A Tale of the Christ* did not deter either Griffith or Biograph. General Lew Wallace, a Union Civil War hero, wrote *Ben-Hur* in 1880. It sold at least two million copies in his lifetime. The book tells the story of Judah Ben-Hur, a Jew wrongly accused of plotting to kill the Roman governor of Judea. Ben-Hur is sentenced to the galleys, and Roman authorities imprison his sister and mother. He escapes, disguises himself as a Roman officer, and wins a chariot race against the rival who framed him. Ben-Hur rescues his family, who have contracted leprosy. After Christ cures their disease, the entire family converts to Christianity.[20]

Wallace died in 1905. His wife, author Susan Arnold Wallace, died two years later. But Wallace had assigned the publishing rights to Harper and Brothers publishing house and assigned the dramatization rights to a stage production company called Klaw and Erlanger. The dramatization, by William Young, was published and copyrighted in 1899. Kalem Company, unaware of the authorized dramatization, employed a writer to read the novel *Ben-Hur* and submit a treatment of it. The film that came from that treatment portrayed only select scenes from the novel, such as the chariot race.

While considering the case between the authorized publisher and the unauthorized filmmaker, the federal appeals court had to answer two questions: Did this film constitute a "dramatization" under federal copyright law? And was the projection of the film for public consumption and profit a "public performance"? In other words, the court separated the two modes of possible infringement, saying that a film could infringe on the book without infringing on the dramatization, or on the dramatization without infringing on the book. Strangely, the court ruled that the film did not infringe on the book copyright because "pictures only represent the artist's idea of what the author has expressed in words." Answering the second question, the court ruled that the film was exhibited for "public performance" and therefore did infringe on Klaw and Erlanger's exclusive rights to dramatize the story. So the judge ruled that the motion picture was not a dramatization of the novel, but that its exhibition did constitute a public performance of the play, despite the facts that the film had no spoken dialogue and the screenwriters had not read the play. Judge Ward wrote, "[W]e have no difficulty in concluding that moving pictures would be a form of expression infringing not the copyrighted book or drama, but infringing the author's exclusive right to dramatize his writings and publicly to perform such dramatization." Such a confusing ruling could hardly be expected to clearly guide the actions of the motion picture industry. Confusion reigned.[21]

It took the pragmatic mind of Supreme Court Justice Oliver Wendell Holmes Jr. to clarify the *Ben-Hur* saga and make sense of what may be protectable when a story is transferred from print to film. Holmes was more familiar with the evolution of copyright law and the idea/expression dichotomy than were most federal judges. As executor of his father's literary estate, Holmes had been a frustrated plaintiff in several copyright cases. In addition, Holmes had by 1911 issued Supreme Court opinions in two landmark copyright cases that altered the course and current of American copyright law. The most significant Holmes decision was in the 1903 case *Bleistein v. Donaldson Lithograph Co.* The defendant had copied three circus posters the plaintiffs had originally created. Lower courts had ruled against the plaintiffs, stating that advertisements were not protected by copyright laws. But Holmes trumped decades of case law—not to mention the statute—by bluntly stating, "Certainly works are not the less connected with the fine arts because their pictorial quality attracts the crowd and therefore gives them a real use—if use means to increase trade and to help to make money. A picture is none the less a picture and none the less a subject of copyright that it is used for an advertisement. And if pictures may be used to advertise soap, or the theater, or monthly magazines, as they are, they may be used to advertise a circus." In one fell swoop, Holmes, the frustrated copyright plaintiff and literary executor, had substantially expanded copyright protection beyond its intended purpose, without legislative consideration.[22]

By the time the Supreme Court heard the appeal of the *Ben-Hur* case, *Kalem Co. v. Harper Bros.*, Holmes had already declared himself willing to personally rewrite copyright law as he saw fit. Most of the other justices were willing to go along with him, despite Holmes's possible bias against "second takers," or those who would create derivative works. As if to invite Holmes to substantially overhaul film and derivative works law, the appeals court had handed up a messy and useless decision concerning *Ben-Hur*. Holmes did not disappoint the plaintiffs. "So, if the exhibition was or was founded on a dramatizing of *Ben-Hur* this copyright was infringed," Holmes wrote.

> Action can tell a story, display all the most vivid relations between men, and depict every kind of human emotion without the aid of a word. It would be impossible to deny the title of drama to pantomime as played by masters of the art. . . . The essence of the matter in the case

last supposed is not the mechanism employed but that we see the event or story lived. The moving pictures are only less vivid than reflections from a mirror.

Since this decision, new media and forms of expression and reproduction have not escaped from or threatened the practice of copyright law. Congress has not had to go back and add language to the code every time someone invented a new machine.

In anticipation of complaints that the Court went beyond its duty in substantially expanding copyright protection, Holmes confronted the idea/expression dichotomy by evading it. "It is argued that the law construed as we have construed it goes beyond the power conferred upon Congress by the Constitution to secure to authors for a limited time the exclusive right to their writings," Holmes wrote.

> It is suggested that to extend the copyright to a case like this is to extend it to the ideas as distinguished from the words in which those ideas are clothed. But there is no attempt to make a monopoly of the ideas expressed. The law confines itself to a particular, cognate and well-known form of reproduction. If to that extent a grant of monopoly is thought a proper way to secure the right to writings this court can not say that Congress was wrong.

Certainly, by defining a film as a dramatization, Holmes was simply employing common sense. And since Congress had since 1870 reserved the right to dramatize to copyright holders, Holmes was not by himself shredding the idea/expression dichotomy, because Congress had already cut a big hole in it. However, the financial and cultural power of motion pictures made the hole even wider, which would not have troubled Holmes.[23]

D. W. GRIFFITH: LEGAL PIONEER

Despite a handful of court rulings, film copyright and derivative works law occupied unplowed legal territory during the first few decades of the film industry. Even as late as 1918, Griffith and his partners were unclear to what extent filmmakers had to secure the rights to stories, and what of their works would be protected from use by others. *Kalem v.*

Harper Bros. had been a clear-cut case of the appropriation, with little alteration, of a major novel still protected by copyright. But most works and the films based on them inhabited gray areas in the law. There is no available evidence that suggests Griffith asked for or received permission from Twain to dramatize "The Death Disk." However, Griffith occasionally produced films that were authorized retellings of protected works.

Before 1910, Biograph released a series of films based on literary works in the public domain such as *Resurrection: Free Adaptation of Leo Tolstoy's Powerful Novel* (1909), *Leather Stocking: Freely Adapted from the Tales of James Fenimore Cooper* (1909), and *A Fair Exchange: Free Adaptation of George Eliot's Silas Marner* (1909). Griffith also made several films that were unacknowledged dramatizations of popular works then under copyright protection. In addition to *The Death Disc* in 1909, Griffith made *For Love of Gold* (1908), an adaptation of the Jack London story "Just Meat" (1907), a film version of London's *The Call of the Wild* (1908), and a film entitled *A Corner in Wheat* (1909), which was based on an unacknowledged Frank Norris short story called "A Deal in Wheat." Griffith biographer Robert Henderson wrote that officials at Biograph were cavalier about using unauthorized literary sources for their treatments and shooting scripts. Biograph produced films so quickly and pulled them from circulation so fast that they seemed unconcerned by any legal ramifications. In addition, Biograph employed several writers, including Griffith (before he moved to directing), to write three-hundred-word "original" treatments for short films. Most of the Biograph films between 1908 and 1913 were based on treatments and scripts that Biograph commissioned.[24]

At least one of these attempts to adapt a popular story to film without permission did generate legal ramifications. In the year Jack London died, 1916, he lost a lawsuit against Biograph concerning his story "Just Meat" and the subsequent film *For Love of Gold*. The story and the film share a similar plot and setting: Two thieves steal some money and jewelry. They argue over how they will divide the loot. Each poisons the other. They both die. The film differs from the short story in the manner of the original crime and the beverages that the criminals use to kill each other. Reflecting on the plot similarities, the judge wrote that the central plot to both tales is older than the London story. Chaucer's "Pardoner's Tale," Rudyard Kipling's *Second Jungle Book,* and many ancient folktales contain similar "crime does not pay" scenarios. "The plot is common

property," the judge wrote. "No one by presenting it with modern incidents can appropriate it by copyrighting." The judge allowed that London added much to his version of the story, not least a glimpse of psychological insight and motivation for the thieves. However, Griffith was
unable or unwilling to pursue such issues. "The copyright can not protect the fundamental plot, which was common property long before the
story was written; it will protect the embellishments with which the author added elements of literary value to the old plot, but it will not operate to prohibit the presentation by some one else of the same old plot
without the particular embellishments," the judge ruled. Therefore,
even if Twain had pursued a complaint against Griffith or Biograph for
using "The Death Disk," he would not have fared better than Jack London did.[25]

Biograph bulletins and records indicate an end to reckless unauthorized adaptation in May of 1910, when Biograph released an authorized version of Helen Hunt Jackson's best-seller *Ramona*. The film
starred Mary Pickford and used the gentle and consistent climate of
Southern California for its expansive outdoor shots. Biograph purchased the rights for *Ramona* from the publishing house of Little, Brown
and Company for $100, four times what Biograph paid its own writers
per treatment. The advertisement for the film boasted of its authorized
status: "Adapted from the novel of Helen Jackson by arrangement with
Little, Brown & Company." There is a good chance that Griffith's *Ramona* was the first film to rely on a literary source secured with permission and payment. Perhaps Griffith, Biograph executives, and their
lawyers developed an institutional concern for copyright issues in the
wake of the passage of the copyright law of 1909, which attracted substantial press attention. Coincidentally, at least, Biograph changed its
behavior around the same time Congress changed the law.[26]

Film copyright in the early years of the industry was guesswork.
All that filmmakers and their lawyers could be sure about was that their
final product could enjoy protection from piracy, but they weren't always sure of the procedures needed to ensure that protection under the
rapidly changing laws. Even then, filmmakers wanted to have the law
work both ways for them: low protection of original printed works that
they could exploit for dramatic adaptation, and high protection for their
own finished products.

In the wake of the early film copyright cases, advances in technology, and the growing popularity and profitability of narrative film,

Congress set about rewriting American copyright laws. The first attempt at wholesale revision, in 1906, had failed, despite the testimony of luminaries such as Mark Twain in support of the bill. But by 1909, Congress was ready to undertake the effort and President William Howard Taft was willing to sign it. To Congress, copyright was still mainly about books, magazines, and the prevention of piracy of both. The new law did not concern itself with film, idea protection, or the dynamics of transferring a story from one medium to another. The chief change instigated by the 1909 law was the extension of the copyright term from fourteen years (renewable for another fourteen years) to twenty-eight years (renewable for another twenty-eight years). It also extended copyright to the mechanical reproductions of music, and clarified the registration process.

The most significant change in the 1909 revision, however, was largely unexpected. The new law created a new definition of authorship: corporate authorship. By 1912, Congress acknowledged that courts needed guidance and confidence when ruling that films were a worthy subject of traditional copyright law. So in a brief revision to the law, Congress added "motion picture photoplays" to the list of protected methods of representation in the law.[27]

Coincidentally, D. W. Griffith left Biograph in 1913 to establish his own company. Then he set about trying to figure out how to capitalize on these changes. First, his lawyers had to learn the formalities of the new copyright law. On September 5, 1914, Frank Woods, the story editor of Griffith's new Mutual Film Corporation, wrote to Griffith's New York lawyer to inquire how best to protect the new films from both piracy and derivative works such as plays or novels based on the original films. Woods suggested that the studio was willing to prepare and register short stories based on the proposed shooting scripts, so they would at least have some minimal idea protection. The lawyer, Albert Banzhaf, immediately wrote to the Librarian of Congress to request the text of the copyright law so that he could register Griffith's upcoming films.[28]

After receiving an unhelpful reply from Thorvald Solberg, the registrar of copyrights at the Library of Congress, Banzhaf again wrote to Solberg. This time Banzhaf wanted to know whether the copyright office would require complete reels of film to register the film, or whether a treatment or script would suffice. Banzhaf also asked Solberg whether a copyright on a particular film would also protect the story of the film, preventing a "second taker" from writing a short story based on it. If not, Banzhaf wondered whether he could register a separate short story to preempt such a derivation and thus protect the underlying story. Solberg replied to Banzhaf with an explanation that seemed to endorse the notion that a copyright holder could register a story in each medium in which she or he desired protection. "Whether copyright for a motion picture would secure the right to prevent the reproduction of a story based upon the motion picture is a question which the Copyright Office could not authoritatively decide," Solberg wrote. "The proprietor would have the privilege of claiming copyright for the story, however, and could register the claim by proceeding as in the case of a book; that is, by publishing the story with the copyright notice and afterward depositing the necessary copies, application, and fee in this office for registration." We can infer from Solberg's letter that at the time story protection worked only one way: from print to dramatization. Registering a film would not necessarily prevent someone from staging a play or publishing a novel based on a film, as the text of the law still privileged printed text and no courts had ruled on the issue. However, since 1870, the text of the law had allowed authors of printed works to control translations and dramatizations.[29]

As Griffith became more successful, his obsession with protecting his stories and titles increased, even though the law at the time generally failed to support copyright protection for either. In 1914, Banzhaf wrote to Frank Woods to explain the copyright procedure. It was Banzhaf's understanding, from his correspondence with Solberg, that protecting a story was as easy as registering a short story or treatment, then submitting two copies of the final film to the Library of Congress. Banzhaf explained to Woods that Griffith could hope to control the rights only to the film version of *The Clansman*—later retitled *The Birth of a Nation*—because the rights to the story would remain under the control of Thomas Dixon, who wrote the book and play. In other words, Griffith could prevent piracy of his film, but not subsequent use of a similar story by another writer. Banzhaf also told Woods that films based on treatments or scripts made "in house" could enjoy a higher level of protection. Specifically, Banzhaf declared that Griffith could possibly protect both the film itself and the underlying story of his pictures such as *Home Sweet Home* (1914), which was based on an original Griffith treatment, and *The Avenging Conscience* (1914), which was an adaptation of Edgar Allan Poe's "The Tell-Tale Heart" (1843). Banzhaf suggested that for every picture Griffith planned to make, he submit a treatment to the copyright office long before the actual reels of film could be registered.[30]

Griffith's lawyers apparently believed that copyright law granted exclusive use of a title for a work. It never has. In 1918, Banzhaf wrote a threatening "cease and desist" letter to another studio—World Film Corporation of New York City. Banzhaf had seen an ad in an issue of *Moving Picture World* for a film called *Heart of a World,* but had not seen the film or read a treatment about it. Griffith had released a twelve-reel film about the war in Europe called *Hearts of the World* in March of 1918. It became a great success for Griffith, but there is no reason to believe that the World Film Corporation production of *Heart of the World* either detracted from Griffith's audience or even resembled Griffith's film in any way.[31]

By the fall of 1918, Griffith's lawyers and business managers concluded that they needed to hire a lawyer in Washington, D.C., who might have some expertise in the arcana of copyright law, which seemed to be changing almost daily. They retained the services of Washington lawyer Fulton Brylawski. With Brylawski handling all the registration and deposit duties that the copyright office required, the Griffith team continued its practice of sending treatments to be registered and deposited, often months before the respective films were ready for registration and release. Brylawski apparently raised no questions about the utility of trying to protect stories by registering treatments. He simply followed orders. For each film in production, the studio would send Brylawski a synopsis of the story, and then two sets of reels for the film six to eight weeks later. He would dutifully register and deposit them with the copyright office of the Library of Congress, then send the registration receipts back to the Griffith studio.[32]

Griffith also pioneered—or at least mastered—two business methods that made the rapid growth of the American film industry possible. The first exploited one of the most significant changes in American copyright law from the 1909 revision: corporate copyright and "works made for hire." The second involved rights acquisitions for musical scores.

Corporate copyright was an accidental Revolution. Before 1909, only individual authors could claim copyright in a work. Authors licensed their work to publishers, but the flesh-and-blood author was the primary agent and thus beneficiary of copyright law. But the 1909 revision contained a small section that made it possible for a corporation such as a newspaper publishing company to retain copyrights in its name for a limited period of time, even if its employees had produced the actual work. Therefore, the publisher had the same rights in the courts and the marketplace as the author. The creation of corporate copyright in 1909 was the real "death of the author." Authorship could not be considered mystical or romantic after 1909. It was simply a construct of convenience, malleable by contract.[33]

The provision was intended to aid the publishers of encyclopedias and periodicals, but its effects were much more powerful in other industries. In the case of film production companies, corporate copyright allowed studio control of content, distribution, advertising, and derivative products. Directors, producers, screenwriters, and even actors— all of whom could philosophically claim "authorship" of a film—regularly sign away control of their work to a studio, and cannot claim the benefits and privileges of legal authorship.

Griffith used the new corporate copyright provisions creatively. He hired a small stable of writers, led by a former newspaper reporter named S. E. V. Taylor, who had written treatments for Biograph years before. Under the agreement Taylor signed with Griffith in 1919, Griffith paid Taylor a retainer of $100 per week as an advance against the payment of $1,000 for each original story he produced. That meant that Taylor earned as much in a week from Griffith as Biograph had paid for the rights to *Ramona* in 1910, back when Biograph was paying Taylor and others $25 per treatment. While working for Griffith, Taylor wrote treatments such as *The Great Love* (1918), *The Greatest Thing in Life* (1918), *Scarlet Days* (1919), *The Girl Who Stayed at Home* (1919), and *The Idol Dancer* (1920). In addition to his per-treatment commission, Taylor received between 3 and 5 percent of all profits above production and distribution expenses. In exchange for this relatively high salary for a writer, Taylor relinquished his personal stake in the legal authorship of the stories and agreed that he would work exclusively for Griffith. In this way, Griffith enjoyed a consistent stream of filmable stories from a veteran writer, and he was able to control every element of the copyright bundle.[34]

Even with Taylor's productivity and Griffith's own prolific writing, Griffith often went out-of-house for stories. Between 1915 and 1919, Griffith produced film versions of Paul Armstrong's play *The Escape* (1914), Daniel Carson Goodman's novel *The Battle of the Sexes* (1914),

Dixon's *The Clansman* (1915), and Thomas Burke's story "The Chink and the Child," which became *Broken Blossoms* (1919). A 1919 rights transfer contract between writer Edward Roberts and Griffith shows the terms under which studios acquired such works. Griffith gave Roberts $500 for the "world's motion picture rights" to Roberts's story "Thou Art the Man." In addition, Griffith received the power to change anything in the story and a pledge that Roberts would not publicize the deal. Roberts also received a promise that he would be given credit in the film for his authorship of the story. Despite the successful transfer of rights, Griffith never made the film. Under the new practice of corporate copyright, Griffith could acquire the rights to a story for a fairly cheap price and ensure that his company controlled the content, distribution, and performance rights to the more lucrative film version. Griffith was well on his way from being copyright-poor to copyright-rich.[35]

Producing a motion picture involves almost all elements of that "bundle" of rights we call copyright. The Copyright Act of 1909 and earlier practices established by the *Ben-Hur* case, Biograph's arrangement with Little, Brown, and Griffith's deal with Dixon allowed authors to sign away rights in one medium while retaining them in all others (or the only others at the time, book and serial rights). But silent films needed music, too, and sheet music compositions were also protected by copyright law. Before 1909, silent films shown in theaters were accompanied by musicians who would improvise along with the action on the screen. Predictably, the value of the film-watching experience varied widely with the improvisational skills of the bands. While Griffith was at Biograph, struggling to control every aspect of filmmaking, he employed a popular composer named Joseph Carl Breil, who had written the hit "The Song of the Soul." Breil composed "cue sheets" for many of Griffith's Biograph releases. The cue sheets were not quite compositions. They were more like road maps or outlines that modestly tempered and standardized the improvised music in theaters. The cue sheets listed the major scenes of the film so that the musicians would not be surprised by plot twists and mood changes. They also suggested some popular music that might accompany the scenes. There is no reason to believe that Griffith arranged for any rights transfers for those suggested songs, nor is it likely that theater owners paid royalties to the composers of popular ballads the orchestras might play because the notion of "performance rights" did not exist until 1913. But by 1919, Griffith was contracting with some independent composers. One agreement that acquired "Chinese themes" for the film *Broken Blossoms* required the composer, Lee Johnson, to relinquish only the theater performance rights to Griffith, while retaining the right to publish sheet music and make recordings or piano rolls for general sale. Most of all, Johnson received valuable publicity for his "Chinese themes."[36]

While Griffith would occasionally contract out for music, the major scoring for his films had to be done in-house to ensure continuity and consistency. By the time Griffith made *Home Sweet Home* in 1914, Breil was composing—as "works made for hire"—complete film scores for small orchestras. The greatest challenge for Breil's composition skills was the 1915 epic *The Birth of a Nation*. The score for the twelve-reel film had 214 cues and 1,500 scenes. The score required a forty-piece orchestra with vocalists. Griffith biographer Richard Schickel cited works by Schubert, Dvořák, Schumann, Mozart, Tchaikovsky, Mahler, Wagner, and Stephen Foster in the score. Breil also employed public domain songs such as "Turkey in the Straw" and "Home Sweet Home." Some of the material in the *Birth of a Nation* score was original to Breil, Schickel explained, including tom-toms in the film's opening scene of slaves arriving in America and the piercing "rebel yells" that stirred audiences nationwide. The score is appropriately credited to both Breil and Griffith, for Griffith approved every measure and insisted on certain expressive elements over Breil's opposition. Griffith grew so skilled at the intricacies of film scoring from his work with Breil that he later composed the theme for *Broken Blossoms* (1919), a song called "White Blossoms." Breil did manage to generate one hit song for himself from the score. It was published as "The Perfect Song," and went on to serve as the theme for the radio program *Amos 'n' Andy*.[37]

The Birth of a Nation also served as the site of a brilliant business move Griffith made using the new corporate copyright. Griffith had raised the money to make *The Birth of a Nation* through a company called Majestic Pictures. The major investors in the film, through their instrument Majestic, expected to have some leverage in directing the publicity and distribution for the film. But when the reels of developed film were finally in their cans, ready for registration and deposit in the Library of Congress, Griffith ensured that the film was copyrighted in the name of the D. W. Griffith Corporation. Griffith and Dixon also formed a company called Epoch Productions and arranged to have the D. W. Griffith Corporation lease the rights of the film to Epoch, which would distribute it. Therefore, Griffith retained complete control over not only the images and music of the film, but its impact on the motion picture market as well.[38]

Just after *The Birth of a Nation* made its splash, and the D. W. Griffith Corporation made its legal presence known, Griffith began work on his next picture, *Intolerance* (1917). This time, Griffith registered the copyright in his own name, not a corporate name. Then he assigned distribution rights to a new corporation called Wark Producing Corporation. This was his normal registration practice for many years after. Griffith's reasons for this new practice are unclear. Perhaps he liked the idea of having a title of personal authorship attached to his films. Perhaps his lawyers advised him that this method would allow a distribution company to go broke and fold, yet let the rights revert to Griffith personally. In just ten years—from *The Death Disc* in 1909 to *Broken Blossoms* in 1919—Griffith had moved from being someone interested in maintaining only minimal protection of others' works to someone who had a vested interest in encouraging maximum copyright protection for his own work. He had moved from being copyright-poor to copyright-rich.[39]

LEARNED HAND AND THE "WEB" OF EXPRESSION

No jurist or legal scholar has had a greater effect on the business and content of American culture than Judge Learned Hand. For most of his career, Hand served on the U.S. Second Circuit Court of Appeals in New York City. A student of William James and George Santayana at Harvard, Hand was passionate about matters of freedom, creativity, and intellectual progress. Through copyright and speech cases that confronted him on the court, Hand exhibited a rare combination of mastery and modesty. When Congress started writing the revisions that would become the Copyright Act of 1976, it codified many of the principles that Hand had articulated in his opinions from the bench. Hand was a biting critic, and he expressed disdain for some of the works that came before him, especially trite songs and plays. Still, he kept his aesthetic opinions from impinging on his judgments about authorship and originality. As Hand wrote in his earliest copyright opinion (echoing one of his legal heroes, Justice Holmes): "While the public taste continues to give pecuniary value to a composition of no artistic excellence, the court must continue to recognize the value so created. Certainly the qualifications of judges would have to be very different from what they are if they were to be constituted censors of the arts." Hand was a great fan of musical theater, yet some of America's best and best-known composers lost copyright cases before him, including Jerome Kern, Sigmund Romberg, Irving Berlin, and Cole Porter. Hand took very seriously the incentive principle behind the copyright clause of the Constitution, and just as seriously the limitations it prescribes. For Hand, copyright was for the public, not for the producers. Most of his copyright decisions emanate from a concern to ensure a rich and diverse array of artistic expressions from which the public may choose.[40]

Perhaps Hand's most significant legacy in copyright law was that he clarified and reinforced the idea/expression dichotomy, which was in danger of eroding as judges frequently and without guidance considered whether motion pictures had infringed on novels or plays or new songs had taken too much from old songs. Hand not only reminded his colleagues of the free speech implications of the dichotomy. He outlined tests for infringement that they could use. In this way, Hand brought some consistency and predictability to copyright law that had not existed since the rise of commercial film and would not survive the expansion of media in the last three decades of the twentieth century.[41]

As a judge on the appeals court responsible for cases from New York City, the center of American publishing, music composition, and theater, Hand played a part in most of the major copyright decisions in the 1920s and 1930s. His first declaration on the importance of the idea/expression dichotomy came in 1930, in the case *Nichols v. Universal Pictures Corp.* Anne Nichols, playwright of the long-running Broadway play *Abie's Irish Rose,* claimed that Universal had relied on her play when it produced the film *The Cohens and the Kellys* (1927). Both the play and the film concerned "star-crossed lovers" from feuding families, one Jewish, one Irish. But as Hand concluded when he analyzed the two works, "the only matter common to the two is a quarrel between a Jewish and Irish father, the marriage of their children, the birth of grandchildren and a reconciliation." Hand wrote,

> If *Twelfth Night* were copyrighted, it is quite possible that a second comer might so closely imitate Sir Toby Belch or Malvolio as to infringe, but it would not be enough that for one of these characters he cast a riotous knight who kept wassail to the discomfort of the house-

hold, or a vain and foppish steward who became amorous of his mistress. These would be no more than Shakespeare's "ideas" in the play, as little capable of monopoly as Einstein's doctrine of Relativity, or Darwin's theory of the Origin of Species.

Hand was concerned that if courts ruled too strictly on such cases, "second comers," who might do a much better job than the originator of an idea, could be forbidden from or punished for improving a plot. Hand concluded: "A comedy based upon conflicts between Irish and Jews, into which the marriage of their children enters, is no more susceptible of copyright than the outline of Romeo and Juliet." Hand was careful, however, to state that drawing a thick and clear line between what is an idea in a narrative and what is an expression of that idea would never be easy, if possible at all. Hand conceded that the line between ideas and expressions is instinctual, but said it should rely on impressions of the total works in question. Hand hoped that judges would use common sense on a case-by-case basis yet adhere to some ill-defined general principles.[42]

Hand delineated those general principles in his next major idea/expression case, *Sheldon v. Metro-Goldwyn Pictures Corp.*, in 1936. The case concerned the Joan Crawford vehicle *Letty Lynton* (1932). The film tells the story of a young woman who has an affair with a young man, then meets a rich, older, single man and decides to marry him instead. The jilted young lover then threatens to expose the aborted affair by showing the new prospect their love letters. Letty, the young woman, considers suicide but opts instead for murder, poisoning her young lover.

The plaintiff's play, *Dishonored Lady*, shared the basic plot with the film. In addition, both the play and the film were set in upper-class New York society and involved a South American lover as the extortionist and murder victim. Metro-Goldwyn officials had seen the play, starring Katherine Cornell, in 1930 and had considered buying the film rights to it, but were dissuaded by censors. In 1931, Metro-Goldwyn executive Irving Thalberg (who engineered the complex script-borrowing machinations for the Marx Brothers) purchased the rights to a British novel, *Letty Lynton* (1931), that had the exact same plot as *Dishonored Lady*. To complicate issues further, both the novel and the play derived their stories from a true incident, the 1857 murder trial of a Glasgow woman named Madeleine Smith. The studio, of course, argued that it justifiably used both the plot, which was in the public domain by virtue of its historical antecedent, and the details of the novel, to which it controlled the film rights.

Using Hand's opinion in the *Nichols* case, the federal district court judge ruled that the film did not infringe on the play, despite similarities in setting and character. Judge John Woolsey had done what any other trial court judge would have done in the wake of the *Nichols* decision: he examined the details of the two works in question, identified what he called "common denominators," and eliminated those that qualified as unprotectable ideas and those that came from the public trial record in the Madeleine Smith case. But narratives are not always reducible to lists of "common denominators." Hand's understanding of how novels, plays, and motion pictures actually work for an audience motivated him to reverse Woolsey's decision. It was not the similarities of recipes, but the similarities of flavors of the final products, that mattered to Hand.[43]

Citing the suit Jack London lost against Biograph for the film based on "Just Meat," Hand wrote, "At times, in discussing how much substance of a play the copyright protects, courts have indeed used language which seems to give countenance to the notion that, if a plot were old, it could not be copyrighted." Hand again declared that a plot in and by itself cannot be protected by copyright, but the "value added," the extra aspects and layers and twists that a new creator imparts to the work, can be. Certainly, there was more to this case than a common plot among several similar works: "In the case at bar there are then two questions: First, whether the defendants actually used the play; second, if so, whether theirs was a 'fair use.'"

Because the play was based on a true story, "the plaintiff's originality is limited to the variants they introduced." Stepping around the plot similarities, which Hand found to be irrelevant, he outlined the elements of the film that corresponded with elements of the play that he found to be "original" to the playwright. First Hand examined the setting, then the characters.

> The defendants took for their mise-en-scène the same city and the same social class; and they chose a South American villain. The heroines had indeed to be wanton, but Letty Lynton "tracked" Madeleine Cary [the character from the play] more closely than that. She is overcome by passion in the first part of the picture. . . . This is the same weakness as in the murder scene of the play, though transposed.

Hand continued to delineate four more traits the characters shared, including the trait that in both the play and the film, the protagonist was ultimately "redeemed by a higher love." Hand then distinguished them from the historical Madeleine Smith and the fictional Letty from the novel, who were throughout their tales manipulative and greedy, never "redeemed by a higher love."

Examining the elements of the story that drove the plot, Hand concluded: "[T]he threat scene is carried out with almost exactly the same sequence of event and actuation [in both the play and film]; it has no prototype in either [historical] story or novel. . . . Surely the sequence of these details is pro tanto the very web of the authors' dramatic expression; and copying them is not 'fair use.'" Hand delivered four conclusions from his reading of the evidence: The prior existence of a plot in history or the public domain does not invalidate a copyright on a later similar work; fair use may permit the taking of an old plot or idea from a copyrighted work, but not its expression in original form; unconscious appropriation of original elements of expression is still infringement; and dissimilar dialogue does not invalidate a claim of infringement.

But Hand's central point was that when judging the extent of infringement between works that tell similar stories, one must distill the "very web of the authors' dramatic expression." This "web" he defined as "the sequence of the confluents of all these means (plot, character, means of revelation, setting, themes), bound together in an inseparable unity; it may often be most effectively pirated by leaving out the speech, for which a substitute can be found, which keeps the whole dramatic meaning." Using such a test, searching for a "web" of expression that can determine the "whole dramatic meaning," Hand would have ruled differently than the presiding judges did in the German translation case of *Stowe v. Thomas* and the derivative works case of *London v. Biograph*. Under the criteria set forth by *Sheldon v. Metro-Goldwyn*, Twain could have successfully sued Biograph and Griffith for infringing on "The Death Disk," despite the changes Griffith made and the public domain source of the story in the work of Carlyle.[44]

Sheldon v. Metro-Goldwyn could be read as a blatant rejection of Hand's own argument—made in *Nichols v. Universal*—for a thick wall between idea and expression. Hand seemed to be retreating or contradicting himself, collapsing the distinction. In fact, it is just the opposite. What Hand accomplished in his opinion—reading each of the four relevant plots and analyzing the similarities and differences—was to show that while particular ideas cannot be protected, a pattern of ideas can be, because a pattern is an expression. It's the analysis of patterns, Hand argued, that is the key to allowing ideas to flow freely and expressions to be protected. In its most basic form, Hand's argument states that the elements of communication are (and should be) common, but the order and arrangement are where the work lies, where the creativity shows, and where the infringement can occur. It's as if Hand took each unit of meaning in the stories—plot devices, setting, tension, characters—and viewed them as letters of a narrative alphabet. Because an alphabet is common property, the law can protect only a specific string of letters in a particular order that perform a particular function—the "web of the authors' dramatic expression."[45]

The play, the novel and the motion picture that Hand considered in the *Sheldon* case all rested on a true story that was well-known in both Britain and North America. Because of this, the case has served as a significant precedent for the resolution of other cases in which films have been based on nonfiction, yet subject to litigation nonetheless. The first of these cases arose in 1943 and concerned a 1936 book called *We Who Are Young*, an economic treatise that discussed problems in the United States against the backdrop of the Franklin Roosevelt-Alf Landon presidential campaign. The book sold about seven hundred copies, mostly in its first year. Four years later, writer Dalton Trumbo, who had never heard of the book *We Who Are Young*, sold a screenplay to Loew's motion picture studio about the hardships young married couples face on a small salary. Trumbo called the screenplay *To Own the World*. The studio later changed the title to *We Who Are Young*. Harry Becker, the author of the nonfiction book, sued Loew's, trying to protect both his title and his "original thoughts and ideas," "central themes," and "material portions," even though there was no evidence that Trumbo used his book in any way. The very idea of an economic treatise contributing anything protectable to a narrative film offended the judge in the case, who cited both the *Nichols* and the *Sheldon* decisions while ruling for the studio. Becker tried to protect his book's title not through copyright law, which clearly avoids protecting titles, but through an appeal to unfair competition law. He argued that the film title would cause confusion in the marketplace. The judge stated that competition would be unfair only if the studio were doing business in a way that would deceive the public. Becker lost on both attempts. Although most cases involving the influence of nonfiction works on fictional works are more troublesome and complex than the case of *We Who Are Young*, courts have consistently granted second takers broad freedoms to use historical and nonfiction works.[46]

One recent example of this concerned the 1997 film *Amistad*. The parallels between the *Amistad* case and the *Letty Lynton* case, *Sheldon v. Metro-Goldwyn*, are striking. Like *Letty Lynton*, *Amistad* is a dramatized retelling of a historical event. Also, as in the 1934 case, another writer claimed to have suffered infringement from a major motion picture studio and cited specific aspects of her work that appeared in the film, yet were not part of the historical record. Also like *Letty Lynton*, the film studio had purchased the rights to another version of the story before proceeding with production. Unlike *Sheldon*, the *Amistad* case never made it to trial, so a judge could not employ the complex narrative analysis that Hand prescribed. *Amistad* is based on an incident that occurred in 1839. A ship by that name carrying captured West Africans was headed toward Cuba. The Africans were to be sold as slaves. But they rebelled, killed some of their captors, and took over the ship. The surviving crew tricked the Africans by sailing northeast instead of due east. U.S. officials captured the ship off the coast of Long Island, and the Africans faced murder charges and possible deportation to Cuba. Former President John Quincy Adams argued their case before the U.S. Supreme Court, and the Africans were eventually freed and returned to West Africa in 1841. At least eleven books recount these episodes with varying degrees of narrative license. But two of these books—William O. Owens's nonfiction account, *Black Mutiny* (1953), and Barbara Chase-Riboud's novel *Echo of Lions* (1989)—mattered in the *Amistad* case. After her friend and editor, Jacqueline Kennedy Onassis, sent the *Echo of Lions* manuscript in 1988 to Stephen Spielberg's production company, Amblin Entertainment, Chase-Riboud flew to Los Angeles to meet executives of the company. Amblin later sent Chase-Riboud a letter declining to pursue the project. However, in 1997, Spielberg's new production company, DreamWorks SKG, announced the imminent release of *Amistad*. DreamWorks claimed it based the film on the well-known historical record of the case and purchased the rights to *Black Mutiny*.

Chase-Riboud filed suit for copyright infringement and asked for a preliminary injunction against the release of the film until the suit came to trial or reached a settlement. Chase-Riboud argued that the film used several narrative devices and one fictional character that exist in her novel and the film but are absent from any other accounts, fictional or historical. After a federal judge denied Chase-Riboud's motion for an injunction the week the film was to premiere, the author and the studio settled their suit out of court in early 1998. Had the suit gone to trial and through the appeals process, it might have shown how effectively Hand's method of measuring infringement applies to the commercial climate of the 1990s. Instead, writers and producers remain wary of each other, unsure of the extent to which laws protect either of their interests, let alone the public's interest.[47]

THE IDEA OF IDEA PROTECTION

While Judge Learned Hand's complex and sophisticated reasoning in the *Sheldon* case served the dual purposes of allowing a wide berth of freedom for "second takers" to exploit, revise, or comment on previously expressed ideas while confounding those who would resort to simple tweaks and trickery to evade paying for rights and permissions, it did not solve all derivative works problems. In fact, in the hands of less careful or talented jurists, the notion of protecting a work's "web" of expressions often resulted in rulings that blew huge holes in the wall between idea and expression and helped carve out a new area of law: idea protection.

By the 1970s, American film and television products were transmitted around the world, and the commercial stakes in each work were higher than ever. Substantial investments demanded exorbitant returns, and as much predictability as possible. Creating and enforcing a monopoly over an idea became a shrewd, if not essential, business move. As the most profitable and controversial elements of American expressive culture emerged from California, the major decisions in copyright and idea protection law soon ceased to come from the chambers of the Second Circuit Court of Appeals in New York City and instead came from the Ninth Circuit in San Francisco.

In 1977, the Ninth Circuit considered a case that pitted a children's television production company, Sid and Marty Krofft, against the fast food company McDonald's. The Kroffts specialized in creating live action shows for children with minimal cartoon animation. Their shows generally had a preteen or early-teen boy as protagonist, who found himself in strange predicaments with stranger creatures in imaginary settings. One of their most successful series of the early 1970s was *H. R. Pufnstuf*. In this series, a Cockney boy named Jimmy had a magic flute that talked to him (in a high, whiny tone, of course). The flute generally resided in Jimmy's breast pocket, as it had no appendages and could do little else. Jimmy was trapped in a place called Living Island. Also on the island were various large creatures of indeterminate genus. One of the friendliest of these creatures was the foam-suited dragonoid H. R. Pufnstuf. All of the books and most of the trees on the island had faces and could talk, and the trees could grab unsuspecting little boys with their scraggly branches. The show was like *The Wizard of Oz* without the happy ending. *H. R. Pufnstuf* went on for many seasons, and poor Jimmy never seemed to get off the island.

Sensing that such a scenario could draw innocent children into begging their parents to take them to such a place, an advertising agency for McDonald's approached the Kroffts in 1970 about basing an ad campaign on the series. They never reached an agreement. Undeterred, and fairly confident that ideas could not be protected, the agency and McDonald's proceeded to produce a series of commercials, starting in 1971, that were set in McDonaldland.

When the case came to trial, McDonald's officials admitted they had borrowed the idea of using a fantasy land with strange characters and talking trees and objects, but they had clearly differentiated the expressions. The Ninth Circuit Court of Appeals, ignoring Judge Hand's carefully structured arguments and concern for erring on the side of full and rich public speech, set out to list what they considered substantially similar expressions. The court determined that both Living Island and McDonaldland, despite being very different geographical entities (one is an island, the other just a land) operating in different ways on Saturday morning televisions, were both "imaginary worlds inhabited by anthropomorphic plants and animals and other fanciful creatures. The dominant topographical features of the locales are the same: trees, caves, a pond, a road and a castle. Both works feature a forest with talking trees that have human faces and characteristics." The judge continued by analyzing the characters, based on very general phrenological criteria. "Both lands are governed by mayors who have disproportionately large round heads dominated by long wide mouths. They are assisted by 'Keystone cop' characters. Both lands feature strikingly similar crazy scientists and a multi-armed evil creature." The facts that the show lasted thirty minutes and the commercials only thirty seconds, and that the show had a narrative drive and line and the commercials only amusing snippets of action and dialogue, did not play into the court's decision. The court did not weave a "web," as Hand had urged. It simply made a list of abstract traits. Hand had clearly stated in *Nichols v. Universal Pictures Corp.* that precisely defined characters are protectable if the infringer borrows those precise definitions, but vaguely drawn characters could and should not be. The Ninth Circuit, in the *Krofft* case, did not take Hand's advice and ruled against McDonald's.[48]

But the court did more than rule in a single case against a handful of commercials. It extended to the realm of visual and narrative entertainment a new principle of idea protection: "total concept and feel." Seven years before it considered the *Krofft* case, the Ninth Circuit had reviewed a copyright case concerning two greeting card companies. The plaintiff had printed decorated cards with copyrighted art and simple, common phrases such as "I wuv you" and "I miss you already . . . and you haven't even left yet." The defendant made similar cards, but with different art. The defendant argued that the words on both cards were too common and vague to be considered "original" under the law, and that they had not infringed on the copyrighted artwork because they used different art. The Ninth Circuit accepted both of those propositions from the defense but then trumped them by ruling that the new cards did infringe on the old ones by sharing their "total concept and feel." The criteria for the court in this case had nothing to do with the specific expressions on the cards but depended on the "mood they portrayed."[49]

By introducing moodiness into the law through these two cases, the Ninth Circuit effectively eroded the already fragile wall between ideas and expressions. The television shows *The Addams Family* and *The Munsters* portray the same moods and share some other facile traits, but they are not the same show. American culture would be poorer if one had prevented the other from reaching people's homes because they shared a "total concept and feel." Some courts, including the Ninth Circuit, would hear similar cases in the twenty years following *Krofft v. McDonald's*, but would choose not to employ the "total concept and feel" notion. But the damage was done. A concept as vague and subjective as "total concept and feel" was bound to cause confusion among writers and artists, if not lawyers. Fear of infringing can be as effective a censor as an injunction. At the dawn of the twentieth century, film copyright was unpredictable because the industry was experimental, its financial returns uncertain, and its practices untested. With Hand's decisions in the 1930s, industry habits stabilized. Clearly, however, after 1970 film copyright law became more unpredictable as ideas grew more protectable.[50]

The unpredictability of motion picture copyright and the possibility of winning an idea protection suit have increased in the 1990s, since Art Buchwald's victory in his suit over the idea he submitted for an Eddie Murphy film that ultimately became *Coming to America* (1989). The Buchwald case received substantial media coverage, but was almost always referred to as a "plagiarism suit." Besides the fact that "plagiarism" is not a legal cause of action, most press accounts ignored the fact that Buchwald's attorneys knew that a copyright infringement suit would be hard to win on idea protection grounds. So instead, they sued in a state court charging a violation of contract. They won. The plot, characters, themes, motivations, setting, and details of *Coming to America* do not at all resemble the two-page treatment Buchwald submitted to Paramount. From 1996 through 1998, copyright infringement, right of publicity, or idea protection suits have been filed against the companies that produced the films *Amistad, Seven, The Devil's Advocate, The Full Monty, Booty Call, Rumble in the Bronx,* and *The Truman Show.* The absurdity of litigation in the film industry reached its apex in 1995, when a visual design artist, noticing similarities between a chair used in one scene of the two-hour science fiction drama *12 Monkeys* and one he had designed, succeeded in delaying the nationwide release of the film by getting a preliminary injunction against it. While fear of lawsuits can substantially change the nature of artistic expression, injunctions against publication or distributions are prior restraints on speech, and should be prescribed rarely and carefully. In the *12 Monkeys* case, one chair designer had a say in when—or whether—audiences could see the film, despite the fact that the infringing chair was only in one scene of a movie that had little or nothing to do with furniture.[51]

Although the film industry has pushed for thicker copyright protection to protect its dominant place in the global cultural marketplace, it should be clear that thin copyright protection, a rich public domain, and a strong legal distinction between idea and expression made the American film industry powerful and creative in the first place. Bending all decisions on the legality of derivations in favor of original authors violates the spirit of American copyright. Bending the law toward "second takers" would as well. Somewhere between the two extremes there must be a formula that would acknowledge that all creativity relies on previous work, builds "on the shoulders of giants," yet would encourage—maximize—creative expression in multiple media and forms. But because twentieth-century copyright law has been a battle of strong interested parties seeking to control a market, not a concerted effort to maximize creativity and content for the benefit of the public, we have lost sight of such a formula along the way.

4

Hep Cats and Copy Cats

American Music Challenges the Copyright Tradition

SHIRLEY DIXON WAS thirteen years old in 1976, when she first played the Led Zeppelin song "Whole Lotta Love" for her father. Shirley had borrowed the 1969 album *Led Zeppelin II* from a friend because the hit song from it had reminded her of one of her father's compositions.[1] Her father was the legendary blues composer, performer, producer, and bass player Willie Dixon. Young Shirley was well versed in the "property talk" of copyright law. She had been typing her father's lyrics and filling in copyright registration forms since she was eight years old. Shirley applied her keen ear and mind to the Led Zeppelin song and concluded "Whole Lotta Love" reminded her of her father's writing style. He agreed that "Whole Lotta Love" sounded like his obscure song "You Need Love," which was recorded by Muddy Waters in 1962.[2]

Willie Dixon filed suit in 1985 against the British rock group. They settled their dispute in 1987. Although this case never made it as far as a court hearing, the tensions between an older blues composer and younger hit makers illustrate many of the contradictions and complications of American music copyright.

Music, more than any other vehicle of culture, collapses the gap that separates idea from expression. Is the string of six notes that initiates "Happy Birthday to You" an idea, an expression, or both? If it is an idea, there must be another way to express the same idea. Would playing the same notes at a different tempo constitute a new expression of the same idea? Would playing it in a different key be an exercise in novel expression? Is there an idea behind a particular arrangement of musical notes? Is there an idea behind a tone, texture, timbre, or "feel" of a song? Are these features of a song ideas in themselves?

If copyright law is charged with protecting a particular arrangement of notes, should it protect the melody, the harmony, the rhythm, or all of the above? How long must that string of notes be to constitute a protectable segment of expression? Should music copyright law be most concerned with the "total concept and feel" of a protected work, or particular elements such as solos, riffs, or choruses? The twelve-bar I-IV-V chord pattern runs through most songs within the blues tradition, so that pattern is generally considered unprotectable. It is considered "common property," drawn from the "deep well" of American blues. However, an identifiable one-measure guitar riff—such as the opening to the Rolling Stones song (and Microsoft Windows advertisement) "Start Me Up"—could be protectable. At what point between general chord patterns and specific strings of notes does repetition constitute an infringement of a protectable expression? None of the answers to these questions is clear. Creative infringement cases have been interpreted on an almost ad hoc basis. Maintaining a healthy measure of freedom for "second takers" to build upon an expressive tradition demands other strategies, because the traditional safeguard of the idea-expression dichotomy does not operate the same way in music as in other fields.

Because these questions yield unsatisfying answers, many disputes among artists get expressed in moral or ethical terms. Led Zeppelin, like many rock groups, did not have an unsullied reputation for granting credit to blues artists. The group had covered and properly credited two other Dixon compositions, "You Shook Me" and "I Can't Quit You Baby," on its first album in 1968, Led Zeppelin I. During the early 1970s, the group had befriended the Dixon family on its visits to Chicago and had publicly paid homage to American blues pioneers. The group had failed to credit two other songs from Led Zeppelin II, "Bring It on Home" and "The Lemon Song," which resembled other Dixon compositions. Unbeknownst to Dixon, his publishing company, Arc Music, had negotiated a settlement with Led Zeppelin over those uncredited songs, but had neglected to inform Dixon or pay him the recovered royalties until long after the settlement. By the late 1980s, Led Zeppelin would not eagerly grant either writing credit or royalties to Dixon over "Whole Lotta Love." The proceeds of that settlement helped Dixon start the Blues Heaven Foundation, dedicated to helping aging composers and performers recoup some of the rewards for their work in years before they had a chance to develop sophisticated business and legal acumen. When Dixon passed away in 1992, his legend had grown from brilliant composer and performer to brave business pioneer. Dixon was among the first blues artists to wrest control of rights and royalties from exploitative record and publishing companies.[3]

The relationship between blues composers and rock artists is complex. There are rarely obvious good guys and bad guys in the stories of disputes over credit, influence, and royalties. In 1956, Elvis Presley revolutionized popular music by introducing stripped-down, high-power southern rhythm and blues to mainstream white audiences around the world. He did so by recording some songs that African American artists had distributed to lesser acclaim just a few years before, such as Big Mama Thornton's "Hound Dog." While Thornton's version gained legendary status among blues fans in the 1950s, it barely scratched the white pop market. Presley's version, on the other hand, sold two million copies in 1956 and simultaneously topped the pop, country, and rhythm and blues charts. Presley's appeal transcended racial and regional lines and opened up several generations of young people from around the globe to the power of African American music.[4] Yet Presley remains a controversial figure to many critics, who consider his work "inauthentic" because he reaped far greater rewards than previous or contemporary black artists whose work was just as exciting. Music journalist Nelson George has called Presley "a damned lazy student" of black culture and a "mediocre interpretive artist." Chuck D, the leader and lyricist of the rap group Public Enemy, sings "Elvis was a hero to most, but he didn't mean shit to me." Whether in good faith or bad, white performers almost always reaped larger rewards than their black influences and songwriters. As Tricia Rose has argued, whiteness matters in the story of the commodification of black cultural expression. By virtue of their whiteness, many artists participated in styles and subcultures that emerged from the rhythm and blues tradition and "crossed over" what was until only recently a gaping social and economic chasm between black music and white consumers. White rockers went where black artists could not. Even when blacks could cross over, white artists have had better opportunities to capitalize on the publicity and distribution systems. For instance, many "alternative" or "rock" radio stations will occasionally play rap music, but only if it is by white artists such as the Beastie Boys, Limp Bizkit, or Kid Rock.[5]

But the politics and economics of cultural exchange and translation are not simple and unidirectional. Like Elvis, many later blues-rock stars such as Eric Clapton, the Rolling Stones, and Bonnie Raitt helped publicize the work of almost forgotten blues artists. Others, such as Led

Zeppelin and the Beach Boys, have granted credit to composers such as Dixon and Chuck Berry under legal duress. There is very little difference in the passion or sincerity behind the work of Muddy Waters and that of Eric Clapton. However, there is an indisputable chasm between the reception of Waters's work in the 1950s and that of Clapton's hits of the 1970s: Because he is white, Clapton was in a better position to exploit vastly better business conditions and broader consumer markets than Waters was. Clapton emerged at a very different time. Nonetheless, many music fans now know and appreciate the work of Willie Dixon, Muddy Waters, and Robert Johnson because of Elvis Presley, Eric Clapton, Jimmy Page, and others.

The simplistic story of the relationship is that younger white performers "stole" material from aging "authentic" composers such as Willie Dixon, Sonny Boy Williamson, or Son House. But tracing influence through something as organic and dynamic as American music is never simple. Blues-based music is often the product of common and standard chord structures and patterns. Relying on or referring to a particular influence can be as important as any "original" contribution to a work. A composer might employ a familiar riff within a new composition as a signal that the new song is part of one specific tradition within the vast multifaceted canon of American music. Influence is inspiration, and songs talk to each other through generations. As Willie Dixon wrote: "When you're a writer, you don't have time to listen to everybody else's thing. You get their things mixed up with your ideas and the next thing you know, you're doing something that sounds like somebody else." Because repetition and revision are such central tropes in American music, rewarding and encouraging originality is a troublesome project in the music industry.[6]

In 1948, Muddy Waters released a song for the Chess brothers' Aristocrat label called "Feel Like Goin' Home." It was Waters's first national rhythm and blues hit. "Feel Like Goin' Home" was a revised version of a song Waters had recorded on his front porch in Mississippi for the folklorist Alan Lomax in 1941. After singing that song, which he told Lomax was entitled "Country Blues," Waters told Lomax a story of how he came to write it. "I made that blue up in '38," Waters said. "I made it on about the eighth of October, '38. . . . I was fixin' a puncture on a car. I had been mistreated by a girl, it was just running in my mind to sing that song. . . . Well, I just felt blue, and the song fell into my mind and it come to me just like that and I started singing." Then Lomax, who knew of the Robert Johnson recording of a similar tune called "Walking Blues," asked Waters if there were any other blues songs that used the same tune. "There's been some blues played like that," Waters replied. "This song comes from the cotton field and a boy once put a record out—Robert Johnson. He put it out as named 'Walking Blues.'. . . I heard the tune before I heard it on the record. I learned it from Son House. That's a boy who could pick a guitar."[7]

In this brief passage, Waters offers five accounts of the origin of "Country Blues." At first, Waters asserts his own active authorship, saying he "made it" on a specific date under specific conditions. Then Waters expresses the "passive" explanation of authorship as received knowledge—not unlike Harriet Beecher Stowe's authorship of *Uncle Tom's Cabin*—that "it come to me just like that." After Lomax raises the question of Johnson's influence, Waters, without shame, misgivings, or trepidation, says that he heard a version of that song by Johnson, but that his mentor Son House taught it to him. Most significantly, Waters declares in the middle of that complex genealogy that "this song comes from the cotton field."

What might seem to some observers a tangle of contradictions might instead be an important complication. Waters had no problem stating, believing, and defending all five accounts of the origin of "Country Blues." To Waters, one explanation did not cancel out the others. Blues logic is neither linear nor Boolean. Blues ideology is not invested in some abstract notion of "progress" and thus does not celebrate the Revolutionary for its own sake. The blues compositional ethic is complex and synergistic, relying on simultaneously exploring and extending the common elements of the tradition. Blues artists are rewarded for punctuation within collaboration, distinction within a community, and an ability to touch a body of signs shared among all members of an audience. While Muddy Waters used the metaphor "from the cotton field," other artists say that inspiration comes to them "from the air." They call their songs "air music." The elements and themes float and flow, ready for any skilled and practiced performer to borrow and put to use. Each performer can revise the common tropes and expand the cultural commons. As blues scholar David Evans explains, blues composition relies on concepts to which we usually assign the terms tradition, inspiration, and improvisation. But blues singers do not see these as separate and distinct factors. They are one process. Because blues composers do not ask themselves what is particularly traditional about their tradition, they do not feel bound to tradition. Because they do not isolate a process called "improvisation," they feel no compulsion to improvise every time they play a particular song. Blues artists often express "newness" passively, as if the original or improvisatory elements "just came" to them from the air or the cotton field.[8]

Whether the basis of the song came from the cotton field or not, Johnson recorded it before either House or Waters. But were all of these recordings really of the "same" song? Johnson's 1937 recording of "Walking Blues" and Waters's 1941 "Country Blues" share many qualities. The verse-and-chorus structures of both songs (ABAB) are identical, but that structure is common if not standard for country blues songs. Both songs employ similar guitar solos using a bottleneck slide. And as music scholar John Cowley has demonstrated, they both share a common ancestor in Son House's "My Black Mama," which House sometimes called "Walking Blues."[9]

Many of the lyrics of Johnson's "Walking Blues" also resemble those of Waters's "Country Blues." Both songs feature the classic blues line "I've been mistreated baby, and I don't mind dying." Consider Johnson's first two verses:

> *I woke up this morning, feeling round for my shoes*
> *Tell everybody I got these walking blues*
> *Woke up this morning, feeling round, oh, for my shoes*
> *But you know about that, I got these old walking blues.*
>
> *Lord, I feel like blowing my old lonesome home*
> *Got up this morning now, Bernice was gone*
> *Lord I feel like blowing my old lonesome home*
> *Well I got up this morning, all I had was gone.*[10]

And here are the first two verses to Waters's version:

> *Ah, it gets later on in the evening, child. I feel like, like blowing my home*
> *I woke up this morning to find my, my little baby gone*
> *Later on in the evening man, man, I feel like, like blowing my home*
> *Well I woke up this morning baby, to find my little baby gone.*
>
> *Well now, some folks say the worried, worried blues ain't bad*
> *That's the miserablest feeling child I most, most ever had*
> *Some folks tell me man that the worried blues ain't bad*
> *Well that's the miserablest old feeling, honey now, ooh now gal, I most ever had.*[11]

Both songs deal with the same story. The singer's love has left him, so he feels like "blowing" his home and he doesn't mind dying. A legal claim to authorship over these lyrics would require an argument that one person deserves monopoly control over these very common expressions of an almost universal experience: frustration and resignation over a failed love affair. The "feel" of these two versions is very distinct. Waters, for instance, syncopates his lyric delivery in "Country Blues" much more than Johnson does in "Walking Blues."

Waters recorded versions of this song several more times in his career, each time changing the order of certain stanzas. Each version tells the same story, contains a slide solo, and shares the verse structure. Yet each is a very different song. Waters's 1948 version "I Feel Like Going Home," is electrified, up-tempo, and "rocks" more than his acoustic version that Lomax recorded. Waters's voice lacks the gravelly growl of the earlier versions. It occasionally almost squeals—more like Bobby Blue Bland than Robert Johnson or Son House—yet distinctly Muddy Waters. The 1948 hit version established Waters's "signature" sound, which no artist, black or white, American or British, would ever capture or imitate. For Waters, originality and authenticity were not in the lyrics or chord sequence. They were in his voice, his passion, his presentation, his motion. There was no reason for Waters to seek a legally granted monopoly over his style. Muddy Waters already enjoyed a natural monopoly.

These are aesthetic and ethical issues more than legal ones. What if Robert Johnson—had he lived—had filed suit against Muddy Waters over composer's rights for "Walking Blues"? Waters's best defense might have been that the elements of both songs came "from the cotton field" and were thus already part of the public domain long before Johnson recorded his version. Yet these same issues of style and presentation mark the dispute over Willie Dixon's composition and Muddy Waters's recording of "You Need Love" and Led Zeppelin's "Whole Lotta Love." Dixon and Led Zeppelin never met in a courtroom. The case was settled for undisclosed terms after two years of negotiation. Both songs do share some lyrics, but they both take elements from the deep well of the blues tradition. What's more, the two songs have completely different "feels." They do different work, speak to different conditions, and strike different audiences in different ways. They are very different songs. Dixon suffered greatly during his career at the hands of unscrupulous and exploitative handlers who manipulated the copyright laws to deny him long-term rewards for his brilliant work. But Dixon did not "own" the blues aesthetic as expressed through "You Need Love" any more than Robert Johnson "owned" the elements of "Walking Blues." If the case had made it to trial, the results would have been impossible to predict. However, in an era and industry that have grown accustomed to "property talk," lawsuits have become frequent tools for resolving disputes over authorship, ownership, and originality.

While ownership is a sloppy and almost undefinable quality in the blues tradition, there is a real and significant claim to originality in blues music. Blues originality is just very different from the standard European model. Originality in the blues is performance-based. Pen and paper never enter the equation unless the song is considered for recording and distribution. In his 1978 ethnographic study *Blues from the Delta*, folklorist William Ferris argues that blues artists have a notion of authorship and originality that lies not in the raw materials employed for the composition, but in the style and presentation. Ferris states that many blues singers simultaneously admit learning a particular song from another artist and claim authorship for it. Some artists even claim authorship of classic folk ballads like "John Henry." Ferris exemplifies this point through an interview with blues and gospel singer Sonny Matthews:

> I'll hear somebody else sing it and then I'll put my words like I want them in there. . . . I just sing it in my voice and put the words in there like I want them. Them my words there. I spaced them words like that on a contention that so many peoples singing alike, till you know that's just about to put a ruination on the gospel singing in this part. So many peoples is trying to imitate other folks, you know. . . . I will sing their songs, but I will put the words my way.

Ferris also quotes Arthur Lee Williams of Birdie, Mississippi, on the process of blues composition: "You sit down and hum to yourself. You try to see if that fits and if that don't work, you hum you something else. And then too you may pick out a verse from some other song and switch it around a little bit." The blues tradition values "originality" without a confining sense of "ownership." In the blues tradition, what is original is the "value-added" aspect of a work, usually delivered through performance.[12]

Creativity and composition ethics within the blues tradition derive from West African antecedents. While the cultures of West Africa are diverse and complicated, some cultural forms helped form a "cultural commons" that exists today across the Atlantic, linking many of those in the West African diaspora to those on the continent through a web of familiar signs and tropes. Anthropologists and musicologists have emphasized the importance of the "circle" as the site of both creativity and community in African cultures. The music, lyrics, and dance that emanate from the circle often reflect these attributes: rhythmic complexity and syncopation; individual improvisation and stylization; call-and-response; engagement between individuals and the community at large; commentary in the form of satire, parody, or boastful competition; and a sense of group consciousness. The tension between individual improvisation and communal flow produces and celebrates both a balance between individuals and the community and a safe space for individual expression of daring and excellence. Each value depends on the other. The community rewards both individual "stylization" and mastery of a canon. While other traditions around the world employ these dynamics as well, West African aesthetic principles have had a clear and profound effect on American culture through music, dance, prose, poetry, and humor. The "shape" of West African creativity is a circle, not a line.[13]

This has created a cultural value system among West African-derived traditions that differs from the "progressive" value system that emanates from the European artistic tradition and informs European and American copyright law.[14] This does not mean that American copyright law, as designed and employed through most of American history, conflicts with African principles of expression. In fact, when a copyright system is loose and balanced, it can amplify the positive elements of West African aesthetic tradition. In principle, copyright law does not prevent artists from taking from the "commons." It supports the idea that new artists build upon the works of others. It rewards improvisation within a tradition. But originally, copyright regulated only the proliferation of physical and complete copies. Now copyright regulates (but does not necessarily forbid) performance, transformative works, slight and oblique reference, and even access. And copyrights used to expire on definite dates, thus constantly enriching the public domain with new material. Now, copyright terms last far beyond most people's life span, and Congress keeps extending them, making copyright protection virtually perpetual. American copyright as it has been corrupted at the turn of the twenty-first century clearly conflicts with the aesthetic principles of West African music and dance. Yet American copyright regulates West African musical styles more than ever.

Very little American popular music since 1956 has not been influenced by the blues tradition. Therefore a preponderance of the musical products on the American market since 1956 have emerged from the performance-based blues aesthetic. Simultaneously, the stakes for control of publishing and recording (known as "mechanical") rights have climbed exponentially as the record business has assumed a major place in the American economy. And as the companies that control and reproduce the products that carry this creative work have consolidated and grown more powerful, the legal and commercial balance of the copyright system has shifted to heavily favor established works. These shifts have handcuffed newer artists who want to participate in the chain of creativity.

POISONING THE WELL

Just before the Beatles broke up, lead guitarist George Harrison was busy composing songs for his first solo album, *All Things Must Pass*. Harrison and his new band, which included keyboard player Billy Preston, were playing a concert in Copenhagen, Denmark, in 1970. During a backstage press conference, Harrison slipped away, grabbed an acoustic guitar, and started playing around with simple chord structures. He eased into a pattern of alternating a minor II chord with a major V chord. Then he chanted the words "Hallelujah" and "Hare Krishna" over the chords. Soon other members of his band and entourage gathered around him, joining in on the song in four-part harmony. Between choruses of "Hallelujah" and "Hare Krishna" Harrison improvised some verses that included lyrics such as "My Sweet Lord," "Dear, dear Lord," and "I really want to see you; I really want to be with you." Over the next few weeks, Harrison and Preston returned to that jam, composing and recording the entire text of what became Harrison's first solo hit, "My Sweet Lord."[15]

After the song gained wide acclaim and broad distribution, a band called the Belmonts recorded a tongue-in-cheek version of "My Sweet Lord" that appended the chorus lyrics from the 1962 Chiffons tune

"He's So Fine," composed by Ronald Mack and produced by Phil Spector, to the Harrison hit. The similarities between "My Sweet Lord" and "He's So Fine" were not lost on Bright Tunes Music Corporation either. Bright Tunes was the publishing company that controlled the rights to "He's So Fine." Bright Tunes filed suit against Harrison, and the case went to trial in 1976. In his decision, the district judge closely examined the building blocks of both songs. "He's So Fine" consists of two "motifs," Judge Richard Owen concluded. The first motif (A) is the array of notes "sol-me-re." The second motif (B) is the phrase "sol-la-do-la-do." Owen granted that standing alone neither of these motifs is novel enough to qualify for protection.

However, what matters is not the building blocks themselves, but their arrangement and order within the greater structure. "He's So Fine" contains the pattern A-A-A-A-B-B-B-B. The pattern of four repetitions of A followed by four repetitions of B is "a highly unique pattern," Owen ruled. Then, examining "My Sweet Lord," Owen stated that the Harrison song used the same motif A four times, and then motif B three times. In place of the fourth repetition of B, Harrison employed a transitional passage (T) of the same length as B. "My Sweet Lord" goes A-A-A-A-B-B-B-T. In both songs, the composers used a slippery "grace note" in the fourth refrain of B (or in the substituted transitional phrase T, in the case of "My Sweet Lord"). In addition, Owen wrote, "the harmonies of both songs are identical." Harrison's expert witnesses asserted that the differences between the songs mattered more than the similarities. They argued that the lyrics, the syllabic patterns, and syncopations distinguished each song. For instance, the highly meaningful terms "Hallelujah" and "Hare Krishna" in "My Sweet Lord" replace the nonsense word and rhythmic placeholder "dulang" from "He's So Fine."[16]

In stark contrast to the complex and nuanced "web of expression" analysis that Judge Learned Hand prescribed for motion picture cases concerning derivative works, federal courts ask two questions to determine whether a song infringes on the copyright for an earlier song. The plaintiff must show that the second composer had access to the first song and that the second song shows "substantial similarity" to the first. Similarity without access, the result of a random coincidence, would not infringe. There are only eight notes in a major scale, after all. Accidents do happen. The need to establish access necessarily protects hits better than obscure songs. On the other hand, hits are more likely

to stick in people's minds, more likely to flow through musical communities as influences and inspirations, and more likely to add elements to the musical "well."[17]

George Harrison went to the well once too often. He was raised in
the blues tradition, as embodied by the English working class in the
1950s and 1960s. He and his pals spent their youth memorizing riffs
from Chuck Berry, Muddy Waters, and Buddy Holly records. American
rhythm and blues were irresistible sources of powerful stories and emotions, and influenced everything Harrison and his peers did. Both Harrison and Preston testified vehemently that neither one of them considered "He's So Fine" an inspiration for "My Sweet Lord." The Chiffons
song never entered their minds, they said. But "He's So Fine" topped
the pop music chart in the United States for five weeks in the summer
of 1963. It reached the number 12 spot in England during that same
time—a summer when the top song on the British pop charts belonged
to the Beatles. Both Preston in the United States and Harrison in England had ample access to the Chiffons' recording. They both knew of the
song, but neither consciously appealed to it as a source for "My Sweet
Lord." Judge Owen agreed: "Seeking the wellsprings of musical composition—why a composer chooses the succession of notes and the harmonies he does—whether it be George Harrison or Richard Wagner is
a fascinating inquiry. It is apparent from the extensive colloquy between
the Court and Harrison covering forty pages in the transcript that neither Harrison nor Preston were conscious of the fact that they were uti-
lizing the 'He's So Fine' theme. However, they in fact were, for it is perfectly obvious to the listener that in musical terms, the two songs are
virtually identical except for one phrase." Then, precipitously employing the passive voice, Owen leapt to a conclusion that poisoned the well
for subsequent artists:

> What happened? I conclude that the composer, in seeking musical ma-
> terials to clothe his thoughts, was working with various possibilities.
> As he tried this possibility and that, there came to the surface of his
> mind a particular combination that pleased him as being one he felt
> would be appealing to a prospective listener; in other words, that this
> combination of sounds would work. Why? Because his subconscious
> knew it already had worked in a song his conscious mind did not re-
> member. Having arrived at this pleasing combination of sounds, the
> recording was made, the lead sheet prepared for copyright and the

song became an enormous success. Did Harrison deliberately use the music of "He's So Fine?" I do not believe he did so deliberately. Nevertheless, it is clear that "My Sweet Lord" is the very same song as "He's So Fine" with different words, and Harrison had access to "He's So Fine." This is, under the law, infringement of copyright, and is no less so even though subconsciously accomplished.[18]

Under this standard, which makes "subconscious" influence illicit, something an artist must struggle to avoid, Muddy Waters would have had great difficulty keeping up with who had recorded and marketed particular arrangements that were considered common property in the Mississippi Delta, music that came "from the cotton field," or from the well of tradition. The standard used in the Harrison case puts a heavy burden on those who snatch a groove out of the air and insert it as one part of a complex creative process.

Over the next twelve years, emboldened by the Harrison suit, composers and publishing companies that retained rights to classic American songs considered pursuing legal action against more recent songwriters. In 1981, the company that owned the rights to the 1928 Gus Kahn and Walter Donaldson standard "Makin' Whoopee" filed suit against Yoko Ono, collaborator and spouse of former Beatle John Lennon, for her song "I'm Your Angel" on the 1981 album *Double Fantasy*. Jazz pianist Keith Jarrett pursued action against Steely Dan songwriters Donald Fagen and Walter Becker for jazz-tinged cuts from their album *Gaucho*. Actions such as these did nothing to promote originality and new music. In fact, the publicity about such suits probably retarded creativity by generating an aura of fear and trepidation.[19]

Then, in 1988, another artist who "went to the well" of the American rhythm and blues tradition won a major case that was strikingly similar to the Harrison ordeal. Only this time, the songwriter in question, John Fogerty, had written both the original song and the later one. Fogerty was accused of copying from himself. Fogerty had been the leader, driving force behind, and chief songwriter of the successful 1960s country-blues-rock band Creedence Clearwater Revival. Like many young and naive songwriters, including Willie Dixon, Fogerty had signed a contract earlier in his career that granted all rights to his songs to a publishing company, Jondora, which was owned by Fantasy Records. After Fogerty split with his band and Fantasy in the early 1970s, he refused to play hits from his old catalogue because he resented the performance royalties flowing to Fantasy and its president, Saul Zaentz. Those years of bitterness pushed Fogerty out of the rock spotlight. His refusal to play his old songs disconnected Fogerty from his fans. Then, in 1985, Fogerty released his "comeback" album, *Centerfield*. The album yielded a number of hits that generated airplay and sales, including "Rock and Roll Girls," which shares a chord pattern and beat with classics such as Ritchie Valens's "La Bamba" and the Isley Brothers' "Twist and Shout," and the title cut "Centerfield," which quotes a line from Chuck Berry's song "Brown-Eyed Handsome Man," signifying that the album was just the latest link in the rhythm and blues chain. However, two of the songs on the album seemed to be direct attacks on Fogerty's nemesis, Fantasy president Zaentz. "Mr. Greed, why you gotta own everything that you see? Mr. Greed, why you put a chain on everybody livin' free?" Fogerty sang on the song "Mr. Greed." And the final song on the album was called "Zanz Kan't Danz." The refrain includes the line "but he'll steal your money."[20]

Zaentz filed suit. But he had found a stronger claim than defamation or libel on which to attack Fogerty. Zaentz argued that the opening song on *Centerfield*, "The Old Man down the Road," contains a bass line, rhythm, and guitar bridge that are similar to those of the 1970 Creedence Clearwater Revival hit "Run through the Jungle." While Fogerty had written "Run through the Jungle," Zaentz still owned the rights to it. During the jury trial in San Francisco, both sides called a series of musicologists to discuss influence and originality in music. Then Fogerty took the stand with his guitar in hand. Over a day and a half, Fogerty played for the jury such songs as "Proud Mary," "Down on the Corner," and "Fortunate Son" to explain his creative process. Most importantly, Fogerty played tapes of old Howlin' Wolf and Bo Diddley songs, then picked up his guitar and played a Bo Diddley song called "Bring It to Jerome," which contains riffs and rhythms similar to both "Run through the Jungle" and "The Old Man down the Road." The jury found for Fogerty after two hours of deliberation.[21]

The Harrison and Fogerty cases show that the case law concerning the reuse of tropes and elements from older songs makes little or no space for performance-based models of originality—contributions of style or delivery. Judges such as Owen in the Harrison case have tried to employ the structuralist reading method that Judge Learned Hand developed (although Owen's opinion seems to owe something to Freud as well). But these cases have not yielded anything close to a simple or clear standard for determining whether one song in the blues tradition infringes on another. The ruling in the Harrison case seemed to bend in favor of older composers, putting the burden of clearing influences on newer songwriters. Yet the judgment in the Fogerty case seemed to grant "Creedence" to the notion that songwriters should be allowed to draw from the blues tradition well.

The Harrison and Fogerty cases are concerned with how songwriters might trample on the composition rights—that is, the actual notes and structure—of an older song. But there are two other major rights in the "bundle" of rights that make up musical copyright: performance rights and mechanical rights. Performance rights concern public concerts, radio play, jukebox play, and other media exhibitions. Performance rights are usually licensed—and royalties collected—through consortiums such as the American Society of Composers, Authors, and Publishers (ASCAP) and Broadcast Music, Inc. (BMI). Mechanical rights are the rights to reproduce particular recordings of the song or album. Before the 1980s, infringement suits that dealt with mechanical rights generally concerned large-scale pirating of records and tapes. Suits over composition rights dealt with the re-use of melody, harmony, or lyrics.[22]

However, digital technology and the rise of urban hip-hop culture complicated that dichotomy. Rap does not use melody and harmony in the same ways that other forms of music do. In fact, rap artists often "sample" bits of others' melody and harmony, and use those "samples" as part of a rhythm track, completely transforming and recycling those pieces of music. Rap is Revolutionary because it did not emerge directly from the American blues tradition. It is an example of and expression of "Afrodiasporic" black culture, derived in form and function from Caribbean music more than from American rhythm and blues.[23] However, in the United States, rap artists used whatever building blocks they found in their environment to construct an American rap tradition. So instead of playing similar riffs or melodies from other artists on their own instruments, early rap composers weaved samples from familiar songs into a new montage of sound. By the early 1990s copyright cases concerning mechanical rights intersected with the unstable principles of composition rights.

FEAR OF A SAMPLING PLANET: HOW RAP BUM-RUSHED COPYRIGHT LAW

Over the raunchy, driving Jimmy Page guitar chords of the Led Zeppelin song "Kashmir," Philadelphia rapper Schoolly D bellows the words "Way way down in the jungle deep"—signature of the African American folk poem "Signifying Monkey." In the traditional poem, the trickster monkey uses his wits and his command of diction to outsmart a more powerful adversary. The "Signifying Monkey" has appeared in various forms in blues recordings, folktale ethnographies, the poetry of Larry Neal, and the blacksploitation film *Dolomite*. Only this time, the trickster tale turns up as the lyrics to the song "Signifying Rapper" on Schoolly D's 1988 album *Smoke Some Kill*. Jimmy Page did not join D in the recording studio. Nor did Page or Led Zeppelin garner any credit on the label of *Smoke Some Kill*. But the contribution—and the message—is unmistakable. Schoolly D is "signifying" on Led Zeppelin, a more powerful cultural force than he is. Among the raw materials available to creative black youth in the deindustrialized Reagan-era cities were piles of warped vinyl, scraps of sounds. Pretentions to "authenticity" seemed silly. "Credit," in all its various meanings, was not forthcoming to black youth or black culture. Why should they give it when they weren't receiving it? Led Zeppelin did not "credit" the blues masters as often as they could have, so why should Schoolly D do anything but reciprocate? Yet by rapping an updated and unexpurgated version of an African American folktale, Schoolly D was proclaiming his connection to something that was once "real," by constructing a musical work that felt nothing like "real" music. Repeating and reusing the guitar riff from "Kashmir" was a transgressive and disrespectful act—a "dis" of Led Zeppelin and the culture that produced, rewarded, and honored Led Zeppelin.[24]

Schoolly D released "Signifying Rapper" a decade after rap first attracted the attention of young people and music executives around the world. The first rap record to attract radio play and widespread sales, the Sugarhill Gang's "Rapper's Delight" (1979), rode the thumping instrumental track from Chic's "Good Times," a disco hit that also served as the backing track for many free-form rap songs of the 1970s. From the late 1970s through the early 1990s, most rap songs adhered to and improved on the formula popularized by "Rapper's Delight," spoken rhymes punctuating a background montage constructed from unauthorized pieces of previously recorded music. The expansion of the market for rap music was phenomenal. In 1987, rap records represented 11.6 percent of all the music sales in the United States. By 1990, rap was 18.3 percent of the music business.[25]

Rap's rise from an urban hobby to a major industry rocked the status quo of not only the music industry, but the legal world as well. Since the late 1970s, rap artists have pushed the boundaries of free expression with sexually explicit lyrics and descriptions of violence by and against law enforcers. They have raised questions about society's power structures from the ghettos to the Gallerias. In many cases, legal and societal traditions had no way to deal with these fresh and strong sentiments that drove through America in an open jeep, powered by a heavy beat.

That's what happened when an entrenched and exciting hip-hop tradition, sampling, energized by digital technology, encroached upon one of the most ambiguous areas of the American legal tradition: American copyright law. Complicating the clash, the concept of copyright has been deeply entrenched in western literary tradition for centuries, but does not play the same role in African, Caribbean, or African American oral traditions. It's far too simple and inaccurate to declare that copyrighting has been a white thing; sampling, borrowing, or quoting has been a black thing. The turmoil that rap has created in copyright law is more complex than just a clash of stereotypically opposed cultures. It's not just a case of mistrust and misunderstanding. Rap—for a moment—revealed gaping flaws in the premises of how copyright law gets applied to music and shown the law to be inadequate for emerging communication technologies, techniques, and aesthetics.

The tension in the law is not between urban lower class and corporate überclass. It's not between black artists and white record executives. It's not always a result of conflicts between white songwriters and the black composers who sample them. It is in fact a struggle between the established entities in the music business and those trying to get established. It is a conflict between old and new. As the market for rap and the industry that supports it grew and matured through the 1980s and 1990s, the law shifted considerably in favor of established artists and companies, and against emerging ones. So by the late 1990s, rap artists without the support of a major record company and its lawyers, without a large pool of money to pay license fees for samples, had a choice: either don't sample or don't market new music. Copyright law is designed to forbid the unauthorized copying or performance of another's work. Authorization means licensing. Licensing means fees. Violations bring lawsuits. Lawsuits bring settlements. But the practice of digital sampling, having gained access to the airwaves and record stores less than two decades ago, is relatively new to the music business and its lawyers. For the longest time, no one seemed to be able to agree on a fair price for licensing samples. No one seemed to know the best way to structure the fees. No one seemed to know exactly how existing statutes and case law would apply to alleged violations of musical copyrights. And before 1991, no one had pursued a sampling case through to a judicial ruling.[26]

Yet entertainment lawyers, alarmed over these and other issues, reacted with varying degrees of anger and concern. Juan Carlos Thom, a Los Angeles lawyer, musician, playwright, and actor, wrote in 1988:

> Digital sampling is a pirate's dream come true and a nightmare for all the artists, musicians, engineers and record manufacturers. Federal courts must update their view of piracy and interpretation of the [Copyright] Act to meet the sophistication of digital technology. Sounds are not ideas, but expressions, and therefore copyrighted works. . . . Unchecked digital sampling will present the incongruous result of a copyrighted work which is both protected by copyright but is also part of the public domain. By any standard, digital sampling is nothing but old fashioned piracy dressed in sleek new technology.[27]

As it emerged on the American music scene in the late 1970s, hip-hop music was composed of two layers of creative raw material. On the top was the vocalization, the rap itself. The rhymes were—and still are—in heavy dialect, urban African American, Caribbean, or Spanish, and were originally improvised. Rappers focus much of their efforts on boasting of their own abilities in arenas as diverse as sex, sports, money, knowledge, or rhyming ability. Sometimes raps serve to show disrespect for people in authority, or even other rappers. Many of the vocal habits of rappers are easily traced to the African American tradition of "toasting," or "playing the dozens," and ultimately to the African oral tradition of "signifying."[28] In addition, rap styles of the last twenty years bear significant resemblance and owe a heavy debt to scat singers like Cab Calloway, rhythm and blues performers like Otis Redding, and rock precursors like Bo Diddley. A more direct debt should be paid to James Brown, Isaac Hayes, George Clinton, and Muhammad Ali.[29]

Underlying the rap vocal tracks is the bed of music. Because the art was originally performed and perfected by disk jockeys, the rhythms and melodies of the tunes were essentially lifted from records that were popular dance themes at the time. So while the oral traditions of dissing and signifying can be easily linked, the vinyl traditions are of more obscure lineage.[30] Early DJs scratched and sampled whatever records they had, and listened specifically for funky breaks, or at least funny combinations. They fused a mishmash mosaic of samples that would confound anybody trying to assemble a simple ethnic genealogy for the birth and growth of rap.[31]

What developed in rap in the 1970s and 1980s has been compared to what happened to jazz in the 1940s and 1950s, when Dizzy Gillespie and Charlie Parker took it higher by cutting up and improvising on top of stale standards like "I Got Rhythm" and "How High the Moon."[32] If we could trace the tradition of borrowing other people's music, making it one's own, and improvising on top of it, back through African American musical history to Africa, a simple thesis would emerge: The rap on sampling would be that American laws don't deal with African traditions. The history, as we have seen with blues music, is not that simple. In Africa, music and poetry are not simply considered community property. Some cultural anthropologists have claimed that authorship and composition hold little or no value in African societies, but this is an oversimplified and ethnocentric notion.[33]

Instead, it is easier, and perhaps more accurate, to trace this tradition back along two lines: one through mid-century American rhythm and blues and jazz, and the other through more recent immigrant influences from the Caribbean islands. Caribbean islanders, somewhat freer of the special social constraints that American blacks felt, had the ability to build and control their own music industry. They also had the benefit of choosing the best of American, British, and African influences to blend into their music. And in Jamaica, more than in most cultures, the concept of music as community property is important to the development of commercially viable art forms.[34] Dick Hebdige, a music scholar who specializes in how Caribbean music has affected world music in general, claims that "versioning," the repeated borrowing and recycling of a popular standard, is the key to not only reggae, but all African American and Caribbean music. Hebdige writes that often when a reggae record is released, hundreds of dif-ferent versions of the same rhythm or melody will be released in the subsequent weeks. Every new version will slightly modify the original tune.[35]

In the mid-1970s, ska and reggae producers invented a new way to version. They began fading instrumental tracks in and out, playing bass off of vocals, slowing down the rhythm, and throwing in echoes. They called this process "dubbing." It involved different raw materials than sampling, but the same production process.[36] Hebdige writes that while the studio environment spawned dubbing, the dance hall scene incubated the vocal precursor to American rap: the DJ talk-over.[37]

There is a recent and clear link between New York hip-hop in the 1970s and Jamaican "versioning" in the 1960s. His name is Kool Herc.[38] Kool Herc came to the Bronx from Jamaica in 1967. On his native island, he had heard "talk-over" DJs and knew the scat-singing techniques of some of the ska and reggae artists who had churned out international hits during the 1960s.[39] Hebdige explains how Kool Herc imported almost all the necessary precursors to modern rap music: By 1973 Herc owned the loudest and most powerful sound system in his neighborhood. But when he deejayed at house parties Herc found that the New York African American crowd would not dance to reggae or other Caribbean beats. So Herc began talking over the Latin-tinged funk that held broad, multiethnic appeal in the Bronx. Gradually, he developed a popular and recognizable style. Herc began buying records for the instrumental breaks rather than for the whole track.[40] Herc became one of the first—if not the first—to discover that he could sample the hearts out of a pile of vinyl and give a room full of people plenty to taste.[41]

Before too long, other New York DJs picked up on the popularity of Herc's style. The first changes they made were to incorporate classic rhythm and blues riffs and breaks, adding the thrill of recognition to the groove, "scratching" a record to create a new rhythm track, and rapping in an American dialect full of street slang.[42] To complement the linkage of American sampling with Caribbean versioning, there have been suggestions that the vocal styles of American rap may have thicker Caribbean roots than previously thought. Music critic Daisann McLane argues that rap's strongest and most obvious musical and ideological links are not to Africa but to the West Indies and the Afro-Caribbean styles of calypso and reggae. Calypso lyrical style, for instance, overflows with double entendres, verbal duels, and playful boasts. These themes are common in American rap lyrics.[43]

In American popular music, versioning or borrowing is not unheard of, although it has traditionally been white artists versioning the work of black artists. The Beach Boys lifted riffs from Chuck Berry that dominated their songs to the same extent that Van Halen's "Jamie's Crying" guitar riff stands alone as the backing track to Tone Loc's "Wild Thing."[44] The traditional New Orleans rhythm and blues song "Stagger Lee" (which in its original form is called "Stack-o-Lee"), is one American song that has been versioned so many times that it has served as almost a signature song for New Orleans music. Stagger was a bad man, into gambling, drinking, and fighting. His tales of gluttony and bad luck have taken on almost as many plots as voices. It can still be heard covered in live music clubs large and small all over the United States.[45]

Sampling, as opposed to simply imitating, became a big issue in American music after digital technology became cheap and easily available and its products became immensely popular.[46] Digital sampling is a process by which sounds are converted into binary units readable by a computer. A digital converter measures the tone and intensity of a sound and assigns it a corresponding voltage. The digital code is then stored in a computer memory bank, or a tape or disc, and can be retrieved and manipulated electronically.[47]

But why do rap artists sample in the first place? What meanings are they imparting? Some songs grab bits and pieces of different pop culture signposts, while others, such as Tone Loc's "Wild Thing" or Hammer's "U Can't Touch This," which lays lyrics upon a backing track made up almost entirely of Rick James's "Super Freak" instrumentals, hardly stand alone as songs, but are truly "versions" of someone else's hits.[48] Sometimes, as with Schoolly D's sampling of Led Zeppelin's "Kashmir" for his song "Signifying Rapper," it can be a political act—a way of crossing the system, challenging expectations, or confronting the status quo. Often, the choice of the sample is an expression of appreciation, debt, or influence. Other times it's just a matter of having some fun or searching for the right ambient sound, tone, or feel. Certainly Rick James's funky hits of the late 1970s and early 1980s influenced not only artists of the 1990s but their audiences. Sampling is a way an artist declares, "Hey, I dug this, too." It helps form a direct connection with listeners, the same way a moviemaker might throw in a Motown hit in a soundtrack. By the early 1990s, at least 180 recordings by more than 120 artists contained samples by some of funk godfather George Clinton's P-Funk school, which included 1970s bands Funkadelic, Parliament, and various other bands headed by Clinton or his bassist, Bootsy Collins.[49] It's tough to say whether a new song that relies almost completely on some older hit riffs can achieve financial success on its own merits. Two of the best-selling rap hits are entirely dependent on massively danceable older songs and are, sadly, lyrically limited. They are Hammer's "U Can't Touch This" and Vanilla Ice's 1990 single "Ice Ice Baby," which was a stiff and meaningless rap over the backing track to the 1982 David Bowie–Queen hit "Under Pressure."[50] *Village Voice* music critic Greg Tate explained the aesthetic value of sampling: "Music belongs to the people, and sampling isn't a copycat act but a form of reanimation. Sampling in hip-hop is the digitized version of hip-hop DJing, an archival project and an art form unto itself. Hip-hop is ancestor worship."[51]

Sampling helps forge a "discursive community" among music fans. Rap music first made that connection to white audiences—and thus expanded the discursive community exponentially—in 1986, when Run DMC released its version of the 1977 Aerosmith song, "Walk This Way."[52] Within the African American discursive community, rap songs serve, in historian George Lipsitz's words, as "repositories of social memory."[53] Lipsitz particularly credits the matrix of cultural signs highlighted by sampling and realistic lyrics that document the struggles of inner-city life. Sampling can be transgressive or appreciative, humorous or serious. It gives a song another level of meaning, another plane of communication among the artist, previous artists, and the audience.

Digital sampling also had a powerful democratizing effect on American popular music. All a young composer needed was a thick stack of vinyl albums, a $2,000 sampler, a microphone, and a tape deck, and she could make fresh and powerful music. She could make people dance, laugh, and sing along. She might, under the right conditions, be able to make money from the practice. As critic John Leland wrote in *Spin*: "The digital sampling device has changed not only the sound of pop music, but also the mythology. It has done what punk rock threatened to do: made everybody into a potential musician, bridged the gap between performer and audience."[54]

Clearly, sampling as an American expression was raised in the Bronx, but was probably born in the Caribbean. Its aesthetic appeal is deeply embedded in African American and Afro-Caribbean culture, if not for most of this half century, then certainly over the last twenty-five years. More significantly, for a while in the late 1980s, it looked as if transgressive sampling was not going to go away. It made too much money and was too important to the meaning and message of rap. During the first decade of rap, the legal questions surrounding sampling grew more troublesome for both artists and labels as rap became more popular and the economic stakes rose. Sampling seemed to undermine the very definitions of "work," "author," and "original"—terms on which copyright law rests. Consider a song with a backing musical track filled with bits and pieces of other works, others' applications of skill, labor, and judgment. There's a Keith Richards guitar riff here and there. We hear Bootsy Collins's thumb-picked and hand-slapped bass filling in the bottom. The rhythm is kept constant through an electronic drum machine. We hear the occasional moan of a Staple Singer or a shout of James Brown. The new work may exist as an individual work per se. The new, composite, mosaic work is assembled from these samples through an independent application of skill, labor, and judgment. Is each of these samples a copyright infringement? If the artist asks for permission to sample the Keith Richards riff—which might be an expression of Chuck Berry's or Houndog Taylor's idea—does she admit that permission should have been sought for the bass line? How about the moans and shouts, which could easily be considered "signature sounds" and thus marketable qualities? If the artist, the assembler of the mosaic, had hired studio musicians to imitate these distinctive sounds, instead of splicing digital grafts onto a new tape, would she be lifting unprotected "ideas," instead of tangible products of actual skill, labor, and judgment? If a person recorded an entire song based upon the music to "The Boogie-Woogie Bugle Boy of Company B," and a court found the use of the score to be outside the domain of fair use, then the defendant would be expected to pay the appropriate penalty for violating the letter and spirit of the copyright law. But what if the defendant used only the notes and words of the "Boogie-Woogie" portion of the refrain, and repeated them throughout a song that had other creative elements in it? Has the right to the original "work" been infringed? Courts have varied in their rulings of how much one may take before a "work" has been violated. Legal scholars agree there is no clear guideline, and the text of the law simply does not deal with the issue.[55] After examining this confusion, David Sanjek, director of the Broadcast Music, Inc., archives, concluded that the rise of digital sampling had removed whatever claim musicians had to "an aura of autonomy and authenticity." Sanjek wrote: "If anyone with an available library of recordings, a grasp of recorded material history, and talent for ingenious collage can call themselves a creator of music, is it the case that the process and the product no longer possess the meaning once assigned to them?"[56]

In many sectors of the law, we would expect courts to clarify issues like these. Ideally, federal courts would slowly sift through the competing arguments and seek a balance that would ensure freedom for the emerging artists while protecting the risks and investments of established ones. But from 1978 through 1991, the courts were silent on most of these issues.

THE ILLIN' EFFECT: HOW COPYRIGHT BUM-RUSHED RAP

All was not well for the creative process before courts weighed in on sampling issues. Anarchy was not paradise. Artists also suffered because of the confusion the practice caused in the record business. Record companies were understandably risk averse. Because sampling raised so many questions, labels pushed their more successful acts to get permission for samples before releasing a record. The problem was that no one knew what to charge for a three-second sample. As a 1992 note in the *Harvard Law Review* stated: "Consequently, the music industry has responded with an ad-hoc, negotiated licensing approach to valuing music samples."[57] As industry leaders and lawyers, and older songwriters, grew more aware of the prevalence of sampling and of the potential monetary gain from challenging it, artists became more concerned with the potential costs of sampling. This certainly retarded the creative process. Artists chose to sample less-well-known works, works published or produced by their own companies and labels, or works with a lower licensing price. When the Beastie Boys wanted to sample the Beatles song "I'm Down," Michael Jackson informed them that he owned the rights to the song and denied them permission to use it. The Beastie Boys eventually opted against using that song.[58]

Until 1991, no one in the rap or licensing businesses knew what the guidelines for digital sampling were. This means that on any given day, an artist may have been ripped off by an overpriced licensing fee, or a publishing company may have gotten burned by charging too little for a sample that helped produce a top hit.[59] That's why several legal scholars in the late 1980s and early 1990s tried to formulate licensing systems based on the use, length, and type of sample. Still, the industry was waiting for a court to weigh in so there could be some predictability and stability in the system.[60]

Several sampling cases were settled out of court before December of 1991, postponing the inevitable guidance a judicial decision would bring. Nonetheless, the publicity surrounding these cases made older artists hungry to cash in on the potential sampling licensing market. A song that had ceased bringing in royalties decades ago could suddenly yield a big check. In 1991 Mark Volman and Howard Kaylan of the 1960s pop group the Turtles sued the rap trio De La Soul for using a twelve-second piece of the Turtles' song "You Showed Me" in the 1989 rap track "Transmitting Live from Mars." Volman and Kaylan sued for $2.5 million, but reached an out-of-court settlement for $1.7 million. De La Soul paid $141,666.67 per second to the Turtles for a sliver of a long-forgotten song.[61]

Then in December 1991 a federal judge issued a terse sixteen-hundred-word ruling that all but shut down the practice of unauthorized sampling in rap music. In August of 1991, Warner Brothers Records distributed an album released by a small record label called Cold Chillin' Records. The artist was a young New Jersey rapper named Biz Markie. The album was called *I Need a Haircut*. There was nothing particular, unique, or special about the album. It was pretty substandard fare for rap albums from the late 1980s and early 1990s. The rhymes were simple. The subject matter was juvenile. The production was pedestrian. The choice of samples was neither funny nor insightful. *I Need a Haircut* might have been a trivial footnote in rap history but for the second-to-last cut on the album: "Alone Again." For that song, Biz Markie took the first eight bars of the number one single of 1972, Gilbert O'Sullivan's "Alone Again (Naturally)." Markie used only about twenty seconds of piano chords from the original song, which he looped continually to construct the musical background of the song. O'Sullivan's song was a sappy ballad about family loss. Markie's song was about how the rapper received no respect as a performer back when he played in combos with old friends, but since he had become a solo performer his career had been satisfying. Markie's use of O'Sullivan's sample did not directly parody it, but it was essential to setting the minor-chord mood of Markie's tale of determination and self-sufficiency.[62]

So while Biz Markie's song did not "cut on" O'Sullivan's song, or revise O'Sullivan's song in a way that would replace it in the marketplace or even generate confusion for record buyers, O'Sullivan pursued the case with righteous indignation. O'Sullivan's attorney, Jody Pope, stated after the case ended that O'Sullivan would not allow his song to be used in a humorous context, and would license it to be used only in its complete, original form. Even though Markie had requested permission to use it, O'Sullivan failed to grant permission because the use did not maintain either the integrity or the original meaning of the song. Markie's attorneys launched two strategies for defense, neither particularly effective. The weaker was that O'Sullivan himself was not the copyright holder, and thus could not seek relief from the court. The fact that Markie's lawyers had mailed a tape of the song to O'Sullivan asking for permission (they received no reply) persuaded the judge that it was clear to everyone that O'Sullivan was the holder of the original copyright. The other defense was that everybody in the music industry was doing it. This did not score points with either the judge or others in the music industry. Biz Markie's lawyers did not claim that sampling in this context was fair use. They could have argued that only a small section of O'Sullivan's song contributed to a vastly different composition that did not compete with the original song in the marketplace. This fair use defense probably would not have swayed the judge either. But they didn't even attempt to mount one.[63]

O'Sullivan requested an injunction against further sale of the song and album. U.S. district judge Kevin Thomas Duffy gladly granted O'Sullivan his wish. Duffy wrote in terms loaded with hints of moral rights, natural rights, and property talk:

> "Thou shalt not steal" has been an admonition followed since the dawn of civilization. Unfortunately, in the modern world of business this admonition is not always followed. Indeed, the defendants in this action for copyright infringement would have this court believe that stealing is rampant in the music business and, for that reason, their conduct here should be excused. The conduct of the defendants herein, however, violates not only the Seventh Commandment, but also the copyright laws of this country. . . .
>
> . . . From all of the evidence produced in the hearing, it is clear that the defendants knew that they were violating the plaintiff's rights as well as the rights of others. Their only aim was to sell thousands upon thousands of records. This callous disregard for the law and for the rights of others requires not only the preliminary injunction sought by the plaintiff but also sterner measures.[64]

Duffy concluded by referring the case to a U.S. district attorney to consider criminal prosecution. What Duffy did not write is as important as what he did write. Duffy's ruling did not articulate any nuanced standard by which a song could be sampled, manipulated, or revised without permission. It left no "wiggle room" for fair use. It did not consider whether the new use affected the market of the original song in any way. It did not try to clarify how long a sample must be to qualify as an infringement. The fact that the sample in question was a mere twenty seconds did not bode well for fair use. Duffy's brevity clarified these issues by ignoring them: "how much?" and "for what purpose?" need not even be asked after Duffy's ruling. It was safe to assume that any sample of any duration used for any purpose must be cleared.

Soon after Duffy's ruling, Markie's attorneys realized they would not have much chance to win the case before Duffy. They settled. The record company agreed to remove the offending song from subsequent printings of the album, and O'Sullivan received monetary compensation. Reaction to Duffy's ruling was also extreme. One of O'Sullivan's lawyers declared an end to sampling: "Sampling is a euphemism that was developed by the music industry to mask what is obviously thievery. This represents the first judicial pronouncement that this practice is in fact theft." Mark Volman of the Turtles said, "Sampling is just a longer term for theft. Anybody who can honestly say sampling is some sort of creativity has never done anything creative." On the other side, Dan Chamas, an executive with the rap label Def American Records, warned that Duffy's ruling would "kill hip-hop music and culture."

While Chamas's fears were exaggerated, they were not unfounded. The case did not kill the music. It just changed it broadly and deeply. Rap music since 1991 has been marked by a severe decrease in the amount of sampling. Many groups record background music and then filter it during production so it sounds as if it has been sampled. Other groups—the well established—pay for and extensively credit all the sources of their samples. Many established songwriters—including Led Zeppelin—often refuse requests for samples. Others deny sampling requests if the new song tackles controversial subject matter like sex, drugs, or violence. What sampling did occur in the late 1990s was nontransgressive, nonthreatening, and too often clumsy and obvious. The signifying rapper had lost his voice. The 1991 ruling removed from rap music a whole level of communication and meaning that once played a part in the audience's reception to it. The Biz Markie case "stole the soul" from rap music.[65]

The death of tricky, playful, transgressive sampling occurred because courts and the industry misapplied stale, blunt, ethnocentric, and simplistic standards to fresh new methods of expression. The trend could have gone the other way. Courts and the music industry could have allowed for limited use of unauthorized samples if they had considered taking several tenets of fair use and free speech seriously—especially the question of whether the newer work detracts from the market of the original. In fact, as has been shown repeatedly, sampling often revives a market for an all but forgotten song or artist. The best example is the revival of Aerosmith since Run DMC's version of "Walk This Way" reminded young listeners of the power of the original song. Aerosmith, almost forgotten after a string of hits in the 1970s, collaborated on that project. But even an unauthorized use of the original song would have revived interest in Aerosmith, one of the most successful bands of both the 1970s and the 1990s.

Beyond fair use, courts and the record industry could have considered actually employing the idea-expression dichotomy in a new way. Music copyright has traditionally protected melody, sometimes harmony, almost never rhythm. Rhythm has been considered either too common or too unimportant to warrant protection.[66] But what actually happens when a rap producer injects a sample into a new medium is this: an expression of melody becomes a building block of rhythm. The claim that samples cease transmitting their original meanings—cease operating as expressions once they are taken out of context—is best expressed by Chuck D of Public Enemy, who sang:

> *Mail from the courts and jail*
> *Claim I stole the beats that I rail*
> *Look at how I'm living like*
> *And they're gonna check the mike, right? Sike*
> *Look how I'm livin' now, lower than low*
> *What a sucker know*
> *I found this mineral that I call a beat*
> *I paid zero*
> *I packed my load 'cause it's better than gold*
> *People don't ask the price but it's sold*
> *They say I sample but they should*

Sample this, my pit bull
We ain't goin' for this
They say I stole this
Can I get a witness? [67]

For Chuck D, a sample is a "mineral." It is raw material for a new composition. Sampling is a transformation: using an expression as an idea; using what was once melody as a beat, an element of rhythm. Sampling is not theft. It's recycling. If we define an expression by what it does, instead of what it did, it no longer counts as an expression (or that particular expression) in the new context. The expression does not do the same work in its new role. Context matters to meaning. An old expression is no longer the same expression, and not even the same idea, if the context changes radically.

There could be room for unauthorized sampling within American copyright law. It could and should be considered fair use. Digital samples are more often than not small portions of songs. These portions are being used in completely different ways in the new songs. Because they are not working in the same way as in the original song, they are inherently different from their sources. But most importantly, samples add value. They are pieces of language that generate new meanings in their new contexts. The new meanings are clear and distinct from their original meanings. A new song that samples an old song does not replace the old song in the marketplace. Often, it does the opposite. Despite all the panic digital sampling generated among legal experts in the late 1980s, sampling does not threaten the foundation of the law. In fact, if copyright law is to conform to its constitutional charge, to "promote the progress of science and useful arts," it should allow transgressive and satirical sampling without having to clear permission from original copyright owners. A looser system—and a broader definition of fair use—would encourage creativity. A tightly regulated system does nothing but squeeze new coins out of old music and intimidate emerging artists.

AS FUNNY AS THEY WANNA BE

There is social value in allowing transformative uses of copyrighted music without permission. The U.S. Supreme Court in 1994 articulated this principle in a landmark case that involved rap music. But it was not a case about sampling per se. It was the case that made America safe for parody.

Despite its brief tenure on the music charts, no group in the history of rap has been as controversial as the 2 Live Crew. A Broward County sheriff prosecuted a record store owner for selling the group's 1990 album *As Nasty As They Want to Be*, which relied on sexist and explicit lyrics and a complex montage of digital samples. Scholars and musicologists lined up both for and against the group and its leader, Luther Campbell. Within a year, Campbell had recast himself from nasty rapper and talented producer to a hero for the First Amendment. But it was 2 Live Crew's "nice" version of the album, *As Clean As They Want to Be* that brought the group to the U.S. Supreme Court. It contained a cut entitled "Pretty Woman" that relied heavily on the melody and guitar riff of Roy Orbison's 1964 hit "Oh, Pretty Woman." Orbison's publishing company, Acuff-Rose Music, Inc., had denied 2 Live Crew permission to parody the song. Campbell decided to do it anyway, and relied on a fair use defense when the lawsuit came. The U.S. district court granted a summary judgment in favor of 2 Live Crew, ruling that the new song was a parody of the original and that it was fair use of the material. But the Sixth Circuit Court of Appeals reversed that decision, arguing that 2 Live Crew took too much from the original and that it did so for blatantly commercial purposes. The U.S. Supreme Court ruled unanimously that the appeals court had not balanced all the factors that play into fair use. The Supreme Court reversed the appeals court and ruled in favor of Campbell and 2 Live Crew.[68]

Besides failing to understand the playfulness of parodying a canonical white pop song in a black rap context, the Sixth Circuit Court of Appeals showed that it's not always clear that a silly song that sounds like an old song is parodic. For a work to qualify as a parody, it must make some critical statement about the first work. It's not good enough to be just funny. The critical statement must be directed at the source text itself. If the second work does not clearly target the original work, the second work more likely operates as satire, not parody. For example, the Second Circuit Court of Appeals ruled in 1981 that a song from the off-Broadway erotic musical *Let My People Come* called "Cunnilingus Champion of Company C" was not a parody of the song "Boogie Woogie Bugle Boy of Company B." The court ruled that the infringing song did not make sufficient fun of the original, but instead satirized sexual mores in general. The court argued that the show's writers could have made the same satirical point by either revising a song in the public domain or writing an original song. There was no need to revise the "Bugle Boy" song.[69]

Courts have had a difficult time carving out the fair use exemption for parody. One of the first significant parody cases, *Loew's Inc. v. Columbia Broadcasting System*, had a stifling effect on parody. The plaintiff stopped comedian Jack Benny from televising a parody of the motion picture *Gaslight* in 1956. The court ruled that the parody could not be a form of criticism because of the defendant's strong profit motive.[70] Slowly, throughout the 1960s and 1970s, courts began recognizing that parody had cultural value. In 1964 *Mad Magazine* published parodic versions of the lyrics to some songs written by Irving Berlin. The Second Circuit rose above the decision that had stopped Jack Benny and held that *Mad* was not liable for infringement. The court stated that "we believe that parody and satire are deserving of substantial freedom— both as entertainment and as a form of social and literary criticism."[71] By the late 1970s, televised parody was a staple of American comedy. In 1978, the NBC show *Saturday Night Live* ran a parody of the pro–New York jingle "I Love New York." It was called "I Love Sodom." The district court found that "I Love Sodom" neither competed with nor harmed the value of "I Love New York."[72] Music parodies had also proliferated during the 1970s and 1980s with the popularity of Weird Al Yankovich and others. In 1985, disk jockey Rick Dees produced a twenty-nine-second parody of the Johnny Mathis song "When Sunny Gets Blue" called "When Sunny Sniffs Glue." The Ninth Circuit Court of Appeals ruled that the parody would not compete in the market with the original. The court also concluded that a parody necessarily takes a large portion—perhaps even the heart—of the original, or else fails in its effort. Most significantly, the court ruled that "copyright law is not designed to stifle critics."[73]

Rick Dees's success at defending his parody made 2 Live Crew's eventual success a little more likely. Relying on recent precedents such as the Dees case, Justice David Souter criticized the Sixth Circuit for basing its judgment on a presumption that, since the parody was produced for commercial sale, it could not be fair use. The Sixth Circuit had decided on the same faulty basis on which the Jack Benny case had been decided. Souter also concluded that a parody is unlikely to directly compete in the market with an original work because it serves a different function—criticism. Souter wrote,

> Suffice it to say now that parody has an obvious claim to transformative value, as Acuff-Rose itself does not deny. Like less ostensibly humorous forms of criticism, it can provide social benefit, by shedding light on an earlier work, and, in the process, creating a new one. Parody needs to mimic an original to make its point, and so has some claim to use the creation of its victim's (or collective victims') imagination, whereas satire can stand on its own two feet and so requires justification for the very act of borrowing.

Souter concluded that 2 Live Crew did target Orbison's song, not just society at large. But Souter also warned that this case should not be read as an open license to revise others' works for merely satirical purposes, and that each case should be considered individually. "The fact that parody can claim legitimacy for some appropriation does not, of course, tell either parodist or judge much about where to draw the line. Accordingly, parody, like any other use, has to work its way through the relevant factors, and be judged case by case, in light of the ends of the copyright law."[74]

While Souter was careful not to send too strong a message to potential parodists, his ruling set down some pretty firm principles upon which future cases might be decided. Significantly, Souter declared from the highest perch that parody has social value, and that courts must take such fair use claims seriously. But the U.S. Supreme Court has not considered a case in which transgressive or parodic sampling in rap music was defended as fair use. Based on the principles Souter outlined, it's not likely that the court would smile upon unauthorized digital sampling that indirectly commented on the culture at large—that is—most sampling. But sampling that directly comments upon its source, positively or negatively, might have a chance for consideration. Fundamentally, courts, Congress, and the public should consider how creativity happens in America. Ethnocentric notions of creativity and a maldistribution of political power in favor of established artists and media companies have already served to stifle expression—the exact opposite of the declared purpose of copyright law.[75]

5

The Digital Moment

The End of Copyright?

THE JAZZ PIANIST Herbie Hancock started his career in Chicago in the 1960s, playing with such legends as Donald Byrd, Wes Montgomery, Quincy Jones, Sonny Rollins, and Dexter Gordon. By the late 1960s, Hancock had moved beyond blues and bop, experimenting with the avant-garde sounds of Eric Dolphy. Most of Hancock's notoriety came from his mid-1960s work in the legendary Miles Davis Quintet. Hancock and Davis split in 1968. But in separate groups they both soon pushed the rhythmic foundations of jazz into new areas through the late 1960s and early 1970s, embracing funkier rhythms and more lively, colorful arrangements than the hard bop that had dominated the scene for most of the decade. As a keyboard player, Hancock soon discovered the creative potential of a new instrument—the electronic synthesizer. Synthesizers offered Hancock and other composers a new set of sounds and new ways to manipulate them. Keyboard players could generate thousands of new sounds: buzzes, chirps, whistles, solid tones (with unlimited sustain), crashes, and sirens. Players could alter the pitch, duration, and timbre of a song by tweaking a few knobs or dials.[1]

Early synthesizers were huge and ungainly, difficult to employ for live performances. They used analog technology. Different electric voltages created and controlled the sounds. Higher voltages generated higher notes and lower voltages created lower notes. The first generation of synthesizers could play only a single note at a time. To get more musical depth and texture and to play simple chords, musicians stacked several expensive synthesizers to play at once or layered parts on tape, mixing it later in the studio. By the mid-1970s, several companies had introduced polyphonic analog synthesizers with attached keyboards. Soon synthesizer companies added computer memory to their systems, making it easier to use smaller synthesizers in live shows. By 1979, keyboards came with computer interfaces installed. If all of a musician's synthesizers were of the same brand, they could operate together through a single keyboard. But there was no standard of compatibility. Each company's equipment offered different features and abilities. Hancock, enchanted by the new gadgets, customized connections for his various synthesizers so they would work in concert. Hancock's hacking inspired the next Revolutionary move in electronic music: the creation of an open compatibility standard known as the Musical Instrument Digital Interface, or MIDI, in 1982. MIDI software protocols tell a synthesizer the duration of a note, the shape and pitch of a sound, and its volume.[2]

MIDI transforms the analog signal of a synthesizer into a digital stream, representing all the variances of sounds in a string of zeros and ones. And MIDI allows that information to flow over a network of musical instruments and input and output devices.

Within a couple of years, MIDI became the universal standard for digital music. And its success opened the music industry to the potential of converting every step in its production process to digital technology. The MIDI standards are now used by home computers to generate, share, and play music and video files. At its heart, MIDI is like the blues-based music that inspired Herbie Hancock's career—portable, widely compatible with a variety of instruments, open for anyone to improve, and thus powerfully adaptable.[3]

The parallels between jazz and open technology were not lost on Hancock, who had been an engineering student at Grinnell College in the 1950s. In 1983, Hancock released an electronic album called *Future Shock*. It featured a single called "Rockit" that soon climbed to the top of dance and soul charts and garnered a Grammy award for best rhythm and blues single. The song featured sampled sounds and "scratches" such as rap artists were using over a bed of jazzy electronic keyboard riffs. "Rockit" had an infectious beat. Most Revolutionary, Hancock released a video of the song at a time when MTV was in its infancy. The video featured a group of robots with dismembered appendages dancing around while Hancock performed on his electronic keyboard. Hancock not only inspired the digitization of music in general and the daring fusion of pop music styles but helped establish the music video as a site of intense creativity in the early 1980s.

Hancock was also instrumental in making digital sampling acceptable as an artistic technique within the African American musical tradition. Few jazz musicians have embraced sampling as eagerly as Hancock has. In 1993, Hancock allowed the rap group Us3 to sample his 1964 classic "Cantaloupe Island." Us3 worked with the Blue Note jazz catalogue to create the hit album *Hand on the Torch*, which opens up with the funky dance single "Cantaloop."[4] To sample a piece of music, one must convert it from analog to digital signals. We live in an analog world. The sensations we experience are manipulations of light and matter, interpreted by our organs and mind as waves. These waves have several aspects to them, most significantly frequency and amplitude. When someone plucks a guitar string, her finger vibrates the string, the string vibrates the air, and the air vibrates our eardrums. We can represent the pluck in many ways, including a drop of ink on music staff paper. This is an analog representation. The musician's eyes can scan the paper, sense the difference in light reflecting off the staff paper, and relay a signal to her mind. Her mind then signals her finger to pluck the same string for the same duration. We can record the pluck as a series of magnetic flakes on plastic tape. We can carve grooves into plastic or wax to replicate the sound.

Or we can convert the manipulations of matter that make up an analog signal into digital form—a series of ones and zeros—by running the sound through computer software. The computer measures the frequency and amplitude of each sound and generates a string of Boolean signals to represent each sound and shift. A computer can store these digital signals in a variety of media. It can then play the signals back with something close to perfect reproductive quality. Of course this method of representing analog signals in digital form does not limit itself to sound. Reflections of light can be represented the same way, allowing for the conversion of all sorts of images into strings of digits. As Paul Goldstein explains, digital formats offer three powerful advantages for creativity and economy: fidelity, compression, and malleability. At first glance, these features seem terrifying to the copyright-rich and exciting to the copyright-poor. But that is not necessarily so.

DEFINING THE DIGITAL MOMENT

Herbie Hancock was present at the dawn of the digital moment. From the early 1980s through the late 1990s, artists, musicians, hackers, intellectuals, policy makers, and business leaders embraced the transformative potential of digital technology. Besides the digital representation of all forms of expression, the other, perhaps more significant process inherent in the "digital moment" is the rise of networks. The ability for people to share ideas, information, expressions, truths, and lies over vast distances in virtually no time (and at no discernible marginal cost) has deeply frightened the powerful and empowered those blessed with a connection to the network.[5]

The synergistic relationship between these two processes—digitization and networking—has collapsed some important distinctions that had existed in the American copyright system for most of the twentieth century. Converting Mozart's *Jupiter Symphony* into a series of ones and zeros has collapsed the idea-expression dichotomy. Ones and zeros are the simplest possible grammar through which we can express anything. A living, breathing symphony orchestra may be the most complex medium one could choose to express the same notes. And the analog vibrations in the air that fills a symphony hall might be the most complex grammar one could use to express those ideas. Perhaps the ones and zeros are ideas, and the analog versions we inhale are the expressions. But if strings of ones and zeros operate as an alphabet, a code, for representing ideas, shouldn't they enjoy status as expressions? Are strings of digital code expressions worthy of both copyright protection and First Amendment protection?

The digital moment has also collapsed the distinctions among three formerly distinct processes: gaining access to a work; using (we used to call it "reading") a work; and copying a work. In the digital environment, one cannot gain access to a news story without making several copies of it. If I want to share my morning newspaper with a friend, I just give her the object. I do not need to make a copy. But in the digital world, I do. When I click on the web site that contains the news story, the code in my computer's random access memory is a copy. The source code in hypertext markup language is a copy. And the image of the story on the screen is a copy. If I want a friend to read the story as well, I must make another copy that is attached to an e-mail. The e-mail might sit as a copy on my friend's server. And then my friend would make a copy in her hard drive when receiving the e-mail, and make others in RAM and on the screen while reading it. Copyright was designed to regulate only copying. It was not supposed to regulate one's rights to read or share. But now that the distinctions among accessing, using, and copying have collapsed, copyright policy makers have found themselves faced with what seems to be a difficult choice: either relinquish some control over copying or expand copyright to regulate access and use, despite the chilling effect this might have on creativity, community, and democracy.

The third distinction that the digital moment collapsed is that between producers and consumers of information and culture. The low price of network-ready computers and digital equipment in the United States has reduced the barriers to entry into music, literature, news, commentary, and pornography production and distribution. For less than $5,000 in 2000, a young person could record, produce, edit, advertise, and distribute hundreds of new songs. Of course, the ease of distribution and the low barriers of entry have created a cacophony of "white noise" in the digital environment. Creativity has been democratized, but it's that much harder to attract an audience or a market.

Digitization and networking have also collapsed the distinctions between local and global concerns. The U.S. Congress can outlaw gambling on the Internet. But the U.S. government has no authority to regulate a server on a small island in the Caribbean Sea. As with all questions of digital regulation, what jurisdiction should rule on copyright concerns?

The distinctions among the different types of "intellectual property" have also eroded, if not collapsed. They have certainly collapsed in the public mind and generated much confusion in public discourse. The distinctions also have collapsed in practice. For instance, computer software was until the late 1980s the subject of copyright protection. Then the U.S. Patent Office started issuing patents for algorithms. As the industry has grown, so have the stakes in its legal protection. Now software can carry legal protections that emanate from copyright, patent, trademark, trade secret, and contract law. So while the phrase "intellectual property" was merely a metaphor and an academic convention in the 1960s, by 2000 it was a reality.[6]

THE "DIGERATI" AND "COPYLEFT"

The digital moment inspired a flurry of intellectual work about copyright. Not since the American literati campaigned for international copyright protection in the 1870s and 1880s had so many important writers and thinkers waxed about copyright policy. Most influential among the "digerati" was John Perry Barlow, a founder of the Electronic

Frontier Foundation and former lyricist for the Grateful Dead. Barlow wrote that the application of traditional copyright laws to the digital environment was a fundamental misunderstanding and mistake. In an influential 1994 essay in *Wired* magazine, Barlow wrote that copyright was designed to protect ideas as expressed in fixed form, but not the ideas or bits of information themselves. He chose the metaphor of wine and bottles: copyright protects the bottles, not the wine. But now the bottles have all overflowed, so the system seems to make no sense, Barlow wrote. Barlow did not prescribe a solution to the digital dilemma. He only named and outlined the problems that large portions of the global economy would confront over the next five years.[7]

While Barlow diagnosed a problem inherent in the digital moment and celebrated what he thought might be a powerfully libertarian moment, Richard Stallman sensed just the opposite trend in the late 1980s. Stallman, a programmer who was then working for the Massachusetts Institute of Technology, saw the rise of proprietary software systems as a severe threat to freedom and creativity. In fact, Stallman argued, too much control over software through contract, trade secrets, or copyright impeded the development of the best possible software. The software industry was born out of collaboration among the academy, the government, and private industry. And in the 1960s and 1970s, much of the culture of software reflected the openness and spirit of community and inquiry that exist within the academy. But once the industry outgrew its own incubators, a different, conflicting value infected its practices. What was once public, shared, collaborative, and experimental became secret, proprietary, and jealously guarded. Back in the 1960s and 1970s, only computer programmers used computers widely. Software companies (which were more often than not also hardware companies such as AT&T and IBM) released the source code with their software so that programmers could alter and customize it to their needs. Source code is the set of instructions that human beings write in languages such as Fortran, Pascal, COBOL, and C++. Programmable computers have a feature called a "compiler" that translates source code into "machine language," or object code. In general, only humans can read source code. Only machines can read object code. As the software industry blossomed in the 1980s, companies realized there was commercial value in keeping the source code secret. If a buyer needed a particular feature, he or she had to order it from the software company. In addition, competing software companies would have a difficult time replicating the effects of the object code without access to the source code. Before the rise of Windows, UNIX was one of the most common and powerful operating systems available. It was flexible, powerful, and stable. But it was hardly user-friendly. Only professionals dared to play with UNIX. When AT&T, which distributed UNIX (although it was developed in collaboration with universities, especially the University of California at Berkeley), bottled up its source code in the 1980s, it angered many computer programmers who had considered themselves part of the UNIX team. Among these was Richard Stallman. Stallman grew frustrated that he could not customize a particular printer driver and other peripherals. If he could only get a peek at the source code, it would take him minutes or hours to create a patch and make the system work better. Instead, every time users had a problem, they had to wait months or years for the company to roll out another version and fix it.[8]

Frustrated by the unwillingness of university computer administrators to stand up for their values in the face of increasing corporate control, Stallman left MIT and founded the Free Software Foundation in 1984 to promote the use of "free software," programs unencumbered by proprietary restrictions on alterations, revisions, repairs, and distribution. Also in 1984, Stallman wrote the "GNU Manifesto." GNU stands for "Gnu's Not UNIX!". In the manifesto, Stallman wrote,

> I consider that the golden rule requires that if I like a program I must share it with other people who like it. Software sellers want to divide the users and conquer them, making each user agree not to share with others. I refuse to break solidarity with other users in this way. I cannot in good conscience sign a nondisclosure agreement or a software license agreement.[9]

Stallman went to great lengths to define the freedom he valued. It was not the "give it away for free" freedom that idealized the foolishly generous. Stallman said that "Free Software is a matter of liberty, not price. To understand this concept, you should think of 'free speech,' not 'free beer.'" Stallman outlined four specific freedoms central to the Free Software movement:

- The freedom to run a program for any purpose.
- The freedom to examine and adapt a program (and thus to get access to the source code—it would be "Open Source").

- The freedom to distribute copies.
- The freedom to improve any program.[10]

Stallman started coding free programs that would work with UNIX. But he hoped for a better yet open operating system to emerge. In the 1990s, some other programmers generated LINUX, the operating system Open Source champions needed to make free software important and powerful. The Free Software movement had grown to be a major force in the software world by the year 2000. But for this phenomenon to occur, Stallman had to come up with a way to ensure that no one company could corner the market on the work that Free Software programmers produced. If Stallman and his collaborators released their programs without any copyright protection, declaring them in the public domain, then any company such as AT&T or Microsoft could bottle up that work by adding a few proprietary and highly protected features. So instead, Stallman came up with an ingenious license that he called "Copyleft."

Copyleft licenses require that anyone who copies or alters Free Software agree to release publicly all changes and improvements. These changes retain the Copyleft license. Thus the license perpetuates itself. It spreads the principle of openness and sharing wherever someone chooses to use it. This prevents any company from trying to release proprietary versions of free software. If a company were to release a "closed" or "unfree" version of the software, it would be violating the original "GNU General Public License" (or GPL) that it agreed to in the first place. The code and the freedoms attached to it become inalienable. The proliferation of free software could not have occurred without this license, which uses the power of the copyright system to turn copyright inside out. Copyleft's power and popularity have allowed many people to examine the foundations upon which copyright rests and ask whether its powers have actually worked to impede creativity. By the year 2000, the principles behind Free Software and Copyleft remained fringe views, even though the software they inspired and enabled had worked its way into the mainstream of the computer industry.[11]

Among those in the 1990s to make sense of the digital moment, Stanford law professor Paul Goldstein was the most prescient observer of copyright issues and trends. In his 1994 book *Copyright's Highway: The Law and Lore of Copyright from Gutenberg to the Celestial Jukebox*, Goldstein outlined an optimistic vision of the digital moment and its potential for both producers and consumers. Goldstein saw on the local horizon a day when all cultural content—text, music, video, software, video games, virtual reality environments—could be streamed into our homes through one wire and out of one box. Each consumer would have instant access to huge and substantial private libraries of culture and information.

Goldstein saw three vestiges of traditional copyright policy imped-ing his pay-per-view utopia: fair use; private, noncommercial, nonin-fringing copying; and the idea-expression dichotomy. Goldstein had fallen under the sway of the fundamentalist "Law and Economics" school of copyright analysis. According to this school, broad appeals to values beyond material concerns—culture, beauty, dignity, democ-racy—invite inefficiency into social, political, and economic systems. These extra-economic principles are not bad ideas per se, according to Law and Economics concepts, but proposals that appeal to them should be justified by tests of their utility. Within this school of thought, fair use and home copying have no inherent educational or democratic value. Fair use is not a good idea per se, but only a necessary flaw in what might otherwise be a perfectly efficient and rational market for cultural goods. Fair use exists simply because the "transaction costs" of restrict-ing copying in the home and schools would be too high to justify en-forcement. If Home Box Office or its parent Time Warner had to negoti-ate with a consumer every time she made a videotape copy of *The So-pranos* for later viewing, the consumer would probably not bother recording the show. Perhaps out of frustration she would decide not to watch the show. The transaction costs of time, money, and stress would not justify the small reward the consumer gets from home recording or the small return the company would get from charging each time the consumer recorded the show. Similarly, the transaction costs of regulat-ing every time a teacher makes a copy of a newspaper article for thirty students would be too high to justify the hassle of extracting permission and payment. Imposing high transaction costs would only chill this use. Therefore, the conservative Law and Economics theorists argue, society benefits from fair use and private, noncommercial domestic copying only because producers can't exact transaction costs easily and effi-ciently. They can't monitor every use. They can't send a bill through the mail and expect timely payment every time someone records a show. But Goldstein argued that the digital moment and the potential of the Celestial Jukebox reduces transaction costs to just pennies per use.

Users and producers would negotiate terms just once—upon subscription. Freeloaders and scofflaws would be locked out of the jukebox. And most importantly, producers would have exact measures of consumer demand, even concerning the smallest possible slivers of cultural production such as quotation and raw information. Goldstein saw this as the best possible bargain. It would maximize market efficiency and democratize gatekeeper decisions. It would deliver the maximum number of products in the shortest possible time for the lowest marginal cost to producers.

For the Celestial Jukebox to work at maximum efficiency, fair use would not just be economically unnecessary, it would be a problem. Fair use is copying that occurs outside of the gaze of the market. Despite cold Law and Economics pronouncements to the contrary, fair use has clear albeit unquantifiable social benefits—for public education, for instance. Other forms of fair use assume that the user need not and probably should not request permission from the copyright holder. A highly critical film review or scholarly article demands that the critic or scholar have the confidence to reuse portions of the original work in the subsequent work. If the copyright holder wanted to work the Celestial Jukebox most efficiently, it could extract higher rent for critical use, deny permission entirely, or exact retribution by limiting access to other works in the future. And if parodists had to extract permission and make payment for the original work they targeted, they would probably all give up. A rare and brave copyright holder would willingly allow its works to be viciously ridiculed. Although Goldstein did not consider this problem in *Copyright's Highway*, the potential for corporate censorship under the Celestial Jukebox is unlimited. And, as Goldstein pointed out, for the market to work as efficiently as he hoped, producers would have to monitor use and demand precisely. This not only raises serious privacy concerns but renders transgressive fair use impossible. This potential social and cultural cost did not trouble Goldstein. He argued that only the strongest possible corporate protections could generate incentives to justify the investments in bandwidth infrastructure necessary to pipe all that digital content into our homes. Toward this end, Goldstein endorsed controversial database protection efforts, applauded the recapture of "leakage" caused by educational fair use copying, and proposed strong proprietary software protection through copyright and trade secrets law.[12]

Aware of the potential effects of the digitization of all cultural production and the potential for an unstable copyright system, policy makers in the late 1990s set about strengthening and expanding copyright and making Goldstein's vision of a Celestial Jukebox possible. They used alarmist rhetoric and claimed that they had to act to strengthen copyright lest they invite anarchy. In 1995 the Clinton Administration released its manifesto on copyright and information policy. It was called "Intellectual Property and the National Information Infrastructure: The Report of the Working Group on Intellectual Property Rights," usually referred to as the "White Paper." The White Paper summarized what it considered to be the state of the copyright regime in the early 1990s, just as digitization and digital networks rose to prominence and revealed their promise. But its summary ignored all moves in the history of copyright that extended or protected the public, or users' rights. In fact, the paper referred to fair use and other users' rights as a "tax" on copyright holders, as if copyright were not granted carefully by the citizens of a nation to copyright holders as part of a carefully balanced deal. So it overstated—in fact distorted—the status quo. Then the White Paper suggested ways to "extend" copyright to cyberspace, as if the traditional principles of copyright did not apply in the new medium. The White Paper paid no attention to the public interest concerns of the copyright system. In fact, the subsequent legislative moves—including the Digital Millennium Copyright Act of 1998—essentially nullified the role of deliberation and legislation in determining copyright. It let copyright holders be copyright cops.[13]

FOUR SURRENDERS

At the behest of content industries and with little public discussion, the Clinton Administration used the White Paper as the blueprint to engineer four surrenders of important safeguards in the copyright system:

- The surrender of balance to control. As a result of the chief piece of legislation in recent years, the Digital Millennium Copyright Act, content providers can set the terms for access to and use of a work. There is no balance if the copyright owner has all the power.
- The surrender of public interest to private interest. The rhetoric of "intellectual property" in the 1990s was punctuated by

appeals to prevent theft and efforts to extend markets. There was little public discussion about copyright as a public good that can encourage a rich public sphere and diverse democratic culture.

- The surrender of republican deliberation within the nation-state to unelected multilateral nongovernmental bodies. Copyright issues went global. Ancillary markets for music and motion pictures became central to marketing efforts. So the World Intellectual Property Organization and the World Trade Organization assumed a greater role in copyright policy as multinational media companies sought global standards that satisfied their ambitions.

- The surrender of culture to technology. The Digital Millennium Copyright Act forbids any circumvention of electronic locks that regulate access to copyrighted material. Before 1998 copyright was a public bargain between producers and users. It was democratically negotiated, judicially mediated, and often messy and imperfect. Now the very presence of even faulty technology trumps any public interest in fair use and open access.

GOING GLOBAL

One of the major mechanisms behind these surrenders was the World Intellectual Property Organization, or WIPO. Four times in the twentieth century representatives from up to 127 nations met to revise the Berne Convention for the Protection of Literary and Artistic Works. They first met in 1886 after a group of European authors, led by Victor Hugo, convinced political leaders that Europe should standardize its copyright laws to prevent rampant piracy from neighboring states. Before Berne, for example, many popular French works were pirated in Belgium and sold cheaper than the originals.

Although the United States agreed in 1891 to share copyright protection with the British Empire, it refused to join the Berne Convention until 1989. The reasons for the United States' century-long resistance to Berne are complex, but they boil down to the fact that for much of American history, the United States has been a net copyright importer, while Europe has been a net copyright exporter. European countries in general have afforded broader and deeper protection to authors and publishers than the United States has. For the most part, American copyright theory has leaned toward making books cheaper and more available and—when it appeals to its Madisonian republican roots—encouraging free and rich speech.[14]

But all that has changed. The United States by the late twentieth century had become a net copyright exporter. Software, compact discs, and American films are among its strongest exports. Recent moves—initiated by the European Union and the Clinton Administration—have jeopardized the good things about American copyright law: that its relatively loose fair use provisions and limited duration have through most of its history acted to the benefit of science, education, democracy, creativity, and freedom. Specifically, these recent moves at the latest meeting of the Berne Convention in Geneva in December 1996 threaten one of the bedrock principals of American copyright law: the idea/expression dichotomy.

The delegates in Geneva considered three treaties. They approved two of them and tabled the other for further consideration in pending meetings. The two treaties that passed Berne, as the WIPO Copyright Treaty and the WIPO Performances and Phonograms Treaty, have some major problems. The third treaty they considered, which would have created a whole new area of "intellectual property" law, would have protected databases from piracy and unauthorized use. The database proposal is the most dangerous of the three. It could limit scientific exploration. It could severely restrict debate on public policy. It could render information a resource available only to wealthy people in wealthy nations.[15]

The WIPO Copyright Treaty provides that computer programs will be considered "protected as literary works." This is consistent with U.S. case law and with standard procedure around the world. However, the protocol clearly considers copying software into Random Access Memory, or RAM, potentially liable copying. This is consistent as well with U.S. case law. On my laptop, as on many other models, I can create an imaginary RAM disk, so I can load a program like Microsoft Word into it and run the computer on its battery without spinning the hard drive, which eats up time and energy. Whenever I look at a web page, it gets copied into RAM until I exit the browser. And JAVA plug-in modules, little programs embedded in web pages that you load into RAM to use briefly but then discard when you move on, could be the source of future lawsuits. Most of this copying would not really become a problem because I am not trying to sell the RAM copy, but potential complications and conflicts lie beneath the surface. If I send a pirated piece of software to you via e-mail, it gets copied into your Internet service provider's computer. Then, when you open it up, not knowing what it is, you have made a copy in RAM. This could be a violation by both your provider and you, without your even knowing about it. The treaty could have contained language that would exempt copies made while "browsing" and transferring data. Delegates from underdeveloped nations pushed for it, but the American representatives objected. They settled on broad, foggy language that individual nations will consider differently.[16]

The second Berne treaty, the WIPO Performances and Phonograms Treaty, deals with music. In the commotion over database protection proposals and moves to better protect software, few have examined the implications of this treaty. Through the Performances and Phonograms Treaty, U.S. copyright law would for the first time adopt a codification of a composer's "moral rights." Moral rights represent a position in copyright theory by which the author, composer, or director has almost complete control over the ways in which his or her works shall be presented or manipulated. Moral rights have been part of the European copyright tradition since the first Berne Convention in 1886 but had never been part of American law. There have been cases in which moral rights crept into the discourse of American law, but this was usually because the judges did not know what they were doing. Thus European law has for the last hundred years served the interests of artists and publishers, while American law has purported to serve the interests of the public at large.[17]

Through the WIPO Performances and Phonograms Treaty a composer or even a performer can claim a right to be identified as the performer and can prevent any "distortion, mutilation or other modification of his performances that would be prejudicial to his reputation." In other words, performers would have veto power over parodies of their work. This provision directly speaks to the recent landmark case *Campbell v. Acuff-Rose Music, Inc.*, in which the Supreme Court ruled that the rap group 2 Live Crew was within fair use guidelines when it parodied Roy Orbison's song "Oh, Pretty Woman." If the U.S. Congress adopts this provision, making fun of other people's songs will be precarious.[18]

BOTTLING UP INFORMATION

Just as Berne delegates used this treaty to attack a recent U.S. Supreme Court case that defends parody and fair use, *Cambell vs. Acuff-Rose,* they used the convention to attack another landmark case, *Feist Publications, Inc. v. Rural Telephone Service, Inc.,* in 1991, and the fundamental principal behind it. In the *Feist* case, the U.S. Supreme Court ruled that a phone book company, regardless of the time, effort, and money it invested in compiling a directory, could not claim copyright protection over the mere information in the text: alphabetized names, addresses, and phone numbers. Conforming to the alphabet is not considered "creative" enough to qualify as an act of "authorship," the Court ruled. However, it's safe to assume that the "Now I know my ABCs; next time won't you sing with me" part could be protected by copyright. But in *Feist,* the Court clearly stated the bedrock principal of American copyright law: You can protect specific expressions of ideas, but not the underlying ideas themselves. You can protect the style and structure of "Casey at the Bat," that "there was no joy in Mudville," but not the awful truth that Casey did strike out.

To evade the "problem" that the U.S. Supreme Court generated for database companies—that others might feel entitled to copy their data electronically and sell it cheaper than they could—European and American negotiators have been trying for several years to create a new form of intellectual property law that would consider databases protectable outside the constraints of American copyright law. They would base this new form of intellectual property not on the idea of "creativity" or "authorship," as in copyright law, but instead on the "sweat of the brow" principal: that any investment of time, effort, and money warrants protection. The delegates at Berne delayed considering this third treaty to protect databases. But the European Union has already moved to protect them, and the U.S. Congress considered database legislation in 1997, 1998, and 1999.

By the late 1990s, data services were the sixth largest segment of the information industry. Database companies sell texts of legal cases, government filings, telephone and address lists for direct marketing, voter profile lists, consumer profile lists, chemical information, geological data, and much more. Database providers collect more than $100 billion per year for their services—and that's without specific legal protection.[19] Bruce Lehman, President Clinton's commissioner of patents and trademarks, led the American delegation to Berne and helped write and push the enabling legislation on Capital Hill. He is on record supporting these changes as essential to the growth of a new and emerging American industry. Lehman told the *New York Times* in February 1997, "We are protecting people against theft of their intellectual property, not trying to stop fair use. If you're going to have people making large-scale investments in this new digital environment, they have to have some sense of security that they are going to be protected and make money on it." In other words, Lehman wanted to use federal and international law as protectionist measures to support one sliver of American industry. Protecting one industry raises costs and limits opportunities for everyone else. This is exactly what is happening with the data industry.[20]

Opposing the database protection measures were representatives of underdeveloped nations who are concerned by the concentration of database access in western nations, scientists concerned about easy and inexpensive access to data, and, of course, librarians. The proposed legislation, which is similar to but in fact more stringent than the European Union pact, contains the following provisions:

- A database is subject to legal protection "if it is the result of a qualitatively or quantitatively substantial investment of human, technical, financial or other resources in the selection, assembly, verification, organization or presentation of the database contents, and the database is used or reused in commerce, or the database owner intends to use or reuse the database in commerce."
- Although government databases are not protected, and are free for anyone to use, privately owned databases compiled from government-generated statistics are to be protected.
- No person shall "extract, use, reuse a substantial part, qualitatively or quantitatively, of the contents of a database subject to this act in a manner that conflicts with the database owner's normal exploitation of the database or adversely affects the actual or potential market for the database."
- No person shall "engage in the repeated or systematic extraction, use or reuse of insubstantial parts . . . in a manner that cumulatively conflicts with the database owner's normal exploitation of the database."

It's important to remember a few things when weighing whether this industry should get this special form of protection. First, the database industry has grown rich and powerful without a special law to protect it. Second, consumers will always pay more for the delivery—quick and easy access to information—than they will for the data itself. Delivery systems are proprietary and protectable by trade secret and unfair competition laws. And as more databases go on-line and link themselves to the Internet, they do so with elaborate and expensive gates. We cannot enter them without a permission and usually payment. They already have big gates to keep most of us out. They are almost perfect monopolies already. Further, much of the "data" these services provide is already protected by American copyright laws. For instance, a database of periodical articles has protection over the specific expression in each article. Another layer of protection simply limits their potential uses.

How can this move to protect databases impinge on the way information is used in the world? Let's examine one small yet significant area that would be severely cramped by database protection: scholarship. Let's pretend I'm writing a book about American life between the World Wars, and I want to use some popular icons to represent major trends in American culture. I pick baseball commissioner Kennesaw Mountain Landis to represent the puritanical progressivism that drove the anti-immigration and antiliquor movements. I pick Washington Senators pitcher Walter "Big Train" Johnson to describe the rising industrial and technological timbre of the times. I choose Yankee first baseman Lou Gehrig to exemplify the immigrant work ethic and the generational tensions alive in immigrant families. And, of course, I use George Herman Ruth to illustrate the excesses of the times. To write this book, and mainly because I would really be looking for an excuse to write about baseball, I would use a lot of statistics: how Babe Ruth did against Walter Johnson; how Lou Gehrig did against Johnson; how Ruth and Gehrig made each other better hitters and became bitter rivals over time. In other words, I would have to dip time and time again into the database of Major League Baseball statistics. This database is easy to get and easy to manipulate. You can get it on CD-ROM or in small, handheld computers. Under traditional copyright law, my repeated use of information for a commercial purpose in this case would normally demand no permission and no payment. Information, at the end of the twentieth century at least, was free and reusable. Only by reprinting in their entirety the statistical tables from the baseball record books and using the exact same format would I be infringing on a copyright.

Under the proposed treaty and law, however, I would have to request permission for each statistical cross-reference I made; I would have to pay a fee for each search I did, perhaps sign a contract that gave Major League Baseball a cut of my meager book royalties. I might even find permission to use the information denied if the commissioner's office found out that I oppose realignment, expansion, artificial turf, and expensive ballpark food. Imagine every newspaper, every sports magazine, every radio and television broadcast that covers major league baseball having to seek permission and pay a fee for statistical data on players.

Let's say a geologist at a private university gets a major grant through his institution and private foundations to do geological research off the coast of Alaska. This research could be valuable to both oil companies and environmental interests. However, lawyers for the private university have insisted that databases compiled by university employees are the property of the university itself, so it can license the information to oil companies for a hefty fee. Regardless of the geologist's best intentions, her work could not be used freely, accessed easily, criticized, or tested. Her research would produce a small short-term gain for the institution, but no long-term gain for science or the environment. And if her work is imperfect and no one verifies her findings, it might even mess up the oil companies. If Jane's handbooks of military vehicles, weapons, and equipment become restricted databases, debate over military expenditures might dry up.

As John Dewey wrote, "No scientific inquirer can keep what he finds to himself or turn it to merely private account without losing his scientific standing. Everything discovered belongs to the community of workers. Every new idea and theory has to be submitted to this community for confirmation and test."[21]

This process of collecting raw material from a group of people, processing, refining, and arranging it, and then selling it back to them at monopolistic prices is intellectual mercantilism. Just as the East India Company used the British government to support its program to collect Indian rock salt and sell table salt back to Indians, the database company Reed-Elsevier has been using the power of the U.S. government to achieve an operational monopoly around the world so that the world must turn to Reed-Elsevier to find out about itself. This is a new imperialism—an imperialism without borders. Companies with the resources to assemble and license facts and data can control dissemination to those unblessed with capital. Whether the unblessed includes a fifth grader in South Africa who walks ten miles to a library with an Internet connection or researchers at universities, these companies will be able to price most consumers out of the information to encourage scarcity and drive up demand. In addition, these companies will be able to choose who may gain access to and use their information.

So what we are seeing on the horizon is the potential perfection of monopolies. Database companies will not only charge for any repeated use of their information, but hold the keys to it as well. On an international level, "intellectual property" law is being used as a weapon in protectionism. We've seen several moves in this direction in the last ten years: digital audio tape legislation, the Semiconductor Chip Protection Act of 1984, European Union database protection, and the subsequent American response with even stronger database protection.

And there is one more scary aspect of database protection. The duration of protection under both the European and American proposals is potentially infinite. Databases would be protected for twenty-five years under the American plan, but that term is renewable every time more data are added. In other words, the baseball statistical database would renew its protection every season, possibly every game. This directly violates the enabling clause of the Constitution that governs "intellectual property." The clause specifically calls for a "limited" duration of protection for patents and copyrights.[22]

The electronic networks that should be the great democratizers could just as easily kill inquiry, expression, and debate around the world. Fortunately, Congress balked at passing the enabling legislation for the unsigned database protection treaty through the late 1990s.

"RECYCLING" THE IDEA-EXPRESSION DICHOTOMY

In the bottom-right corner of the computer screen on which I am writing this sentence sits the image of a garbage can. It's an icon, a functional part of the "graphical user interface," or GUI, that the Apple Computer Company developed for its Macintosh line in the early 1980s. Even though this icon resembles any common aluminum trash can one might see on a curbside or around Oscar the Grouch on Sesame Street, it is a highly protected part of Apple's array of copyrighted materials. If you are like nine out of ten personal computer users in the United States, you have a different icon on the left side of your computer screen. You have a green "Recycle Bin," a functional part of the Microsoft Windows operating system since 1995. Both of these operating systems share other icons such as folders, drop-down (or pop-up) menus, and dog-eared documents. And both GUIs have bins into which one can drag unwanted items. Yet one bin is marked "Trash" and the other is marked "Recycle Bin." This is a trivial, superficial difference between the systems. But the difference is a vestige of a string of controversies and cases that marked and perhaps determined the development of the personal computer and the proliferation of digital technology in daily life.

While recent global moves to protect data with sui generis intellectual property protection threaten the foundation of the idea-expression dichotomy, the conflicts that created more recycling bins than trash cans on our computer screens have actually worked to revive and reinforce the dichotomy—at least in the area of software design.

The tenuous revival of the idea-expression dichotomy began with the phenomenal success of Pac-man, a video game that Midway Manufacturing Company licensed and introduced to the United States at the dawn of the Reagan era. Within months of its arrival from Japan, the "wocka-wocka-wocka" sound of upright Pac-man machines rang through the corridors of shopping malls and bowling alleys across North America. The idea behind Pac-man was rampant consumption. The player controlled a joystick that guided a yellow circle around a maze. As the circle moved, it opened up like the jaws of an egg-snake, gobbling small points of light. Each point of light yielded minimal points for the player. Many more points came from eating the larger "power pill" that sat in four corners of the maze. When the Pac-man image ate a power pill, the four ghosts that were charged with chasing the Pac-man and defending the maze turned colors and became edible as well. If the ghosts—Inky, Blinky, Pinky, and Clyde—were in their normal state and color, they would chase the Pac-man. If the ghosts caught the Pac-man, the Pac-man would wither and die with a pathetic "woo-woo-woo-woo" sound. If the Pac-man were energized, he would chase the ghosts. If the Pac-man consumed one of the four ghosts, the player would earn bonus points. If a Pac-man cleared a maze of all the points of light, he would move up a level to a more difficult maze with faster ghosts. Within a few weeks of regular play, young people discovered that there were certain patterns that would allow easy victory. There were even "blind" spots programmed into the maze, where a Pac-man could hide unmolested by the aggressive ghosts. For a twenty-five-cent charge, a skillful and devoted young person could play the game infinitely.[23]

Pac-man wizards ruled the video game parlors in the early 1980s. The skilled players monopolized the machines to such a degree that Midway—yearning for more quarters—soon had to roll out other versions of the game with different patterns to success. Chief among these new authorized versions was the oddly named "Ms. Pac-man." And soon Midway licensed the home version of Pac-man for the popular Atari home game system. But just after the authorized Atari version hit store shelves, another company, North American Philips Consumer Electronics Corp., released a similar game cartridge for the long-forgotten Magnavox Home Entertainment Center game system. It was called "K. C. Munchkin." The Philips version featured a maze, points of light, power pills, and monsters that would chase and flee from K. C. Munchkin. There were some minor aesthetic differences between K. C. Munchkin and Pac-man. K. C. Munchkin was green, not yellow. And he had horns and eyes. Pac-man was a simple, elegant yellow circle—and a ruthlessly efficient munching machine.

With fond memories of H. R. Pufnstuf and McDonaldland fresh in their minds, lawyers for Atari and Midway filed suit against Philips and Magnavox, expecting the trial court to invoke the troublesome "total-concept-and-feel" principle immediately and issue a preliminary injunction against the sale of K. C. Munchkin. But the trial court instead focused on the minor differences between the two interfaces and ruled that the general idea of a "maze-chase" game is not protectable. Reviewing the request for an injunction, the Seventh Circuit Court of Appeals also ruled that Atari could not protect general attributes such as mazes, dots, and scoring systems. But the court ruled that maze-chase games did not necessarily require the presence of ghosts and the act of gobbling such ghosts. The court concluded that any ordinary observer would see that K. C. Munchkin was substantially similar to Pac-man. Therefore, it issued a preliminary injunction against K. C. Munchkin. The Seventh Circuit seemed to be making the world safe for maze-chase games. But in fact, no other competitors to Pac-man's dominance emerged in ensuing years. Mazes without Inky, Blinky, Pinky, and Clyde seemed empty, soulless, and silly.[24]

Video games were among the most lucrative and popular software products in the early 1980s. But personal computer operating systems were clearly emerging as valuable business tools, and thus potentially worthy of high levels of protection as well. Congress had in 1976 added computer programs to the list of copyrightable works, but courts had not sorted out the limits and principles that would guide software developers. Specifically, was an operating system—the guts, heart, and mind of a computer—protectable as an original work of authorship or was it part of the machine itself, and thus purely functional?

Among early personal computer operating systems, the Apple II had a clear edge. It was cool, flexible, useful, and fun. It had brand recognition over such early competitors as Commodore and Tandy. Many hobbyists were developing business and game software for the Apple. By 1981, Apple employed more than three thousand people at its headquarters in Cupertino, California, and enjoyed $335 million in sales. The code for the Apple II operating system was inscribed on silicon chips inside the processor, in what is called read-only memory, or ROM. Unlike its cousin random access memory, or RAM, ROM can't be modified, deleted, or upgraded by users. With the success of the Apple operating system, the company had little incentive to license it to other computer makers. If customers wanted to use an Apple, they had to buy the whole box. And just like with the Pac-man phenomenon, soon a second-comer decided to compete directly with Apple.[25]

Franklin Computer Corporation had the idea to market a cheaper version of an Apple II. The Franklin Ace 100 looked like an Apple II, and it had a similar operating system. Unfortunately for Franklin, the system was so similar that the code contained several clues to its origin. Clearly, the engineers at Franklin had gone farther than reverse-engineering the Apple operating system. They had copied major portions of it.[26]

Apple lost the first round in its copyright suit against Franklin. The trial court refused to grant an injunction against the Ace 100 because it was confused about whether both source code and object code were protectable expressions. Programmers produce source code in commonly used languages such as COBOL, Pascal, or C++. Then the computer uses its "compiler" to translate those expressions into object code, in what is often called "machine language." The trial court concluded that object code, unreadable by human beings, cannot be "expressive" for the purposes of copyright protection. Being the purest form in which one may render ideas, object code is close to being a collection of ideas themselves. In addition, the court was troubled by the fact that the object code was embedded on ROM chips, which might not count as a "tangible medium of expression" as the copyright law demands. After all, the medium of silicon chips is not immediately "tangible" to human eyes. But the appellate court reversed the trial court decision in August 1983, granting Apple an injunction. The appeals court could not insert a distinction between source code and object code in the language Congress had written into the copyright law, which defined a "computer program" as "a set of statements or instructions to be used directly or indirectly in a computer in order to bring about a certain result." And the appeals court ruled that ROM was just as "tangible" as magnetic disks or tape. Third, the court ruled that even though a computer program is purely "functional," the umbrella of copyright would still cover it. Emboldened by this victory, Apple arrogantly surged on, enjoying its fleeting dominance of the personal computer business, refusing to license its operating system to other hardware companies until well into the 1990s. Had Franklin prevailed, copyright protection for functional software would have been extremely weak. Other competitors to the Apple II would have sprung up immediately, and operating systems based on the core of the Apple system might have become the standard for personal computers for many years.[27]

But instead, a smaller, lighter company—one that dealt exclusively in software, took over desktops all over the world. Microsoft triumphed not only through bullying, intimidation, clear restraint of trade, predatory takeovers, brilliant public relations, a Rolling Stones song, and other deft business moves, but by exploiting what was left of the idea-expression dichotomy at the end of the twentieth century.

Back before 1984, all personal computers relied on textual interfaces. Whether using the archaic CP/M, Microsoft's MS-DOS, or an Apple II, users had to know specific command codes to retrieve and manipulate files. The computer would offer a "prompt," and the user would instruct the computer to "run," "save," or "delete." But some clever engineers at Xerox Corporation's Palo Alto Research Center, or PARC, saw another way. They envisioned—and invented, the graphical user interface, or GUI. A GUI would appear as a "desktop." Users would see open files and running applications as "windows." Pushing a "mouse" on a tabletop would move a "cursor" along the screen. Clicking on an "icon" would launch an application or open a document. Xerox developed the GUI, but it did not exploit it for commercial gain. Instead, it let the revolutionary engineers of Apple in the front door to see how it worked.[28]

In August of 1979, Steve Jobs, the once and present chairman of Apple, led a small crew of his programmers into PARC to check out the new developments within. In exchange for access to the labs, Jobs had sold to Xerox a hundred thousand shares of Apple stock for $1 million. Among all to gadgets and tricks on display, Jobs and his team were transfixed by the demonstration of the GUI. They asked for a detailed explanation of how it worked, and the Xerox programmers explained "bitmapping" to them. What these Xerox computers were doing was assigning each pixel on the screen to a specific bit on the processor's chip. That bit would light up its pixel on command, and the resultant illusion was a cartoon desktop on a screen. Bitmapping required huge assignments of memory to the display function. But if memory and processing speeds could support it, Jobs realized, the GUI could Revolutionize computer use. At least it could be the key to maintaining and extending Apple's dominance in the blossoming personal computer industry. Since the development of the Apple II, giant IBM had agreed to license Microsoft's MS-DOS for its line of business desktop computers. Despite the clear technical and aesthetic superiority of Apple products, the business world steadily gravitated to the familiar blue logo of IBM. But Jobs assumed that if Apple could roll out a marketable graphical user interface, the entire game would change. Many people in the 1980s were still wary of using computers. And the textual interface reminded users of the secret code that computer specialists used. So Jobs sent his programming teams on a Quixotic quest to develop a new way for humans to extend their perceptions through machines.[29]

After the disastrously premature introduction of the $12,000 Lisa computer in 1983, Apple put all its hope in a slicker, more friendly system by 1984: the Macintosh. It changed the world.

Meanwhile, up the Pacific coast in Redmond, Washington, software engineers at Microsoft were busy rolling out inferior versions of other people's inventions. The 1980s and early 1990s not only saw the proliferation of MS-DOS on an increasing number of machines. It saw the introduction of a cumbersome Microsoft version of the superior and popular word-processing program WordPerfect, a Microsoft version of the Revolutionary spreadsheet program Lotus 1-2-3, and ultimately a windows-and-mouse-based graphical user interface with a powerful generic name, Windows.[30]

When Microsoft sought to introduce a GUI as early as 1985, Apple agreed to license some Macintosh design features to Microsoft. But Microsoft did not specifically purchase particular icons such as the trash can. Nor had Apple licensed the use of items such as tiled windows for subsequent upgraded versions of Microsoft Windows. Angry that Microsoft had apparently extended its ambitions beyond their licensing agreement, Apple filed suit in 1988 against Microsoft over its Windows 2.03 and 3.0 versions, claiming specific contractual abrogations and a general copyright infringement on the "total concept and feel" of the Macintosh system. Two trial court judges ruled against Apple, deciding that many of the questionable features were either covered by the license agreement or so common and obvious as to be considered part of the public domain. The first trial judge, Judge William Schwarzer, drew the line of infringement so tightly that an operating system would have to be "virtually identical" to an original system to infringe. The second, Judge Vaughn Walker, ruled that many of the features in dispute between the two operating systems were "purely functional" and intuitively necessary for any graphical user interface. Walker compared the use of file folders and drop-down menus to dials and knobs on a television set. Standardization is not copying. To allow Apple to protect its "total concept and feel" would be to stifle any competing operating system, better or worse.

These court rulings allowed Windows to grow, while just a few years before a very different and much broader decision had killed off K. C. Munchkin and all potential competitors to Pac-man. In 1994 an appeals court agreed with the trial court's ruling, making the computer world truly competitive, at least at the level of interface design. Not coincidentally, by the time the appeals court ruled, Microsoft was almost ready to roll out Windows 95, its most dynamic and user-friendly GUI operating system up to that time. Microsoft clearly felt legally safe competing directly with Macintosh by selling a very Mac-like interface. But just to be safe, Windows still features a recycling bin instead of a trash can. Microsoft started the 1990s relatively copyright-poor. It successfully exploited the idea-expression dichotomy and used it as a wrench to break Apple's hold over the user-friendly computer market. And in 2000 Microsoft—now copyright-rich—continued to recycle other people's ideas into their own monopolistic empire while fighting to maximize copyright enforcement and control around the globe.[31]

CODIFYING THE DIGITAL MOMENT

As the software wars show, the idea-expression dichotomy was still relevant but certainly in flux by the late 1990s. A strong defense of the dichotomy had allowed for healthy (and later unhealthy) competition between Apple and Microsoft. But a strong push on behalf of database companies continued to threaten the principle behind the dichotomy: that facts and ideas should flow freely (in both senses of "free"), while creative arrangement and expression deserve limited monopoly protection. On several other copyright fronts, courts, Congress, and international governing institutions were steadily strengthening the power and scope of copyright protection with little or no regard for the effects these changes would have on democracy and creativity.

The best example of legislative recklessness is the Digital Millennium Copyright Act of 1998, the enabling legislation for the WIPO copyright treaty. The Digital Millennium Copyright Act has one major provision that upends more than two hundred years of copyright law. It puts the power to regulate copying in the hands of engineers and the companies that employ them. It takes the decision-making power away from Congress, courts, librarians, writers, artists, and researchers. The DMCA:

- Prohibits the circumvention of any effective technological protection measure installed to restrict access to a copyrighted work.
- Prohibits the manufacture of any device, composition of any program, or offering of any service that is designed to defeat technological protection measures.
- Orders the Librarian of Congress to conduct rule-making hearings to judge the effects the law would have on non-infringing uses of copyrighted material.
- Specifically allows certain uses such as reverse engineering, security testing, privacy protection, and encryption research.

- Makes no textual change to the fair use provisions of the Copyright Law, despite eliminating the possibility of unauthorized access to protected materials for fair use purposes.
- Limits the liability that on-line service providers might face if one of their clients were circumventing or pirating.

Before congressional committees and in hearings held by the Copyright Office of the Library of Congress, public interest advocates such as law professors, electronic civil liberties activists, and librarians outlined some concerns with and objections to the DMCA. These included the possibility that the DMCA makes it possible to levy fees for various uses that might otherwise be "fair" or "free," such as parody and quoting for news or commentary.

In addition, the DMCA erodes the "first sale doctrine." When a work is sold, the copyright holder relinquishes "exclusive" rights over it yet retains "limited" rights, such as restricting copying or public performance. But under the first sale doctrine, the consumer can highlight a book, copy portions for private, noncommercial use, resell it to someone, lend it to someone, or tear it up, without asking permission from the copyright holder. Because the DMCA allows content providers to regulate access and use, they can set all the terms of use. And as with the database protection proposal, the de facto duration of protection under the DMCA is potentially infinite. While copyright law in 2000 protects any work created today for the life of the author plus seventy years or ninety years in the case of corporate "works for hire," electronic gates do not expire. This allows producers to "recapture" works already fallen or about to fall in the public domain. This also violates the constitutional mandate that Congress enact copyright laws that protect "for limited times." Most dangerously, producers could exercise editorial control over the uses of their materials. They could extract contractual promises that the use would not parody or criticize the work in exchange for access. Many web sites already do this. Just as dangerous, the DMCA allows producers to contractually bind users from reusing facts or ideas contained in the work. If a user wants to hack through access controls to make legitimate fair use of material inside—perhaps facts, an old film in the public domain, or pieces of the work for commentary or news—that user is subject to civil and criminal penalties under the DMCA.[32]

MAKING AN EXAMPLE OF HACKERS

As librarians, industry representatives, and copyright office staff at the Library of Congress debated the effects of this law during the summer of 2000, the Motion Picture Association of America was already hard at work trying to make an example out of those who might challenge it. The motion picture industry's newest format, the digital video disc (DVD), has two important access control features: a content scrambling system (CSS) and a region code, which ensures that users can play U.S.-purchased DVDs only on U.S.-purchased DVD players. Without the properly licensed DVD player from the right region of the world, a DVD will not play. Not surprisingly, some companies such as Sony produce both motion pictures and the machines one must play them on. The motion picture industry negotiated licenses with producers of stand-along DVD players and with both Apple and Microsoft so that computers running these operating systems could descramble the code on DVDs. But in 1999, one could not use a computer that runs on the open-source Linux operating system to run DVDs. So some programmers who use Linux created and distributed a small computer program called DeCSS, which hacks through the CSS and region code protection and deposits unscrambled data from DVD to a hard drive. DeCSS was invented by a team of creative and independently minded European programmers led by Jon Johanson, a sixteen-year-old Norwegian.[33]

Soon after an on-line hacker magazine called *2600* started alerting its readers as to where they could get a copy of DeCSS, the Motion Picture Association of America got an injunction against *2600* in federal court in New York. As the case went through to trial in the summer of 2000, the Electronic Frontier Foundation and the Berkman Center for Internet and Society at Harvard Law School began assisting the publisher's defense counsel to formulate a strategy to protect the journal's First Amendment rights in the face of a suit based on the anticircumvention provisions of the DMCA. Their arguments—which failed to persuade the federal judge—included the argument that DeCSS can be used for noninfringing purposes such as fair use viewings of DVDs from other countries. They also argued that because CSS can be used to protect material in the public domain, the DMCA is too broad.[34]

Public interest advocates also argued that Congress had left the definition of a protective "device" up to the copyright holder. The DMCA lets companies "write" the law, then puts the power of the state behind them. But the Copyright Clause of the U.S. Constitution gives only Congress the right to design copyright laws. It cannot delegate lawmaking authority. Underlying all of these concerns is one that should have dominated the discussion in 1998: If pirating is already illegal, why do we need this law? Congress decided it was easier to regulate machines than people. The DMCA was not only the enabling legislation for the WIPO treaties. It is the enabling legislation for the "Celestial Jukebox," the "pay-per-view universe," and what Neil Postman calls "Technopoly."

A PAY-PER-VIEW WORLD

As Neil Postman wrote, "Technopoly is a state of culture. It is also a state of mind. It consists in the deification of technology, which means that the culture seeks its authorization in technology, finds its satisfactions in technology, and takes its orders from technology." Postman was describing a condition, technopoly, which he defined as "what happens to society when the defenses against information glut have broken down. It is what happens when institutional life becomes inadequate to cope with too much information. It is what happens when a culture, overcome by information generated by technology, tries to employ technology itself as a means of providing clear direction and humane purpose." Among the defenses Postman cited are schools, courts, and the family. Postman didn't mention it at the time, and he perhaps had not even considered it, but copyright law is a system—an institution of practices and habits—that regulates information by creating artificial shortages for limited times and for limited purposes. It's an imperfect and sometimes inefficient mechanism to regulate information. But its imperfections and inefficiencies were its strengths, its democratic safeguards. And now, more through political intervention than technological irrelevancy, we find ourselves unwilling to accept the imperfections and inefficiencies inherent in copyright law. Now we turn to technology. We turn to code.[35]

As Lawrence Lessig writes, when code, not human beings, regulates copyright, the system forfeits its checks and balances.

> As privatized law, trusted systems regulate in the same domain where copyright law regulates, but unlike copyright law, they do not guarantee the same public use protection. Trusted systems give the

producer maximum control—admittedly at a cheaper cost, thus permitting many more authors to publish. But they give authors more control (either to charge for or limit use) in an area where the law gave less than perfect control. Code displaces the balance in copyright law and doctrines such as fair use.[36]

But copyright is already being replaced—or supplemented—by contract. Most commercial software and much digital content comes with what is known as a "Clickwrap" or "Shrinkwrap" license. Users often agree to waive rights, such as fair use and first sale, when they click on a web page button to get access to the content. For example, the site for Billboard.com charges its users $14.95 per month to get access to data on sales within the music industry. For that fee, members get to view five articles for no extra charge. But in addition to the monthly fee, Billboard.com charges its members from 50 cents to $2.50 per article or database view after the five free views. Much of the information within the gated web site is not available in print form. But researchers who use the Billboard.com site are contractually forbidden from disclosing the information they retrieve. The user license agreement states, "Unless separately and specifically licensed to do so in writing and by BPI (Billboard's parent company), subscriber agrees not to re-transmit, disclose, or distribute any of the information received from the service, to any other person, organization or entity." In other words, paying users must sign away their rights to fair use. Because there is no "sale" in the transaction, there is no concept of first sale. And the user is contractually forbidden from exploiting the idea-expression dichotomy. Users who choose not to pay for the information, those who hack through the web site lock to read the articles within, are subject to civil and criminal penalties through the DMCA. The Billboard.com system is protected by copyright plus contract plus code.[37]

Commercial software, even software distributed in compact disc form, is protected by similar licenses. Even though it might seem that when you spend money on software, you are buying a physical compact disc, you are actually only renting a license to use the encoded software. Consumers sign away fair use and first sale rights with regularity. It's a pay-per-install system that potentially allows for metered usage or even the electronic expiration of the software.

Many of our cultural products will soon be "triple protected" by copyright, contracts or licenses, and code. Therefore, they will be "closed systems," limited in their ability to enhance the public domain or enrich the public sphere.

NAPSTER NATION

But citizens are fighting back against these methods of digital and cultural control. The best example of this is the proliferation of peer-to-peer networks. The most famous of these networks is the music-sharing system called Napster. Napster was invented by a teenage college student named Sean Fanning. Fanning was living in Boston and spending a lot of time surfing the Internet in search of MP3 files. He grew frustrated with the sporadic availability of MP3s on the World Wide Web. So he hacked the software that allows people to peer into each other's hard drives to find and copy specific MP3s. The company he founded, Napster, has attracted million of dollars in venture capital, millions of users, and more than its share of lawsuits.

In July 2000 Napster went to U.S. district court in San Francisco to defend itself against a barrage of plaintiffs, including legendary composer Jerry Lieber and all the major record labels. The plaintiffs claimed that Napster is liable for contributory copyright infringement because it enables thousands of people to share and copy MP3s for no cost. The companies hope to plug up this leak in the music distribution system. The companies would like to distribute their music electronically, but in a format they control, under terms they dictate, for a price they can enforce.[38]

While Napster has frightened the music industry and attracted the attention of every major news organization, it is not the whole story. The issue is much larger than the fortunes of Napster itself. Even if a court shuts Napster down, the MP3 movement will thrive. And even if Napster survives, it's not so clear that people will stop buying CDs just because they can get free MP3s one song at a time. But regardless of the outcome of this case, the music industry will never be the same again.

The MP3 movement is a rational revolt of passionate fans. Compact discs cost too much. Cutting-edge fans want the newest, coolest music as fast as possible. So they share music and tips about music where they find each other—over the net. The free music strategy is, for lack of a better term, the Grateful Dead business model: Give away free music to build a loyal following, establish a brand name, and charge handsomely for the total entertainment package. Whole creative movements have established themselves through this process of community building. In the late 1970s, downtown New York punk fans found each other and discussed emerging artists through the handmade fanzines given away at the few clubs willing to host punk shows. At the same time, uptown in the Bronx, the hip-hop movement was spreading through a network of fans who would copy and lend tapes of artists like Grandmaster Flash and Kurtis Blow. Free music has always been essential to the discursive communities that fuel the creative process. These days, some small music labels such as Emusic.com and Chuck D's Rapstation.com are experimenting with "value-added" and "gatekeeper" business models, with modest taxation on consumers and artists (and thus modest profit potential). They depend on open systems, like the Internet itself, to foster creativity and "buzz" about their products and services.

MP3 distribution offers a wonderful opportunity for emerging artists, the very people copyright law is constitutionally charged to encourage and aid. Because the established music industry narrows the pipes of production and distribution, manufacturing scarcity, only established artists profit from the old system.

This new technology evades the professional gatekeepers, flattening the production and distribution pyramid. As Chuck D of Public Enemy says, Napster and other such networks are not pirating machines. He posits that Napster is radio. Fans will continue to download cheap or free music, and will continue to buy CDs if they offer value like documentation, design, arrangement, and convenience at a reasonable price.

There is another metaphor that might explain Napster and its effects better than a copy machine or a user-programmed radio: Napster is a public library.

Regardless of the direct effect on CD sales, MP3 distribution makes music fans more informed consumers. In the long run, the music industry could be more responsive to margins of the market, such as ethnic communities, subcultures, and political movements. Consumers can only express their preferences rationally if they enjoy good information and a fair pricing structure. MP3s let consumers taste before they buy, and let them act in concert with like-minded fans. They let music companies react instantly to changes in the market place. With better feedback, apparent "trends" would not surprise companies in the future. The charm of digital music distribution lies in the thought of capitalist theorists such as Friedrich von Hayek and W. Edwards Deming. The current mainstream music industry is a "planned economy," the sort Hayek railed against. It limits information flow and resists price pressures. And Deming advocated constant change, flexibility, new ideas, flat organizational structures, quick reactions to customer preferences, and maximum creativity.[39]

The MP3 phenomenon is a battle for control of the music and information pipelines, not the music itself. Since December 1999, several other Napster-like services have emerged on the net. Unlike Napster, these are noncommercial and community based. They depend on volunteer programmers to fix and improve the open systems. And unlike Napster, they pretty much assure privacy—for now. No one has any idea who else is using these services.

One of these relatively open systems is called Gnutella. Several versions exist, at least one for every common computer platform. Unlike Napster, it requires no password and has no registration process. Also unlike Napster, Gnutella lets users share all kinds of files—text, video, photos, software, and music. No one "runs" or "owns" Gnutella. Gnutella is a new kind of Internet. But it's really what the old Internet was supposed to be. It's free, open, decentralized, uncommercializable, ungovernable, and uncensorable.[40]

The rise of MP3 formats and free, open networks like Gnutella should have been expected. The culture industries invited them. They have hijacked the copyright system and drained it of any sense of public interest or balance. Copyright is an essential state-granted monopoly that works well when balanced. Thanks to the Clinton Administration and its partnerships with big media companies, it has lost its balance. What the content industries have claimed is a "crisis" of digital reproducibility is actually the opportunity they have been dreaming of.

The music industry has been stalling through litigation until it can establish a standard secure digital encryption format, which is an essential step toward a global "pay-per-view" culture. This technocratic regime will be a severe threat to democracy and creativity around the world.[41]

The important struggle is not bands versus fans, or even AOL Time Warner versus pirates. It involves the efforts of the content industries to create a "leak-proof" sales and delivery system, so they can offer all their products as streams of data triple sealed by copyright, contract, and digital locks. Then they can control access, use, and ultimately the flow of ideas and expressions. The content industries have been clear about their intentions to charge for every bit of data, stamp out the used CD market, and crush libraries by extinguishing fair use. In early July 2000, America Online signed a deal with a digital rights management system called InterTrust. InterTrust will provide the encryption and de-cryption technology to AOL's software so that AOL users will endure metered and regulated use of digital music, film, text, and everything else. And other digital music services are struggling to settle cases with the record industry so they can "partner" to install electronic "digital rights management" controls on their music.[42]

The reason the culture industries can take advantage of the "digital moment" to trump the democratic process and write their own laws is that digital formats collapse the distinction between using material and copying material. Because regulating reading or listening raises deep First Amendment concerns, courts have been unwilling to do so until now. However, copyright law regulates copying. So digital distribution allows a higher level of regulation than we ever imagined. Soon we may have to apply for a license to listen or read, and the rule of law will no longer apply. America Online will be the cop, jury, and judge in matters of copyright.

THE END OF COPYRIGHT?

In the summer of 2000, as the conflicts over Napster occupied front pages of newspapers and magazines across the nation, the public started asking itself some difficult questions about the nature and fu-ture of copyright. One of the most interesting of these discussions hap-pened in the on-line news magazine *Slate*, which is owned by the copy-right-rich Microsoft Corporation. *Slate* writer Robert Wright published two pieces that asked what music and literature might look like in a "post-copyright" age. Wright was not willing to declare copyright dead yet. He still saw that copyright holders had weapons of enforcement at their command. But the thought intrigued him. Flashing back to John Perry Barlow's predictions from 1996, Wright found that Napster and other peer-to-peer networks might actually create the necessary liber-tarian environment that could render copyright irrelevant. Wright pre-dicted that performers would be pressed to add value through liveness, and through high-quality technical delivery, rather than through the enforcement of a temporary monopoly over content. If consumers want stuff, they can get it for free. If consumers want good stuff, they will have to pay for it. And in the book industry, Wright predicted that for authors who could also perform—motivational speakers, for instance—money would still be forthcoming. The postcopyright economy would be brutal to many musicians and writers, and kind to others. Wright did not offer a sophisticated analysis of the role copyright plays in a democratic culture or the matrix of technological initiatives involved in the issue. He viewed it only in terms of the financial reward for artists. But the most interesting observations came from "The Fray," the on-line discussion that follows articles in *Slate*. Many readers who wrote in to "The Fray" were upset that Wright seemed so cavalier about the effects Napster might have on recording artists. Others were indignant about the arrogance of the record companies. Some readers declared that copyright was dead, so we should just forget about it and rejoice in the prospect of a future without big music labels. Others declared copyright untenable in the digital era and called for the strongest possible digital protection schemes. Still others declared copyright a natural right that emanates from the act of artistic creation. Napster had generated more than panic and glee. It had sparked some serious and sometimes nuanced discussion of copyright issues in the public sphere.[43]

Two years before Napster alerted the general public to the turmoil within the copyright system, American University law professor Peter Jaszi gave a speech he called "Is This the End of Copyright As We Know It?" In this talk, Jaszi argued that copyright was being displaced by three much stronger, almost leakproof systems that he called "pseudo-copyright," "paracopyright," and "metacopyright." "Pseudo-copyright" stood for data protection efforts. "Paracopyright" described the technological locks that would soon encase much digital content. And "metacopyright" stood for the system of contractual rights surrender. Jaszi concluded that the American tradition of "balanced" copyright had been very successful. He credited it with stimulating competition among content companies while nourishing a not-for-profit cultural sector that includes libraries, universities, and think tanks. Jaszi did not predict the demise of copyright. He outlined the initiative that content companies had been taking for years before anyone had dreamed of peer-to-peer distribution. The end of copyright was visible long before the general public became aware of it.[44]

What American jurists like James Madison have known for centuries is that a leaky copyright system works best. When properly balanced, copyright allows users to enjoy the benefits of cultural proliferation at relatively low cost through a limited state-granted monopoly. Libraries help that process by letting the wealthy subsidize information for the poor. And a thin, leaky copyright system allows people to comment on copyrighted works, make copies for teaching and research, and record their favorite programs for later viewing. Eventually, a copyright runs out, and the work enters the "public domain" for all of us to enjoy at an even lower cost. But when constructed recklessly, copyright can once again be an instrument of censorship, just as it was before the Statute of Anne.

Epilogue

The Summer without Martha Graham

FOR SOME GOOD reasons, we could call the summer of 2000 "the Summer of Napster." Not a week went by when the Revolutionary music distribution software did not garner headlines in the popular press. Everyone from college students to the U.S. Department of Justice weighed in on the matter. But I prefer to remember 2000 as "the Summer without Martha Graham."

Martha Graham, who died in 1991, was one of the most influential dancers and choreographers in the twentieth century. She collaborated with artists such as sculptor Isamu Noguchi and composer Aaron Copland, and is responsible for such Revolutionary works as *Primitive Mysteries*, *Frontier*, and her 1944 masterpiece, *Appalachian Spring*.[1]

Because of a nasty dispute between the Martha Graham Dance Company and Ron Protas, the director of the Martha Graham trust and the person who claims to control the copyrights on Graham's choreography, the company was not able to perform Graham's work throughout the summer. Protas wouldn't license the work to the company that bears Graham's name. In response, the dancers in the company asked other dance companies to refrain from performing Graham's works as well. So the dancing stopped.

Is this what we want our copyright system to do? Isn't copyright supposed to encourage art? And isn't copyright supposed to be secured only "for limited times"? Instead, more and more, excessive and almost perpetual copyright protection seems to be squelching beauty, impeding exposure, stifling creativity.

At first glance, it seems that we were denied the beauty of Martha Graham's dances because of a series of poorly thought out changes in copyright law—specifically the extension of the duration of copyright. Protection now can extend to the life of the author plus seventy years. This extension does nothing to promote creativity. It rewards the established at the expense of the emerging. From 1909 to 1978, artists enjoyed copyright protection for a fixed term of twenty-eight years. They could renew the copyright for another twenty-eight years if they thought there was still a market for their work. Once copyright expired, a work belonged to all of us. It entered the "public domain." As their copyrights expired, artists had a strong incentive to produce new works to make money. Publishers could issue inexpensive editions of great works. New artists could borrow liberally for their own new creations. But despite what the Constitution says, Congress has decided to extend copyright protection for what might as well be forever. This creates an almost perpetual monopoly over creative works and starves the public domain of raw material.[2]

Martha Graham recognized the value of the public domain for the creative process. She used Greek myths, Native American legends, and the Declaration of Independence as raw material for her dances. She went to the deep well of cultural signs and tropes, and used them in fresh and powerful ways. As dance scholar Brenda Dixon Gottschild explains, Graham incorporated several specific African elements into her style, including pelvic contortions and barefoot performance. And Graham was vocal about her reliance on what she called "primitive sources," African and Native American cultures.[3]

That's how creativity happens. Artists collaborate over space and time, even if they lived centuries and continents apart. Profound creativity requires maximum exposure to others' works and liberal freedoms to reuse and reshape others' material. Graham understood the collaborative creative process better than any lawyer or congressman ever could. She clearly was not interested in fencing in her or anyone else's creativity.

In fact, Graham never bothered to register copyrights over most of her dances created before 1978. She filed to protect only one—the 1946 tale of Medea entitled *Cave of the Heart*. So it turns out the summer without Martha Graham might not have had to happen that way. The best of Martha Graham might just be in the public domain anyway. But by the time lawyers for the dance company discovered the lack of registration, it was too late. The company had canceled its summer shows in the face of legal intimidation.[4]

Reckless "intellectual property" intimidation can have nearly the same effects in the culture as bad laws can. Despite a clear U.S. Supreme Court ruling in favor of the principle that parody is fair use, culture industries and their lawyers still seem to resist the idea. In July 1999, journalist Michael Colton posted an Internet parody of *Talk* magazine, which is a partnership between Hearst Magazines and Walt Disney-owned Miramax Films. Miramax lawyers sent a cease-and-desist letter to Earthlink, the Internet company that owned the server on which the parody sat. Earthlink immediately shut down the parody. It restored the site only after *Talk* editor Tina Brown appealed to the Miramax legal department to let the parody stand. Because of widespread misunderstanding of copyright law, cease-and-desist letters carry inordinate cultural power and can chill if not directly censor expression.[5]

Corporate legal intimidation has even chilled political speech. While running for reelection in the spring of 1999, Dallas mayor Ron Kirk aired a radio commercial that used the words "Four years ago, we chose Kirk captain of the Dallas enterprise. Well four years later, Dallas has become the center of the enterprise. With the largest capital bond program in the history of Dallas, a half a billion dollars, the Trinity toll (road) and the new arena add up to be a Starship Enterprise." The commercial also sampled the voice of William Shatner saying, "Space, the final frontier." Lawyers from Paramount Pictures threatened the campaign with a cease-and-desist letter. The campaign capitulated.[6] And in August 2000, Green Party presidential candidate Ralph Nader parodied a MasterCard advertisement by issuing a television advertisement saying: "Grilled tenderloin for fund-raiser, $1,000 a plate; campaign ads filled with half-truths, $10 million; promises to special interest groups, over $10 billion; finding out the truth, priceless." MasterCard International, Inc., filed a federal suit seeking an injunc-tion against the campaign. The suit claimed trademark infringement and unfair competition, but not a copyright violation. Nader eventually prevailed in court. While neither of these political cases would fall under the parody-as-fair-use defense for a copyright case, they both show how chillingly vigilant the content industries have grown in recent years. These companies firmly believe courts should side with their proprietary interests over those of the electorate. At the turn of the twenty-first century, invoking "intellectual property" is as good as using a trump card in public discourse. All discussion and debate stops.[7]

Following a strategy more pernicious than mere intimidation, media companies are actually pursuing legal action to stifle criticism of themselves. They are also using copyright suits to squelch clearly political speech. In October of 1998, the *Washington Post* and the *Los Angeles Times* filed suit against a conservative news forum web site called FreeRepublic.com. Members of the group had been pasting stories from various newspapers and annotating them, commenting on them. These newspapers brought legal action as an effort to control distribution of the web site's potentially valuable digital content. Other newspapers, including the *Wall Street Journal* and the *New York Times*, have signed contracts with a company called the Copyright Clearance Center so that it can meter, charge for, and regulate distribution of their digital content. The Copyright Clearance Center web site boasts, "CCC's new solution lets publishers and other content owners determine the types of reuse they wish to license. They decide whether to license use of their materials in electronic media such as e-mail, Internet, Intranet or CD-ROM; or in print media such as reprints or for republication. Copyright holders can also specify distinct rights, terms and conditions for different pieces of content." In other words, all electronic access, copying, and redistribution will require permission and payment. There will be no fair use of electronic news stories from the *Boston Globe*, the *New York Times, Barron's,* or the *Wall Street Journal*, arguably the most important news sources in the United States.[8]

In the 1970s, thanks to coverage of the Watergate scandal and the Pentagon Papers, the *New York Times* and the *Washington Post* were considered heroes for free speech and a free press. Now, as major "content providers" in the new digital economy, they are part of the problem. They are private copyright cops. And citizens who wish to gather, discuss, debate, and criticize must do so with one fearful eye on the front door, waiting for the cease-and-desist letter.

Recent expansions of copyright power have clearly stifled artistic creativity as well. Vladimir Nabokov's son, Dmitri Nabokov, succeeded in temporarily blocking American publication of Pia Pera's novel *Lo's Diary*, a revision of *Lolita* from the voice and point of view of the young girl. After some tense negotiation, Dmitri Nabokov agreed to allow publication as long as the American edition contained a nasty preface by the son. "Is *Lolita* to pay this price [the indignity of a transformative work] because it is too good, too famous? Are writers to strive for mediocrity lest their works similarly enter the 'common consciousness'? Are icons of popular culture—*Star Wars* perhaps—to be made subject to plundering by free riders because they have entered the common consciousness?" the younger Nabokov wrote in the preface.[9] Interestingly,

Star Wars screenwriter George Lucas "plundered" the work of Joseph Campbell and the myths of the collective public domain. Despite such an overt and acknowledged reliance on others for his material, Lucas himself has used lawyers to intimidate *Star Wars* fans who distribute their own unauthorized fanzines.[10] Despite entertaining such a narrow, elitist view of the creative process, Dmitri Nabokov had the law on his side. Copyright law grants estates control over transformative uses of their fictional characters. But is this good? Isn't the world better off with more than one perspective on the iconic yet controversial *Lolita* story? Wouldn't creativity flower if unfettered by fears of petty lawsuits by relatives who contributed nothing to the creative process in the first place? What public interest does it serve to enrich the heirs of Irving Berlin, Vladimir Nabokov, Martha Graham, or Gilbert O'Sullivan? Which system would better promote art: one in which anyone with a good idea for a James Bond story could compete in the marketplace of ideas for an audience or one in which those who control Ian Fleming's literary estate can prevent anyone from playing with his toys? A looser copyright system would produce more James Bond books, not fewer. Some might be excellent. Other might be crappy. Publishers and readers could sort out the difference for themselves. The law need not skew the balance as it has.

But there is hope in this story. All this talk of modern dances and MP3 files allows us to have a national—perhaps global—conversation about what sort of copyright policy we want to live with in the twenty-first century. Copyright policy should help—not hinder—the next Metallica, the next Martin Scorsese, the next Vladimir Nabokov, the next Martha Graham.

Maybe some summer not too many years from now a young woman will enjoy a performance of *Appalachian Spring* and will be inspired to borrow from it to construct a life of creativity and beauty. That's how Martha Graham would have wanted it.

Notes

NOTES TO THE INTRODUCTION

1. Groucho Marx to Warner Brothers, undated, 1944, Groucho Marx Papers, Library of Congress. Also published in Marx, *The Groucho Letters: Letters to and from Groucho Marx* (New York: Simon and Schuster, 1967).

2. Marx to Warner Brothers.

3. Marx, *Groucho Letters*, pp. 17–18

4. The best explanation of the democratic basis for copyright law is Neil Weinstock Netanel, "Copyright and Democratic Civil Society," in *Yale Law Journal* (November 1996). Also see Mark Lemley, "The Economics of Improvement in Intellectual Property Law," in *Texas Law Review* (April 1997); Peter Jaszi, "On the Author Effect: Contemporary Copyright and Collective Creativity," in Martha Woodmansee and Peter Jaszi, eds., *The Construction of Authorship: Textual Appropriation in Law and Literature* (Durham: Duke University Press, 1994); James Boyle, *Shamans, Software, and Spleens: Law and the Construction of the Information Society* (Cambridge: Harvard University Press, 1996); J. H. Reichman and Pamela Samuelson, "Intellectual Property Rights in Data?" *Vanderbilt Law Review* (January 1997): 49–166.

5. Jürgen Habermas, *The Structural Transformation of the Public Sphere: An Inquiry into a Category of Bourgeois Society* (Cambridge: MIT Press, 1991). Also see Thomas McCarthy, *The Critical Theory of Jürgen Habermas* (Cambridge: MIT Press, 1978). For an introduction to Habermas's contributions to the broad matrix of recent critical theory, see Seyla Benhabib, *Critique, Norm and Utopia: A Study of the Foundations of Critical Theory* (New York: Columbia University Press, 1986). For assessments of Habermas's critiques of postmodern antifoundationalism, see Maurizio Passerin d'Entreves and Seyla Benhabib, eds., *Habermas and the Unfinished Project of Modernity: Critical Essays on The Philosophical Discourse of Modernity* (Cambridge: MIT Press, 1997). According to Habermas, the "public sphere" includes the aspects of social life in which public opinion is formed. Ideally, access to the public sphere should be as democratic as possible, open to all citizens. In reality, some members of the public are louder than others, amplified by money, credentials, or reputation. Others are silenced by virtue of poverty, marginalized identities, or opinions. Interaction within the public sphere is distinct from legislative, commercial, or professional discourse, and

participants are free from coercion. Since the eighteenth century, instruments such as newspapers, magazines, town meetings, radio, television, and the Internet have operated as the sites of public interaction. But events such as dinner parties and barbecues can serve just as easily as loci for the public sphere. The purpose of the public sphere is to mediate between state and society. While individuals and interest groups can form opinions and promulgate them to the public, they cannot create "public opinion" without free, open, and informed dialogue exercised within the public sphere. As Europe shifted its decision-making habits from the private spheres of feudal states to the more public environs of bourgeois society, the public sphere emerged. Without such a sphere, republics could not have claimed legitimacy in the eighteenth and nineteenth centuries. These sociopolitical shifts were especially powerful in North American colonies in the 1770s and France in the 1780s, when citizens published—at their own expense—periodicals that advocated their views on matters of public policy and philosophy. But by the 1830s in the United States, many of the instruments of the bourgeois public sphere had started changing into purely commercial enterprises that facilitated "public relations" more than they forged consensus or "public opinion," starting a long process of what Habermas calls "the structural transformation of the public sphere." As a result of this transformation, state and commercial institutions have assumed some of the functions of the public sphere, and political institutions, such as parties, assume advocacy roles in support of their patrons. Habermas complains that this transformation has led to a "refeudalization" of the public sphere. Large and powerful organizations such as corporations, labor unions, political parties, professional groups, and interest groups bargain with the state and one another—often out of sight or mind of the public—to allocate resources, opportunities, and patronage. These institutions still seek public support and the marks of legitimacy, but they do this through the exercise of publicity or public relations, not necessarily through contributions to rich public discourse. Whenever an authentic public sphere appeared in the late twentieth century, it did so in an ad hoc fashion, before a specific election or within realms outside of state or commercial influence, such as electronic discussions during the early years of the Internet. These occasional acts of publicness usually occur only with the tacit consent of the interest groups that transformed the public sphere in the first place and are therefore limited by the public's unwillingness to antagonize these powers.

6. Michael Warner, *The Letters of the Republic: Publication and the Public Sphere in Eighteenth-Century America* (Cambridge: Harvard University Press, 1990). An essential corrective to Warner's bold thesis, and one that considers the ramifications of the development of copyright law, is Grantland S. Rice, *The Transformation of Authorship in America* (Chicago: University of Chicago Press, 1997).

7. Walter Lippmann, *Public Opinion* (New York: Macmillan, 1922). My understanding of the Lippmann-Dewey debates comes from several valuable discussions I have had the pleasure of having with James Carey and Jay Rosen. See Carey, *Communication as Culture* (New York: Routledge, 1992), pp. 74–82.

8. John Dewey, *The Public and Its Problems* (New York: Henry Holt and Co., 1927), p. 219.

9. Cathy N. Davidson, *Revolution and the Word: The Rise of the Novel in America* (New York: Oxford University Press, 1986). Also see Woodmansee and Jaszi; Boyle; David Sanjek, "'Don't Have to DJ No More': Sampling and the Autonomous Creator," in Woodmansee and Jaszi; Mark Rose, *Authors and Owners: The Invention of Copyright* (Cambridge: Harvard University Press, 1993).

10. Roland Barthes, "The Death of the Author," in *Image-Music-Text* (New York: Hill and Wang, 1977), pp. 142–48.

11. Michel Foucault, "What Is an Author?" in Josue Harari, ed., *Textual Strategies: Perspectives in Post-Structuralist Criticism* (Ithaca: Cornell University Press, 1979), pp. 141–60. While this analysis of an "author-function" is very useful, especially when trying to make sense of how copyright law operates in western culture, Foucault's essay offers a historical analysis that is suspect. Unfortunately, many critics and historians writing after Foucault have taken his analysis as gospel, without checking to see if it stands up to scrutiny. Foucault briefly outlined a story of the "author-function" in western culture that starts with a time in which there were writers, yet no "authors." Because Foucault's "author" is an author only because it (a function, not a person) has legal and cultural status and power, an "author" could not exist before the eighteenth century, when the first legal codifications of authorship emerged from European courts and parliaments. This invention has been dubbed "Romantic authorship," and the standard scholarly line since the publication of Foucault's essay concedes Foucault's intellectual power and accepts his definition uncritically. However, the cultural power and "authority" that Foucault describes could have and did precede their legal codification. This book is not the proper place to explore the accuracy, uses, and misuses of Foucault's historical claims, but I would urge others to search for examples of the "author-function" that precede 1709. The Apostles, Bhagavan Vyasa ("author-function" of the *Mahabharata*) and English Puritan ministers might be good places to start. Vyasa's authorship of the *Mahabharata* is a fascinating example in the history of authorship. Unlike many to whom authorship of religious texts has been ascribed, such as Mary Baker Eddy, Vyasa was not an earthly scribe for divine words. Instead, the sage enlisted the help (and four arms) of Lord Ganesha as a scribe for Vyasa's narration of the struggle between the Pandavas and the Kauravas and the battle of Kurukshetra. The deal Ganesha struck with Vyasa, however, required the sage to relate the tale in one sitting. If not for this condition, the epic poem might have been even longer. Vyasa, a Brahmin sage who commanded

the elephantine ears of the gods, had and has cultural power, to say the least. He and his Brahman descendants have exercised this power for centuries. Vyasa's role as author of the ninth-century B.C. story matches all of Foucault's criteria for an "author-function." This example of narrative technique demands further examination. See C. Rajagopalachari, *Mahabharata* (Bombay: Bharatiya Vidya Bhavan, 1978).

12. Mark Lemley, "Book Review—Romantic Authorship and the Rhetoric of Property," in *Texas Law Review* (March 1997): 873–906.

13. *Donaldson v. Becket*, House of Lords, 1774, in *Parliamentary History of England*, 17: 953.

14. Lemley, "Book Review—Romantic Authorship and the Rhetoric of Property," p. 895.

15. Henry Louis Gates, *The Signifying Monkey: A Theory of African American Literary Criticism* (New York: Oxford University Press, 1988), p. 66. Gates identifies how the anxiety of influence affected opinions of African and African American expression. Gates notes that David Hume and Thomas Jefferson both accused blacks of being merely imitative rather than creative.

16. Zora Neale Hurston, "Characteristics of Negro Expression" in *The Sanctified Church* (Berkeley: Turtle Island, 1981), pp. 59–60. Also in Gena Dagel Caponi, ed., *Signifyin', Sanctifyin', and Slam Dunking: A Reader in African American Expressive Culture* (Amherst: University of Massachusetts Press, 1999).

NOTES TO CHAPTER 1

1. Adam Moore, ed., *Intellectual Property: Moral, Legal, and International Dilemmas* (Lanham, Md.: Rowman & Littlefield, 1997), pp. 4–6. For a succinct explanation of the issues surrounding the attempted patenting of the human genome, see Siva Vaidhyanathan, "Human Genome," in *Ready Reference: Censorship* (Pasadena: Salem Press, 1997). Patent law emanates from the same section of the U.S. Constitution that empowers Congress to protect copyrights, art. 1, sec. 8. The federal patent law is Patent Act, 35 U.S.C. sec. 101 (1998). Congress added three years to the duration of patent protection in 1995, raising it from seventeen to twenty years.

2. Rosemary Coombe, *The Cultural Life of Intellectual Properties: Authorship, Appropriation, and the Law* (Durham: Duke University Press, 1998), p. 60.

3. Moore, p. 6. See *The Restatement (Third) of Unfair Competition*, sec. 39 (1995). See *Forest Laboratories Inc. v. Pillsbury Co.*, 453 F. 2d 621 (7th cir. 1971).

4. *Black's Law Dictionary*, 5th ed. (St. Paul: West Publishing Co., 1985), p. 304.

5. Harold Nelson and Dwight Teeter, *Law of Mass Communications*, 4th ed. (Mineola, NY: Foundation Press, 1982), pp. 251–261. For a summary of theoretical attacks on the valorization of authorship, see Sean Burke, *The Death and Re-*

turn of the Author: Criticism and Subjectivity in Barthes, Foucault, and Derrida (Edinburgh: Edinburgh University Press, 1992). For the influence of postmodern art on copyright theory, see Lynne A. Greenberg, "The Art of Appropriation: Puppies, Piracy, and Post-modernism," in *Cardozo Arts & Entertainment Law Journal* (1992). For the effects of sampling in rap music on copyright, see David Sanjek, "'Don't Have to DJ No More': Sampling and the Autonomous Creator," in Martha Woodmansee and Peter Jaszi, eds., *The Construction of Authorship: Textual Appropriation in Law and Literature* (Durham: Duke University Press, 1994). For a general historical account of the development of copyright, see Lyman Ray Patterson, *Copyright in Historical Perspective* (Nashville: Vanderbilt University Press, 1968).

6. James Madison, Federalist 43, in Alexander Hamilton, James Madison, and John Jay, *The Federalist* (Cambridge: Belknap Press, 1961), p. 309.

7. The republican virtues of copyright are best explained by Neil Weinstock Netanel, "Copyright and Democratic Civil Society," *Yale Law Journal* (November 1996): 356–86. Washington is quoted in Netanel, p. 357.

8. Thomas Jefferson to James Madison, Paris, July 31, 1788, in *The Writings of Thomas Jefferson*, vol. 7 (Washington: Thomas Jefferson Memorial Association, 1904), pp. 93–99.

9. Jefferson to Madison, Paris, August 28, 1789, in *The Writings of Thomas Jefferson*, 7:444–53.

10. Jefferson to Isaac McPherson, Monticello, August 13, 1813, in *The Writings of Thomas Jefferson*, 13:326–38. Louis Brandeis wrote (dissenting) in *International News Service v. Associated Press*, 248 U.S. 215, 250 (1918).

11. *Feist Publications, Inc. v. Rural Telephone Service*, 499 U.S. 340, 111 S. Ct. 1282, 113 L. Ed. 2d 358 (1991).

12. Victor A. Doyno, *Writing Huck Finn: Mark Twain's Creative Process* (Philadelphia: University of Pennsylvania Press, 1991), pp. 185–98. Also see Aubert J. Clark, *The Movement for International Copyright in Nineteenth Century America* (Washington, D.C.: Catholic University of America Press, 1960).

13. *Campbell v. Acuff-Rose Music, Inc.*, 114 S. Ct. 1164 (1994).

14. Paul Goldstein, *Copyright's Highway: The Law and Lore of Copyright from Gutenberg to the Celestial Jukebox* (New York: Hill and Wang, 1994), pp. 129–64.

15. Melville B. Nimmer, *Cases and Materials on Copyright*, 3d ed. (St. Paul: West Publishing Co., 1985), p. 27

16. Gen. 22:2

17. Bob Dylan, "Highway 61 Revisited," from *Highway 61 Revisited* (New York: Columbia Records/CBS, 1965), side 2.

18. Jonathan Kirsch, *Kirsch's Handbook of Publishing Law for Authors, Publishers, Editors, and Agents* (Los Angeles: Acrobat Books, 1995), pp. 7–8.

19. H.R. Rep. No. 94–1476, 94th Cong. 2d. Sess. 56–57 (1976).

20. *Baker v. Selden*, 101 U.S. 99 (1879).

21. *Feist Publications, Inc. v. Rural Telephone Service,* 499 U.S. 340, 111 S. Ct. 1282, 113 L. Ed. 2d 358 (1991). O'Connor is quoting from *Harper & Row, Publishers, Inc. v. Nation Enterprises,* 471 U.S. 539, 556 (1985).

22. Gen. 4:8.

23. I wish I could ask readers to indulge me in a brief explanation of the search for meaning as it has consumed three of the most influential linguistic philosophers of the nineteenth and twentieth centuries: Ferdinand de Saussure, Jacques Derrida, and Charles Sanders Peirce. However, it would take many pages and I would make many mistakes. For insight into how Saussure's theories of signs work, see Saussure, *Course in General Linguistics,* ed. Charles Bally and Albert Sechehaye, trans. Wade Baskin (New York: McGraw-Hill, 1959). Saussure's structuralism inspired many of the most important thinkers of the twentieth century, including Claude Levi-Strauss, Emile Durkheim, and Thomas Kuhn. Others have reworked or revised Saussure's structuralism. They include Roland Barthes, Stanley Fish, Umberto Eco, and Michel Foucault. Derrida offered the most sweeping revisions of structuralism. See Derrida, *Writing and Difference,* trans. Alan Bass (Chicago: University of Chicago Press, 1978). Also see Derrida, *Of Grammatology,* trans. Gayatri Spivak (Baltimore: Johns Hopkins University Press, 1974). Derrida, more than anyone, collapsed the space between the sign and the signified. However, he relied on the dyadic model of signs that Saussure generated at the beginning of the century. Thanks to the recent work of John K. Sheriff, Stephen Knapp, and Walter Benn Michaels, Peirce's linguistic models have returned to "save" meaning as a pragmatic concept, and for that I am greatly indebted. Peirce, a contemporary of Saussure, imagined a triadic model of signs, objects, and "interpretants." See Sheriff, *The Fate of Meaning: Charles Peirce, Structuralism, and Literature* (Princeton: Princeton University Press, 1989). Also see Knapp and Michaels, "Against Theory," in *Critical Inquiry* (summer 1982).

24. Jefferson, "Declaration of Independence," in David Hollinger and Charles Capper, eds., *The American Intellectual Tradition,* 2d ed. (New York: Oxford University Press, 1993), 1:131.

25. Charles C. Mann, "Who Will Own Your Next Good Idea?" *Atlantic Monthly,* September 1998, pp. 57–63.

26. See Amy Wallace, "It's Lights! Camera! Lawyers?" *Los Angeles Times,* Dec. 10, 1997, p. A1 (thanks to Kent Rasmussen for sending me a clip of this article). See *Art Buchwald et al. v. Paramount Pictures Corp.,* Superior Court for the State of California, County of Los Angeles, No. 706083. Both *Coming to America* and Eddie Murphy's first film, *Trading Places* (1983), were directed by John Landis and are variations on Mark Twain's comedy of manners *The Prince and the Pauper* (1882), which itself has antecedents in folklore. See Twain, *The Prince and the Pauper* (New York: Oxford University Press, 1996). For an example of subsequent "idea protection" suits, some appealing to copyright law, see *Woods v.*

Universal City Studios, Inc., 920 F. Supp. 62, Central District of California, 1995. The case involving *Seven*, which ended in favor of the studio, is *Sandoval v. New Line Cinema Corp.*, 973 F. Supp. 409, Southern District of New York, 1997.

NOTES TO CHAPTER 2

1. William Dean Howells, *My Mark Twain: Reminiscences and Criticisms*, ed. Marilyn Austin Baldwin (Baton Rouge: Louisiana State University Press, 1967), p. 80.

2. "Twain's Fancy Suit: Noted Humorist at Capitol in Cream-Colored Costume," *Washington Post*, Dec. 8, 1906, p. 1. Also see "Mark Twain in White Amuses Congressmen: Advocates New Copyright Law and Dress Reform," *New York Times*, Dec. 8, 1906. For an analysis of Twain's costume and performance at the hearings, see Susan Gillman, *Dark Twins: Imposture and Identity in Mark Twain's America* (Chicago: University of Chicago Press, 1989), pp. 181–88.

3. Lyman Ray Patterson, *Copyright in Historical Perspective* (Nashville: Vanderbilt University Press, 1968), p. 2. The accounts throughout this chapter owe their origins to Patterson's early work. For a lighter account of early copyright with a larger historical sweep of recent American copyright changes, see Patterson and Stanley Lindberg, *The Nature of Copyright: A Law of User's Rights* (Athens: University of Georgia Press, 1991). The most important recent historical revelations about early copyright can be found in a seminal law review article, Howard B. Abrams, "The Historic Foundation of American Copyright Law: Exploding the Myth of Common Law Copyright," in *Wayne Law Review*, (spring 1983): 1119–89. The best historical rendering of the changes in copyright policy in the United Kingdom is John Feather, *Publishing, Piracy, and Politics: An Historical Study of Copyright in Britain* (London: Mansell Publishing, 1994). Also see Harry Ransom, *The First Copyright Statute: An Essay on an Act for the Encouragement of Learning, 1709* (Austin: University of Texas Press, 1956). Also see Ransom, "The Theory of Literary Property: 1760–1775," Ph.D. diss., Yale University, 1938. Another well-written historical account of early copyright debates can be found in Paul Goldstein, *Copyright's Highway: The Law and Lore of Copyright from Gutenberg to the Celestial Jukebox* (New York: Hill and Wang, 1994). While Goldstein's recent opinions about the goals of copyright policy are disturbing, he is a talented writer and one of the world's top authorities on copyright law. John Tebbel, *A History of Book Publishing in the United States*, 2 vols. (New York: R. R. Bowker, 1972), offers a broad but shallow account of early copyright efforts in both the colonies and the early republic, but his bias is toward copyright as a natural or property right, and he evades or misses the antimonopolistic philosophy that tempered American copyright law for more than a century. Tebbel does not see perpetual monopoly control as a threat to democratic speech. Tebbel's biggest problem, however, is that he seems completely unaware of

British copyright law, even of the Statute of Anne of 1709, which clearly inspired the titles and timbre of early American law. A brilliant treatise on British copyright in the seventeenth and eighteenth centuries, from a postmodern perspective, is Mark Rose, *Authors and Owners: The Invention of Copyright* (Cambridge: Harvard University Press, 1993). Rose is inspired by Foucault and other recent theorists, yet does not rely on theory for easy answers. The best account of the struggles for international copyright is still a brilliant dissertation, Aubert J. Clark, *The Movement for International Copyright in Nineteenth Century America* (Washington, D.C.: Catholic University of America Press, 1960). Clark's only major flaw is that the dissertation is embedded with Thomistic natural law theories of property rights. Clark's attachment to natural law does not allow him to consider the policy balances and interest group battles that determined copyright policy throughout the century. To his credit, Clark does not, as most publishing historians do, blame resistance to international copyright and expanded copyright protection on some mysterious "anti-intellectualism" among the American public and its leaders.

4. Abrams, pp. 1135–37. Also see Benjamin Kaplan, *An Unhurried View of Copyright* (New York: Columbia University Press, 1967), p. 5, and Patterson, pp. 65–69. This is not so different from the rights acquisition process that operated in the late twentieth century, except that now copyright is considered a "bundle" of rights, and an author can negotiate to sell all or one of those licenses to exclusively distribute the work. For instance, an author can sell her work as a "work for hire" to a company, which would then own all the rights to it in all media for a ninety-five-year term. Or an author can sell one segment of that bundle, such as hardcover book rights, while retaining serial rights, film rights, CD-ROM rights, audio tape rights, etc. If the author reserves the copyright in her name, the copyright will last seventy years past her death. In either case, the publishing company, for all practical purposes, controls the printing, marketing, design, and distribution of the material, and the author has only contractual guarantees that her wishes will be heeded. Even in modern copyright, the publisher, not the author, is the key player in the legal and commercial marketplace.

5. Patterson, pp. 130–42.

6. Tebbel, 1:45.

7. Tebbel, 1:46

8. William Hening, *The Statutes at Large, Being a Collection of All the Laws of Virginia*, vol. 2 (Wilmington, Dl.: Michael Glazier, 1978), p. 518

9. Patterson, pp. 120–130.

10. Quoted in Kaplan, p. 7, and Abrams, p. 1139.

11. Patterson, p. 142.

12. Patterson, pp. 142–45. Ransom called the Statute of Anne "the first copyright law," because it was the first statute to overtly recognize authorship.

However, more sophisticated readings of the historical record by Kaplan, Patterson, and Abrams have yielded the conclusion that the Statute of Anne was a symptom of change in the political and commercial climates, but not a fundamental change from previous law. For an elaboration of the misnamed "Lockean" theory of copyright, see Grantland Rice, *The Transformation of Authorship in America* (Chicago: University of Chicago Press, 1997), pp. 70–96. For an explanation of how Locke's thought does not in fact necessarily support maximum copyright protection, see Peter Drahos, *A Philosophy of Intellectual Property* (Aldershot: Dartmouth Publishing Company, 1996), pp. 47–72. Fear of monopolies was one of the greatest concerns of the liberals who were exercising increased influence on the British political scene in the late seventeenth and early eighteenth centuries. John Locke, who is sometimes unfairly associated with maximum-protection philosophies of copyright because his theories of real property are misapplied to copyright, was one of the strongest critics of both censorship and monopoly power—both of which were the purposes of the Stationers' Company practice and the licensing acts. In 1709, copyright was not about property, it was about control.

13. For a lucid description of the tensions between the common law and statutory law, see Richard Posner, *The Economics of Justice* (Cambridge: Harvard University Press, 1981), pp. 13–47. In this chapter, Posner describes the conflicts between William Blackstone and Jeremy Bentham. But Posner is too harsh on poor Bentham. Posner describes Bentham as having such a passionate attachment to radical parliamentary reform, representative democracy, and harsh utilitarianism that Bentham's principles could somehow justify fascism. Bentham's devout liberalism (which did need clarification by John Stuart Mill and others) seems not to have allayed Posner's concerns. Posner also avoids consideration of Blackstone's investment in a political status quo that was far from liberal, and not too far from authoritarian. Until the Reform Acts of the nineteenth century, British electoral practices were unrepresentative, corrupt, and stacked against free trade and free speech. Bentham, John Locke, James Mill, John Stuart Mill, and Adam Smith chipped away at the intellectual foundation of the conservative status quo that Blackstone embraced, yet Posner's chapter does not give these thinkers credit for outlining the classical liberal principles that Posner himself has spent his career invoking and defending. Still, the chapter is a magnificent introduction to Blackstone's work, and serves as an effective way to understand the dynamics of the common law. See William Blackstone, *Commentaries on the Laws of England* (Buntingford: Layston Press, 1966). For a more muddled account of the development of common law, see Norman Cantor, *Imagining the Law: Common Law and the Foundations of the American Legal System* (New York: HarperCollins, 1997). Also see Lawrence Friedman, *American Law* (New York: W. W. Norton, 1984), p. 16. An essential text to understanding how American common law differs from English is that of Oliver Wendell

Holmes Jr., *The Common Law* (Cambridge: Belknap Press, 1963). Also see Benjamin Kaplan, Patrick Atiyah, and Jan Vetter, *Holmes and the Common Law: A Century Later* (Cambridge: Harvard University Press, 1981). Also see Edward G. White, *Justice Oliver Wendell Holmes: Law and the Inner Self* (New York: Oxford University Press, 1993).

14. John Locke, *Two Treatises of Government*, ed. Peter Laslett (London: Cambridge University Press, 1960), pp. 303–20. As stated above, Locke himself never applied his "mixing metaphor" or his theory of property to copyright. But since it was far from settled in the late seventeenth century that copyright was a property right, it is unfair to infer that Locke would have considered it so.

15. Goldstein, pp. 44–46.

16. *Millar v. Taylor*, in Burr (4th ed.), p. 2303, 98 English Reports, p. 201 (K.B. 1769). See Abrams, pp. 1152–54.

17. Abrams, pp. 1156–71. Abrams shows that historians and judges have consistently misread the documentation from *Donaldson v. Becket* and incorrectly ruled that there was a common law copyright, but the Statute of Anne supplanted it. In fact, Abrams shows, the House of Lords rejected the idea that there ever had been a common law copyright. Had the historical record been clearer, perhaps the theory behind copyright would be clearly in favor of a strong and broad public domain.

18. Tebbel, 1:138–41.

19. U.S. Constitution, art. 1, sec. 8. Both James Madison and Charles Pinckney introduced versions of the copyright and patent clause. The convention approved the plank unanimously without debate or dissent. See Jonathan Elliot, ed., *The Debates in the Several State Conventions on the Adoption of the Federal Constitution*, vol. 5 (Philadelphia: J. B. Lippincott Co., 1836), p. 440.

20. James Madison, Number 43: "Powers Delegated to the General Government: III," in Alexander Hamilton, James Madison, and John Jay, *The Federalist*, ed. Benjamin F. Wright (Cambridge: Belknap Press, 1961), p. 309.

21. Noah Webster, "Origin of the Copy-Right Laws," in *A Collection of Papers on Political, Literary, and Moral Subjects* (New York: Webster & Clark, 1843). Also see Harry Warfel, *Noah Webster: Schoolmaster to America* (New York: Macmillan Co., 1936), pp. 54–60, 184–85, 393.

22. Hellmut Lehman-Haupt, *The Book in America* (New York: R. R. Bowker Co., 1951), pp. 56, 74–85.

23. Clark,. pp. 30–31. Also see Frank Luther Mott, *Golden Multitudes* (New York: Macmillan Co., 1947).

24. Harry Ransom, *The First Copyright Statute*; Ruth Finnegan, *Oral Literature in Africa* (London: Oxford University Press, 1970), p. 9. For an account of Martial's complaint about *plagium*, see Goldstein, *Copyright's Highway*, p. 39.

25. Rose, p. 1. Mark Rose, in his book *Authors and Owners: The Invention of Copyright*, describes the rise of the author class and the ways it defined itself

within the terms of the liberal notions of property. Rose argues that the distinguishing characteristic of the modern author is proprietorship, not originality or genius. The author is defined as the originator of the work, and that role as originator generates status as an owner of the work. The historiography of "authorship" in America is complex and controversial. See Cathy N. Davidson, *Revolution and the Word: The Rise of the Novel in America* (New York: Oxford University Press, 1986), pp. 29–30. Also see Michel Foucault, "What Is an Author?" in Josue Harari, ed.,*Textual Strategies: Perspectives in Post-Structuralist Criticism,* (Ithaca: Cornell University Press, 1979). In her otherwise excellent history of early American novels and their readership, Davidson asserts that American authorship as an intellectual and economic force was absent just after the Revolution. "The early national era antedated the romantic period's notions of the author as the prime creator of art and a concomitant critical privileging of the artist's intentions," Davidson writes. For evidence that the author is merely a creation of the romantic period, Davidson cites Foucault's essay "What Is an Author?" This essay, while important, is hardly sufficient evidence for such a sweeping statement about authorship in the early republic. Authorship is much older than the romantic movement. While British romantics did promote the idea of authorial genius to pass a new copyright law, they did not "invent" the concept. Literary theorists and historians often confuse this political action with a literary phenomenon, and they simply cite Foucault's essay as proof. But Foucault had no way of knowing, for instance, about the preamble to the North Carolina Copyright Act of 1785, which read: "Whereas nothing is more strictly a man's own than the fruit of his study, and it is proper that men should be encouraged to pursue useful knowledge by the hope of reward; and as the security of literary property must greatly tend to encourage genius . . ." Authorship was not a product of the romantic era. It just reached its apex of marketability and political power in the romantic era. The western notion of authorship, as Ransom noted, is much older than the eighteenth or nineteenth century. Davidson is correct, however, in explaining that American authors were certainly less powerful and had less "cultural capital" in the early nineteenth century than they had soon after. Certainly, by the last quarter of the nineteenth century, American publishing was a big international business and some authors were emerging as stars. The battles that forged modern copyright doctrines were financial and political, not literary and philosophical. Only when authors had money and political power could they fight the battle, and the valorization of the author was merely a weapon. See Patterson, p. 187, and Rose, p. 8.

26. *Wheaton v. Peters,* 33 U.S. (8 Peters) 591 (January 1834). Legal historian Lyman Ray Patterson described the multiple and often conflicting goals of American copyright laws in the early republic. On the one hand, state copyright statutes under the Articles of Confederation declared that copyright was to benefit the author primarily. Yet the U.S. Constitution states that copyright is

necessary for learning and is a public good. The first federal copyright act saw it as a governmental grant or privilege. And that copyright was meant to prevent or limit a dangerous monopoly was central to the case of *Wheaton v. Peters,* the first major American copyright decision.

27. Rose, pp. 111–12

28. Rose, pp. 6 and 110–11. It was clear by 1842 that the British author was powerful. The writing community sowed the seeds of valorization, and the intellectual ground was fertile. Rose explains that the liberal discourse of intellectual property blended well with the eighteenth-century discourse of original genius, such that by the 1770s, the doctrine of originality was orthodox in England.

29. Patterson, pp. 181 and 203–11

30. *Stowe v. Thomas,* 23 Federal Cases 201 (No. 13,514), 2 American Law Register 210, Circuit Court of the United States, for the Eastern District of Pennsylvania, October 1853.

31. George P. Sanger, ed., *Statutes at Large and Proclamations of the United States of America from December, 1869 to March ,1871,* vol. 16 (Boston, 1871), pp. 212–17. Reprinted in Thorvald Solberg, *Copyright Enactments of the United States, 1783–1906* (Washington, D.C.: Government Printing Office, 1906), pp. 46–51. The act was signed July 8, 1870. Section 86 of the law states,

> And be it further enacted, That any citizen of the United States, or resident therein, who shall be the author . . . of any book . . . shall, upon complying with the provisions of this act, have the sole liberty of printing, reprinting, publishing . . . and in the case of dramatic composition, of publicly performing or representing it . . . and authors may reserve the right to dramatize or to translate their own works.

For an invaluable account of the *Stowe v. Thomas* case and the literary and legal issues surrounding the translation of *Uncle Tom's Cabin,* see Melissa J. Homestead, "The Author/Mother in the Marketplace and in Court: Harriet Beecher Stowe and the Copyright in *Uncle Tom's Cabin,*" unpublished, 1996. This paper became part of Homestead's doctoral dissertation, "Imperfect Title: Nineteenth-Century American Women Authors and Literary Property," which she completed in the spring of 1998 for the English Department at the University of Pennsylvania. In the paper, Homestead reveals some fascinating aspects of the case. For instance, the main "Stowe" in *Stowe v. Thomas* was in fact Harriet Beecher Stowe's husband, Calvin Stowe. Under the nineteenth-century legal principle of "coverture," her husband controlled all claims to her wealth and property. She had almost no legal standing. Calvin signed her publishing contract with John P. Jewett. Calvin also had to grant his consent for Harriet to be co-plaintiff in the suit against Thomas. Homestead also reveals that Judge Robert Grier's Third Circuit Court of Appeals in Philadelphia was responsible for enforcing the Fugitive Slave Act of 1850, which was central to the understanding of and popularity of Stowe's book. Homestead has investigated the manner in which Stowe registered for and gave notice of her copyright for the periodical installments of *Uncle Tom's Cabin* before the book came out in one volume, and found that Stowe had not taken the proper legal measures to secure her copyright. Although improper registration was not an issue in *Stowe v. Thomas*, and Stowe did not face any other American legal challenges to her copyright for *Uncle Tom's Cabin*, Homestead makes it clear that she likely would have lost a suit that challenged the registration. Technical problems such as this one inspired Congress to remove the registration requirement in the 1976 copyright revision.

32. Clark, p. 27

33. Clark, p. 40

34. Clark, p. 79.

35. Clark, p. 79. See Charles Dickens, *American Notes* (Philadelphia: T. B. Peterson & Brothers, n.d.). This copy, part of the "People's Edition" library, was a pirated version printed some time in or after the late 1860s, as indicated by the text of "The Uncommercial Traveller," included after *American Notes*. In *American Notes*, Dickens refrained from criticizing American copyright law, and instead focused on two much more repugnant evils: slavery and tobacco spitting.

36. Charles A. Madison, *The Owl among Colophons: Henry Holt as Publisher and Editor* (New York: Holt, Rinehart and Winston, 1966), pp. 21–25. For another excellent example of how courtesy worked (barely) for British authors, see Michael Winship, *American Literary Publishing in the Mid-Nineteenth Century: The Business of Ticknor and Fields* (New York: Cambridge University Press, 1995), pp. 135–40. Usually Ticknor and Fields paid British authors a flat fee upon receipt of proof sheets or advance sheets before the first British printing. Occasionally Ticknor and Fields paid British authors a 10 percent royalty, which was standard treatment for American authors.

37. Charles A. Madison, *Book Publishing in America* (New York: McGraw-Hill Book Company, 1966), pp. 52–57.

38. Clark, pp. 122–24, 137–40

39. *Reports of the Committee of the Senate of the United States*, 1st Session, 49th Congress, VII, No. 1188, pp. 115–20.

40. Clark, pp. 140–48

41. Clark, pp. 100, 163–81

42. Frederick Anderson, William Gibson and Henry Nash Smith, eds., *Selected Mark Twain–Howells Letters, 1872–1910* (Cambridge: Harvard University Press, 1967), pp. 53–54.

43. Mark Twain, "American Authors and British Pirates," in *Life As I Find It* (Garden City, N.Y.: Hanover House, 1961), pp. 219–26.

44. As quoted in Clark, p. 140.

45. Samuel Charles Webster, ed., *Mark Twain, Business Man* (Boston: Little, Brown and Co., 1946), p. 315.

46. Twain, "American Authors and British Pirates," p. 222.

47. See Gillman.

48. Twain, *Roughing It* (Berkeley: University of California Press, 1993), pp. 221–27.

49. Victor Doyno, *Writing Huck Finn: Mark Twain's Creative Process.* (Philadelphia: University of Pennsylvania Press, 1991), pp. 186–91. Detailed and invaluable information about Twain's own literary appetites can be found in Alan Gribben, *Mark Twain's Library: A Reconstruction*, 2 vols. (Boston: G. K. Hall, 1980).

50. Mark Twain to William Dean Howells, October 30, 1880, Mark Twain Papers, Bancroft Library, Berkeley, Calif. Also printed and analyzed in Doyno, p. 187.

51. Twain, part of "Plain Speech from American Authors," in *Century,* February 1886, p. 634.

52. Twain, testimony before the Senate Committee on Patents, January 29, 1886. Reprinted in Paul Fatout, ed., *Mark Twain Speaking* (Iowa City: University of Iowa Press, 1976), pp. 206–9.

53. Anderson, Gibson, and Smith, pp. 53–54.

54. Webster, pp. 353–54.

55. Mark Twain, *Mark Twain in Eruption: Hitherto Unpublished Pages about Men and Events* (New York: Harper and Brothers, 1922), p. 374.

56. Mark Twain, *Christian Science* (New York: Harper and Brothers Publishers, 1907), p. 141.

57. Twain, *Christian Science*, pp. 139–43.

58. Twain, "American Authors and British Pirates: A Private Letter and a Public Postscript," from *New Princeton Review,* January 1888. This piece is a response to Brander Matthews, "American Authors and British Pirates," from *New Princeton Review,* September 1887.

59. Albert Bigelow Paine, ed., *Mark Twain's Letters* (New York: Harper & Brothers, 1917), p. 731.

60. Paine, *Mark Twain's Letters*, p. 732.

61. Paine, *Mark Twain's Letters*, p. 731.

62. Paine, *Mark Twain's Letters*, p. 732.

63. Twain, "A True Story, Repeated Word for Word as I Heard It," in *Atlantic Monthly,* November 1874. Reprinted in Twain, *Sketches, New and Old* (New York: Oxford University Press, 1996). For a full account and analysis of the significance of Mary Ann Cord's influence on Twain's literary development, see Shelley Fisher Fishkin, *Was Huck Black? Mark Twain and African American Voices* (New York: Oxford University Press, 1993), and Fisher Fishkin, *Lighting Out for*

the Territory: Reflections on Mark Twain and American Culture (New York: Oxford University Press, 1997).

64. Twain, "How to Tell a Story," in *Literary Essays* (New York: Harper & Brothers, 1899), pp. 7–15.

65. Twain, *Mark Twain to Uncle Remus, 1881–1885* (Atlanta: Emory University, 1953), p. 11.

66. Ralph Ellison, "Twentieth Century Fiction and the Black Mask of Humanity," in *Shadow and Act* (New York: New American Library, 1964), pp. 42–60.

67. Resisting the temptation to leave this section unattributed, without notes or references, I have opted instead to declare that some of the ideas expressed in it are mine, and others are not. However, I concede that it is valuable to point readers toward three important works that deal with the issue of plagiarism. The most comprehensive is Thomas Mallon, *Stolen Words: Forays into the Origins and Ravages of Plagiarism* (New York: Ticknor & Fields, 1989). The second, more specific yet more poignant, is Jim Swan, "Touching Words: Helen Keller, Plagiarism, Authorship," in Martha Woodmansee and Peter Jaszi, eds., *The Construction of Authorship: Textual Appropriation in Law and Literature* (Durham: Duke University Press, 1994). A comprehensive bibliography of plagiarism (which sadly does not adequately distinguish plagiarism from copyright infringement) is Judy Anderson, *Plagiarism, Copyright Violation, and Other Thefts of Intellectual Property: An Annotated Bibliography with a Lengthy Introduction* (Jefferson, N.C.: McFarland & Co., 1998). For some recent debates over the professional sins of plagiarism, see Denise K. Manger, "History Association to Probe Accusations of Plagiarism against Stephen Oates," *Chronicle of Higher Education*, June 2, 1993, pp. A12–A14. Also see Calvin Reid, "Novel at Center of 'Roots' Plagiarism Suit Reissued," in *Publishers Weekly*, July 12, 1993, p. 13. For the effects of plagiarism on scientific research, see Karen Hopkins, ed., "Scientific Plagiarism and the Theft of Ideas," *Science*, July 30, 1993, p. 631. Also see M. H. Crawford, "Plagiarism and Scientific Communication: A Cautionary Note," *Human Biology*, October 1993, pp. 687–88. A substantial examination of some of the most notorious recent scholarly plagiarism cases—and the misapplication of state power to police them—can be found in Gary Taubes, "Fraud Busters: The Rise and Spectacular Fall of Walter Stewart and Ned Feder, SMI (Scientific Misconduct Investigators)," *Lingua Franca*, September/October 1993, p. 47. An interesting and revealing recent case that conflates the issues of accusations of unethical plagiarism and illegal copyright infringement was the public battle between historian William Manchester and novelist/journalist Joe McGinness. Manchester's *The Death of a President* (New York: Arbor House, 1967) served as a source for McGinness's *The Last Brother* (New York: Simon & Schuster, 1993). See Sarah Lyall, "Enter Manchester, Angrily," *New York Times*, July 21, 1993, p. C17. For a defense, see McGinnis, "Credit Check," *New York*, July 26, 1993, pp.

6–8. Two articles in *New York* magazine explore the ethical and legal ramifications of the Manchester-McGinnis dispute. See John Taylor, "Clip Job," *New York*, July 12, 1993, pp. 22–25. And see John Taylor, "Clip Job II," *New York*, July 26, 1993, pp. 14–15.

68. "Recently discovered" and "unexamined" are strong terms that imply a measure of individual industry or cleverness. I mean no such thing. No one— especially not I—"discovered" the document "The Great Republic's Peanut Stand." Finding this dialogue required no detective work, just curiosity. As a caveat and qualification, I must explain that the manuscript lay for many years at the bottom of a box of materials labeled "Copyright" in the Mark Twain Papers at the Bancroft Library in Berkeley. I am just the first person anyone can seem to remember who bothered to read everything in that box. Robert Hirst, editor-in-chief of the Mark Twain Project at Berkeley, said that to the best of his knowledge, no scholar has discussed the piece with him, written about it, or requested permission to publish it or quote from it. That does not mean that no scholar read it before I did. It does not mean that it was never published in any form. Many of Twain's unpublished works made their way into various collections that his biographers and literary executors assembled after his death. However, I have done what I consider a broad sweep of the later collections, and found only one citation of the dialogue, in a list of works Twain wrote in Austria in 1898. See Carl Dolmetsch, *Our Famous Guest: Mark Twain in Vienna* (Athens: University of Georgia Press, 1992). Dolmetsch does not analyze the manuscript or consider the value of its content. For most of the twentieth century, Twain scholars paid little or no attention to copyright law, despite Twain's own well-documented concerns. There are four exceptions. The first literary executor of Twain's work, Albert Bigelow Paine, had a deep interest in copyright law, which he shared with Twain in his later years. Paine discussed copyright at length in his three-volume biography of Twain, *Mark Twain: A Biography, the Personal and Literary Life of Samuel Langhorne Clemens* (New York: Harper & Brothers, 1912). To my knowledge, only two other published scholarly treatises seriously examine Twain's interest in copyright as a major factor in his life and work. The best is Victor Doyno, *Writing Huck Finn*. Doyno explores in great depth Twain's efforts to secure an international copyright treaty among all English-reading nations to limit piracy. The other is Gillman, *Dark Twins*. Two other unpublished works have dealt with Twain's interest in copyright law. A 1968 University of California doctoral dissertation by Herbert Feinstein, "Mark Twain's Lawsuits," does a wonderful job of describing Twain's life as a litigant. Many of his suits as both plaintiff and defendant concerned alleged copyright violations. Feinstein, a lawyer, also wrote articles on Twain and copyright for the American Bar Association and *The Twainian*, the newsletter of the Mark Twain Research Foundation. Most recently, David Briggs, a graduate student in the School of Library and Information Studies at the University of California at

Berkeley and a staff member at the Mark Twain Project, compiled *A Compendium of Sources concerning Mark Twain's Dilemma with International Copyright, 1867–1883: Emphasis on His Problems with Canadian Pirates*.

69. Mark Twain, "The Great Republic's Peanut Stand," manuscript, Mark Twain Papers, Bancroft Library, p. 1*. This and all other quotes from Mark Twain's previously unpublished works are under the control of Edward J. Willi and Manufacturers Hanover Trust Company as Trustees of the Mark Twain Foundation, which reserves all reproduction or dramatization rights in every medium. Quotation is made with the permission of the University of California Press and Robert H. Hirst, general editor of the Mark Twain Papers. Each quotation is identified in the text by an asterisk (*).

70. Mark Twain, "Concerning Copyright: An Open Letter to the Register of Copyrights," *North American Review*, January 1905, pp. 1–8.

71. U.S. Congress, Joint Committee of Patents. "Arguments before the Committees on Patents of the Senate and House of Representatives, Conjointly, on the Bills S. 6330 and H.R. 19853, to Amend and Consolidate the Acts Respecting Copyright," December 7, 8, 10, and 11 (Washington: Government Printing Office, 1906).

72. Doyno, pp. 184–98.

73. U.S. Constitution, art. 1, sec. 8. "Congress shall have the power . . . to promote the progress of science and useful arts, by securing for limited times to authors and inventors the exclusive right to their respective writings and discoveries." Also see Adam Smith, *An Inquiry into the Nature and Causes of the Wealth of Nations* (1776), ed. R. H. Campbell and A. S. Skinner (Oxford: Clarendon Press, 1976), p. 754. Also see James Madison, Federalist 43, in *The Federalist Papers*, ed. Clinton Rossiter (New York: New American Library 1961), pp. 271–72.

74. Goldstein, pp. 165–96. Also see Jane Ginsburg, "A Tale of Two Copyrights: Literary Property in Revolutionary France and America," *Tulane Law Review* (1990).

75. Twain, "The Great Republic's Peanut Stand," pp. 1–3.

76. Twain, "The Great Republic's Peanut Stand," pp. 6–7.

77. For a full exploration and examples of Twain's frustration with American imperialism from 1898 to 1905, see Twain, *Mark Twain's Weapons of Satire: Anti-Imperialist Writings on the Philippine-American War*, ed. Jim Zwick (Syracuse: Syracuse University Press, 1992), and Louis Budd, *Mark Twain, Social Philosopher* (Bloomington: Indiana University Press, 1962). Thomas Babington Macaulay, *Prose and Poetry*, ed. G. Young (Cambridge: Harvard University Press, 1952), pp. 733–37.

78. Twain, "The Great Republic's Peanut Stand," pp. 32–34.

79. Twain, "The Great Republic's Peanut Stand," p. 43.

80. Twain, "The Great Republic's Peanut Stand," pp. 56–59.

81. Twain, "The Great Republic's Peanut Stand," pp. 56–58.

82. Twain, "Remarks on Copyright," in Fatout, p. 335.

83. Senate Bill 6330, 59th Congress, first session, 1906.

84. *Mark Twain's Speeches* (New York: Harper & Brothers, 1910), p. 324.

85. *Copyright Law Revision* (Washington: Committee on the Judiciary, U.S. Senate, 1960), p. 4.

86. Paine, *Mark Twain's Letters*, 2:831.

87. Siva Vaidhyanathan, "The New Imperialism: The Assault on Fair Use and Free Expression by International Copyright," unpublished. Delivered to the annual meeting of the American Studies Association, Washington, D.C., November 1, 1997. For a brief outline of the three treaties, see Eric Schwartz, "International Outlook: Impact of the Two New WIPO Treaties," in *Intellectual Property Strategist,* January 1997, p. 1. For an in-depth examination of how both dangerous and unnecessary the database treaty is, see J. H. Reichman and Pamela Samuelson, "Intellectual Property Rights in Data?" *Vanderbilt Law Review* (January 1997): 49–166.

NOTES TO CHAPTER 3

1. The Marx Brothers and Metro-Goldwyn lost two and won one of the infringement cases against them. The first Marx Brothers-related suit was *Clancy v. Metro-Goldwyn Pictures Corp. et al,* 37 U.S.P.Q. 406. District Court, Southern District of New York, March 26, 1938. A fellow named Clancy wrote a play he called "Nuts to You." Clancy met in January 1935 with Robert Pirosh, an official of Metro-Goldwyn Pictures Corporation. At the meeting, Clancy summarized his idea for a film based on the play. Two years later, Metro-Goldwyn released the Marx Brothers vehicle *A Day at the Races,* written by Pirosh, George Seaton, and George Oppenheimer. In both "Nuts to You" and *A Day at the Races,* a veterinarian (played by Groucho Marx in the film) runs a sanitarium and also owns a racehorse. In his suit, Clancy did not claim that Pirosh or the Marx Brothers used any of his dialogue, or even that they had read his play. As the judge in the case wrote,

> There is no contention that any of the language has been copied by the defendants, but merely that the general idea or plot was taken. . . . There was nothing particularly original in having a veterinarian act as a psychiatrist in a private sanitarium, and, even if there were, the plaintiff would be entitled to no protection for the idea after he had voluntarily disclosed it to another.

Determining that the similarity was not strong enough to justify a ruling of infringement, the judge dismissed the complaint. The second case was *Marx et al. v. United States,* 37 U.S.P.Q. 380 (96 Fed. 2d 204), Circuit Court of Appeals, Ninth

Circuit, April 12, 1938. This was a criminal copyright case in which the Marx Brothers were convicted of infringing on a dramatic composition called "The Hollywood Adventures of Mr. Dibble and Mr. Dabble." The authors, Garrett and Carroll Graham, mailed their copyrighted script to Groucho Marx, who expressed interest. Soon afterward, the Graham brothers met with one of the Marx Brothers' writers named Boasborg. They never reached a deal on the transfer of rights. On September 1, 1936, the Marx Brothers performed a slightly altered version of the script on a radio show without permission or payment. Their defense was that they forgot about the Grahams' script. The Marx Brothers lost in court and on appeal. The third Marx Brothers case was a state suit filed in California, *Barsha v. Metro-Goldwyn-Mayer et al.*, 32 Cal. App. 2d 556 (90 P. 2d 371), District Court of Appeals, California, May 8, 1939. In this case, the plaintiffs had met with Irving Thalberg, the production manager for the film *A Day at the Races*, and had given him a copy of their scenario called "High Fever," which was written specifically for the Marx Brothers and had a plot substantially similar to that of the film *A Day at the Races*. The plaintiffs prevailed both at the state district court level and on appeal, so the studio paid them $10,000. This chapter owes much of its substance to two brilliant law review articles and an essential short book. See Peter Jaszi, "When Works Collide: Derivative Motion Pictures, Underlying Rights and the Public Interest," in *UCLA Law Review* 28 (1981): 715–815. Also see Mark A. Lemley, "The Economics of Improvement in Intellectual Property Law," *Texas Law Review* (April 1997): 990–1084. Also see Benjamin Kaplan, *An Unhurried View of Copyright* (New York: Columbia University Press, 1967).

  2. *Universal City Studios, Inc., et al. v. Sony Corporation of America, et al*, 480 F. Supp. 429 (203 U.S.P.Q 656), U.S. District Court, Central District of California, Oct. 2, 1979. *Groucho Marx Productions, Inc., et al. v. Day and Night Company, Inc., et al*, 689 F. 2d 317, U.S. Court of Appeals, Second Circuit, Sept. 10, 1982.

  3. The expansion of the list of media that enjoy copyright protection can be traced through the text of the various federal copyright revisions. See Copyright Office, *Copyright Enactments: Laws Passed in the United States since 1783 Relating to Copyright* (Washington, D.C.: Library of Congress, 1973).

  4. Mark Twain *The Death Disk*, in *The $30,000 Bequest and Other Stories* (New York: Oxford University Press, 1996), pp. 430–45.

  5. Robert M. Henderson, *D. W. Griffith: The Years at Biograph* (New York: Farrar, Straus and Giroux, 1970), p. 88. Also see Eileen Bowser, ed., *Biograph Bulletins, 1908–1912* (New York: Octagon Books, 1973), p. 147. The film was released by the Biograph Company on December 2, 1909. As of July 1998, I have not had a chance to see the Griffith film *The Death Disc*. The description of the changes Griffith made to the story come entirely from the bulletin for the film and from Henderson.

  6. Thomas Carlyle, *Oliver Cromwell's Letters and Speeches, with Elucidations*

(London: Chapman and Hall, 1888), part 5, p. 11. Twain owned an edition printed around 1882, but the text of the story was not changed for later editions. See Alan Gribben, *Mark Twain's Library: A Reconstruction* (Boston: G. K. Hall, 1980), 1:129.

7. Gribben, p. 129. Also see Charles L. Crow, "Death Disk, The," in James R. LeMaster and James D. Wilson, *The Mark Twain Encyclopedia* (New York: Garland Publishing, 1993), pp. 210–11. Also see R. Kent Rasmussen, *Mark Twain A to Z: The Essential Reference to His Life and Writings* (New York: Facts on File, 1995), p. 108.

8. I can't be sure that Griffith failed to secure permission for *The Death Disc*. I have searched the Mark Twain Papers in Berkeley for some mention of the film, some letter to Biograph or Griffith, and found none. I have searched microfilm copies of the D. W. Griffith papers from the Museum of Modern Art, and found no evidence that Griffith or Biograph asked for or secured permission for the stories. I have seen a pattern in Griffith's records that indicates he grew more concerned with rights—both his own and those of his sources—as he became more successful in the years immediately following *The Death Disc*.

9. For a brief synopsis of Carlyle's life and work, see Margaret Drabble, *The Oxford Companion to English Literature*, 5th ed. (New York: Oxford University Press, 1985), pp. 170–71. For an excellent and concise summary of the history of British copyright, see Drabble, pp. 1113–25.

10. Tino Balio, *The American Film Industry* (Madison: University of Wisconsin Press, 1976), pp. 3–4.

11. Balio, pp. 5–6.

12. Balio, pp. 7–8.

13. *Edison v. Lubin*, 119 F. 993, Circuit Court, Eastern District of Pennsylvania, Jan. 13, 1903.

14. *Edison v. Lubin*, 122 F. 240, Circuit Court of Appeals, Third Circuit, April 20, 1903. District Judge Buffington's opinion in the case appeals to a theory of communication that prefigures the structuralist ideas of Roland Barthes. As Buffington claimed, the viewers create meaning in a motion picture. The source of the images, the raw product, does not matter at all to him.

15. *Barnes v. Miner et al.*, 122 F. 480, Circuit Court, Southern District of New York, March 30, 1903.

16. Balio, p. 9.

17. *American Mutoscope & Biograph Co. v. Edison Manufacturing Co.*, 137 F. 262, Circuit Court, District of New Jersey, May 6, 1905. I could not determine the final disposition of the case. This ruling only rejects a plea for an injunction against Edison's version. Perhaps Biograph's lawyers did not foresee winning the case on its merits, so settled or dropped the case.

18. Ralph Cassady Jr., "Monopoly in Motion Picture Production and Distribution: 1908–1915," in Gorham Kindem, ed., *The American Movie Industry: The*

Business of Motion Pictures (Carbondale: Southern Illinois University Press, 1982), pp. 25–68. Also see Jeanne Thomas Allen, "The Decay of the Motion Picture Patents Company," in Balio, pp. 119–134. Also see Janet Staiger, "Combination and Litigation: Structures of U.S. Film Distribution, 1896–1917," *Cinema Journal* (winter 1983): 41–73.

19. Balio, p. 105.

20. Lew Wallace, *Ben-Hur: A Tale of the Christ* (New York: Harper and Brothers, 1880). The copyright notice on the first edition is in the name of Harper and Brothers, not Wallace himself. Also see James D. Hart, ed., *The Oxford Companion to American Literature*, 5th ed. (New York: Oxford University Press, 1983), p. 67.

21. *Harper and Brothers et al. v. Kalem Co. et al.*, 169 F. 61. Circuit Court of Appeals, Second Circuit, March 16, 1909.

22. *Holmes v. Donahue et al*, 77 F. 179, Circuit Court, Northern District of Illinois, July 1, 1896. *Holmes v. Hurst*, 76 F. 757, Circuit Court, Eastern District of New York, Nov. 6, 1896. *Holmes v. Hurst*, 80 F. 514, Circuit Court of Appeals, Second Circuit, May 3, 1897. *Holmes v. Hurst*, 174 U.S. 82, 19 S. Ct. 606, U.S. Supreme Court, April 24, 1899. Both *Donahue* and *Hurst* concern a popular collection of Dr. Oliver Wendell Holmes's stories, *The Autocrat of the Breakfast Table* (1858). Starting in 1857, the *Atlantic Monthly* published twelve articles by Dr. Holmes that eventually constituted the chapters of *The Autocrat of the Breakfast Table*. Dr. Holmes did not register them with the Copyright Office until they had been collected into a book in 1858. By 1896, several publishing houses had printed pirated copies of the book, claiming that because Holmes had not registered a copyright for each article before it was published in the *Atlantic*, he held no copyright over them and they were in the public domain. Courts at all levels—right up to the U.S. Supreme Court—agreed with the pirates. Holmes and his lawyers were unable to convince the courts that he should have some common law control over his publications, regardless of the letter of the law. The immediate ramification of these rulings was that pirates searched back issues of magazines for articles that eventually made up chapters of famous authors' books. These included *The Minister's Wooing* (1859) by Harriet Beecher Stowe, chapters of which were also published in the *Atlantic* before they were submitted to the Copyright Office. The Stowe cases include *Mifflin et al. v. Dutton et al.*, 107 F. 708, 112 F. 1004, and 190 U.S. 265 (23 S. Ct. 771), U.S. Supreme Court, June 1, 1903. The frustration over losing these cases—not to mention the income that would have been derived from setting monopoly prices on *The Autocrat of the Breakfast Table*—might have motivated Holmes to radically revise copyright principles in his Supreme Court opinions. My understanding of the Holmes decisions was greatly aided by Paul Goldstein, *Copyright's Highway: The Law and Lore of Copyright from Gutenberg to the Celestial Jukebox* (New York: Hill and Wang, 1994), pp. 60–68. *Bleistein v. Donaldson Lithograph Co.*, 188 U.S. 239, U.S. Supreme Court,

1903. Also see *White-Smith Music Publishing Co. v. Apollo Co.*, 209 U.S. 1, U.S. Supreme Court, 1908.

23. *Kalem Co. v. Harper Bros.*, 222 U.S. 55, U.S. Supreme Court, Nov. 13, 1911. The legal saga of *Ben-Hur* on the big screen did not end with the Supreme Court's *Kalem* decision. Five years later, Harper Brothers sued the dramatic production company that had purchased the rights to *Ben-Hur*. See *Harper Bros. et al. v. Klaw et al.*, 232 Fed. R., District Court, Southern District of New York, Jan. 6, 1916. The publisher claimed it had assigned rights to Klaw and Erlanger only for a stage production. Klaw and Erlanger, however, argued that they owned all dramatic rights, even to those forms of dramatization that had yet to be invented in 1899, such as narrative film or video games. The judge granted an injunction against Klaw and Erlanger's attempts to license an authorized film version of *Ben-Hur*, and urged the publisher and drama company to come to terms on the rights transfer. They never did. No film version of *Ben-Hur* emerged until a Metro-Goldwyn silent production in 1926, eighteen years after the novel entered the public domain and just as the copyright on the dramatization expired. Another version, also by Metro-Goldwyn-Mayer, and starring Charlton Heston in full sound and Technicolor, came out in 1959. Holmes's decision in *Kalem*, while setting a valuable precedent, did not generate any income for the Wallace family, the publisher, or the dramatization company, and denied the viewing public a film version of *Ben-Hur* for two decades.

24. Henderson, p. 10. For summaries of the content and attribution of Griffith's Biograph films, see Bowser. For biographical information on London and Norris, see Hart. Jack London lived from 1876 to 1916, and published his first collection of short stories in book form in 1900. Therefore, assuming he registered the stories properly with the Copyright Office in the Library of Congress, none of London's stories entered the public domain until 1914. *The Call of the Wild* was published in 1903, so would not have entered the public domain until 1917. London first published "Just Meat" in *Cosmopolitan* in March 1907, so it would have entered the public domain in 1928. See Hensley Woodbridge, ed., *Jack London: A Bibliography* (Georgetown, Cal.: Talisman Press, 1966), p. 224. Frank Norris lived from 1870 to 1902. The collection of short stories entitled *A Deal in Wheat* was published posthumously in 1903, but the short story by the same title first appeared in *Everybody's Magazine* in August 1902, two months before Norris died from complications from an appendectomy. See Joseph Gaer, ed., *Frank Norris: Bibliography and Biographical Data* (New York: Burt Franklin, 1935). There is a chance the short stories "Just Meat" and "A Deal in Wheat" were in the public domain if the authors or the magazines failed to register them properly. There are no records in the microfilm edition of Griffith's papers that show that either Griffith or Biograph requested or received permission to base any of these films on London or Norris stories. None of the Biograph bulletins for these films makes any mention of literary sources. For Griffith's literary in-

fluences, see Richard Schickel, *D. W. Griffith: An American Life* (New York: Simon and Schuster, 1984), pp. 637–47.

25. *London v. Biograph Co.*, 231 Fed. Rep., pp. 696–99. Circuit Court of Appeals, Second Circuit, Feb. 15, 1916.

26. Henderson, p. 101. Schickel, p. 152. For the full bulletin advertising the film *Ramona*, see Bowser, p. 197. For information on Helen Hunt Jackson, see Hart, p. 373. Also see Valerie Sherer Mathes, *Helen Hunt Jackson and Her Indian Reform Legacy* (Austin: University of Texas Press, 1990). See Helen Hunt Jackson, *Ramona: A Story* (Boston: Little, Brown and Company, 1913). Little, Brown first published the novel for Jackson in 1884. Jackson died the following year. The original copyright on the novel would have expired in 1898, but Jackson's heirs could have renewed the copyright for another fourteen years. That term would have expired in 1912. Biograph could have waited two years to use *Ramona* as a public domain work, but the company would have saved only $100 and would not have been able to advertise the film's authenticity.

27. "An Act to Amend and Consolidate the Acts Respecting Copyright," March 4, 1909 (in effect July 1, 1909), in Copyright Office, *Copyright Enactments* (Washington, D.C.: Library of Congress), pp. 64–86. "Act of August 24, 1912," in Copyright Office, *Copyright Enactments*, pp. 87–91.

28. Frank E. Woods to Albert H. T. Banzhaf, Sept. 5, 1914, D. W. Griffith Papers, Museum of Modern Art, New York. Albert H. T. Banzhaf to Librarian of Congress, Sept. 19, 1914, Griffith Papers. Woods was responsible for suggesting that Griffith purchase the rights to Thomas Dixon's *The Clansman*, which became the film *The Birth of a Nation* in 1915.

29. Albert H. T. Banzhaf to Thorvald Solberg, Oct. 1, 1914, Griffith Papers. Thorvald Solberg to Albert H. T. Banzhaf, Oct. 2, 1914, Griffith Papers.

30. Albert H. T. Banzhaf to Frank E. Woods, Oct. 3, 1914, Griffith Papers.

31. Albert H. T. Banzhaf to World Film Corporation, June 13, 1918, Griffith Papers. There is no reply from World Film Corporation in the Griffith Papers. For information on the Griffith film *Hearts of the World*, see Schickel, pp. 340–60. Also see Scott Simmon, *The Films of D. W. Griffith* (New York: Cambridge University Press, 1993), p. 11. I could find no information on the World Film Corporation's film *Heart of the World*. I have found no evidence to suggest that Griffith changed the title of *The Clansman* to *The Birth of a Nation* so that he could establish some measure of control of the story or title. For complex and unpersuasive theories about the decision to change the name of the film, see Seymore Stern, "Griffith I: 'The Birth of a Nation,'" in *Film Culture* (spring–summer 1965): 150–57. The most commonly told story about the name change is that Dixon himself thought *The Birth of a Nation* would be a bolder title than *The Clansman*, and convinced Griffith to change it between the Los Angeles and New York releases in February 1915. See Terry Ramsaye, *A Million and One Nights* (New York: Simon & Schuster, 1926), p. 641. American copyright law still does not

protect titles. However, some other areas of the law such as trademark and unfair competition law have evolved to protect titles in some instances. See Melville B. Nimmer, *Cases and Materials on Copyright*, 3d ed. (St. Paul: West Publishing Co., 1985). Also see Jonathan Kirsch, *Kirsch's Handbook of Publishing Law for Authors, Publishers, Editors, and Agents* (Los Angeles: Acrobat Books, 1995).

32. D. W. Griffith Studio to Fulton Brylawski, Sept. 18, 1918, Dec. 14, 1918, March 18, 1919, May 15, 1919, Griffith Papers. Fulton Brylawski to D. W. Griffith Studio, May 29, 1919, Griffith Papers.

33. "An Act to Amend and Consolidate the Acts Respecting Copyright," March 4, 1909 (in effect July 1, 1909), in Copyright Office, *Copyright Enactments*, pp. 64–86. Two sections of this law created corporate copyright. Sec. 3 states: "That the copyright provided by this Act shall protect all the copyrightable component parts of the work copyrighted, and all matter therein in which copyright is already subsisting, but without extending the duration or scope of such copyright. The copyright upon composite works or periodicals shall give to the proprietor thereof all the rights in respect thereto which he would have if each part were individually copyrighted under this Act." And Sec. 23, which established the extended copyright terms Mark Twain fought for, reads:

> That the copyright secured by this Act shall endure for twenty-eight years from the date of the first publication, whether the copyrighted work bears the author's true name or is published anonymously or under an assumed name: Provided that in the case of any posthumous work or of any periodical, cyclopaedic, or other composite work upon which the copyright was originally secured by the proprietor thereof, or of any work copyrighted by a corporate body (otherwise than as an assignee or licensee of the individual author) or by an employer for whom such work is made for hire, the proprietor of such copyright shall be entitled to a renewal and extension of the copyright in such work for the further term of twenty-eight years.

34. Albert H. T. Banzhaf to S. E. V. Taylor, Feb. 13, 1919, Griffith Papers. Taylor to Banzhaf, Feb. 15, 1919, Griffith Papers.

35. Schickel, pp. 643–45. Contract between Edward Roberts and David Wark Griffith, March 18, 1919, Griffith Papers.

36. D. W. Griffith Studio to Lee Johnson, March 21, 1919, Griffith Papers. Also see Schickel, pp. 240–44.

37. Stern, pp. 103–41. Also see Schickel, pp. 240–44.

38. Schickel, pp. 245–46.

39. Roy Gilder to W. H. T. Banzhaf, Jan. 11, 1917, Griffith Papers. Contract between David Wark Griffith and Wark Producing Corporation, Jan. 12, 1917, Griffith Papers. Certificate of Copyright Registration for *Intolerance*, Copyright Office, Library of Congress, Washington, D.C., Jan. 8, 1917.

40. *Hein v. Harris,* 175 F. 875, Southern District of New York, 1910. See Gerald Gunther, *Learned Hand: The Man and the Judge* (New York: Alfred A. Knopf, 1994), pp. 315–43. Also see Kaplan, pp. 87–92. As Gunther explains, Hand's opinions from the bench also aided in the century-long process of relieving authors from government censorship. Hand was instrumental in lifting the heavy hand of censorship from H. L. Mencken's magazine, the *American Mercury,* in 1927, and James Joyce's great novel *Ulysses* in 1934. See *United States v. One Book Called "Ulysses,"* 5 F. Supp. 182, Southern District of New York, 1933. Also see the ruling on appeal by Hand's court, *United States v. One Book Entitled Ulysses,* 72 F. 2d 705, U.S. Second Circuit, 1934. For background on the *Ulysses* censorship cases, see Kenneth R. Stevens, "'Ulysses' on Trial," in Dave Oliphant and Thomas Zigal, eds., *Joyce at Texas: Essays on the James Joyce Materials at the Humanities Research Center* (Austin: Humanities Research Center of the University of Texas, 1983), pp. 91–105.

41. Gunther, pp. 323–28.

42. *Nichols v. Universal Pictures Corp.,* 45 F. 2d 119, Second Circuit Court of Appeals, 1930. See Kaplan, pp. 46–48. For a critique of the weaknesses of Hand's definitions of the idea/expression dichotomy in the *Nichols* decision, see Alfred Yen, "A First Amendment Perspective on the Idea/Expression Dichotomy and Copyright in a Work's 'Total Concept and Feel.'" *Emory Law Journal* (1989): 404–6.

43. The trial court decision is *Sheldon v. Metro-Goldwyn Pictures Corp.,* 7 Fed. Supp. 837, Southern District of New York, 1934.

44. Hand's opinion on appeal is *Sheldon v. Metro-Goldwyn Pictures Corp.,* 81 F. 2d 49, Second Circuit Court of Appeals, 1936. See Kaplan, pp. 48–52. See Gunther, pp. 325–28.

45. The segments of story that Hand had identified among the four tellings of a similar tale are examples of what French literary theorist Roland Barthes would years later call a "lexia," a basic element of a narrative text. See Roland Barthes, *S/Z,* trans. Richard Miller (New York: Hill and Wang, 1974), pp. 13–14. Barthes defines a "lexia" as "the best possible space in which we can observe meanings." In *S/Z,* Barthes outlines and defines five narrative "codes" that a text employs (or a reader interprets) to achieve, receive, or create meaning. These five codes are the "hermeneutic code," which governs disclosure, or how the reader gets to know (or fail to know) things; the "proairatic code," which links plot points into a plot, the sequence of events and actions; the "semic code," which sheds light on characters; the "symbolic code," which explores themes and links the text to abstract concepts; and the "cultural code," which influences what the reader makes of the text in terms of the knowledge the reader brings to it. See Barthes, pp. 18–20. Also see Adam Newton, *Narrative Ethics* (Cambridge: Harvard University Press, 1995). Newton adds a sixth code, the "ethical code," to the methods for unlocking the functions of a text. Clearly,

Hand was playing a structuralist game in his reading of the four narratives involved in the *Sheldon* case. In the near future, I will go through Hand's opinion in *Sheldon* and explain it as an act of narratology.

46. *Becker v. Loew's, Inc.*, 133 F. 2d 889, Circuit Court of Appeals, Seventh Circuit, 1943. A historian who wrote a biography of William Randolph Hearst engaged Orson Welles and RKO Pictures in a long-running suit over the alleged use of his book in the production of the script for *Citizen Kane*. The case dragged on for years because of conflicts over discovery, and I was not able to determine the final resolution of the case, but it seems likely the plaintiff gave up in frustration. See *Lundberg v. Welles et al.*, 11 F.R.D. 136, U.S. District Court, Southern District of New York, 1951.

47. Judy Quinn, "*Amistad:* Tie-ins and Trouble," *Publisher's Weekly*, Nov. 3, 1997, p. 19. Sharon Waxman, "Judge Allows Release of Spielberg's *Amistad;* Plagiarism Suit against Filmmaker to Proceed," *Washington Post,* Dec. 9, 1997, p. D1. Marla Matzer, "Plagiarism Suit Targets *Full Monty,*" *Los Angeles Times,* March 3, 1998, p. A1. Preliminary injunctions in copyright suits are one of the few constitutionally sanctioned methods of prior restraint of otherwise free communication. The threshold for injunctions in copyright suits, unlike other causes of action in free speech cases, is alarmingly low, despite the fact that in commercial fields such as book publishing and motion picture production, remedies for infringement are available long after the release of any work. See Mark Lemley and Eugene Volokh, "Freedom of Speech and Injunctions in Intellectual Property Cases," Duke Law Journal 48 (1998): 147–217.

48. *Sid and Marty Krofft Television Prods., Inc. v. McDonald's Corp.*, 562 F. 2d 1157, Ninth Circuit Court of Appeals, 1977. See Yen, pp. 407–15. *H. R. Pufnstuf* scared me as a child. I used to have nightmares about the trees. On the other hand, McDonaldland did nothing for me. Had I been called as a six-year-old expert witness, I would have testified that no child would be stupid enough to confuse the two habitats. The prime motivation for the plot of the series was that Jimmy was trapped on an island and could not get off. The kids in McDonaldland never wanted to leave, because the charming characters kept feeding them and entertaining them. Besides, any kid could tell you that one was in a show and the other was in a commercial. Commercials last only 30 seconds. Seeing McDonaldland commercials for most of my childhood never even generated for me a loose association with *H.R. Pufnstuf.* Until I read about this case, I had not imagined that anyone could have even assumed the two settings had anything in common. Living Island had monsters, witches, evil trees, and an unhappy boy with an annoying flute. McDonaldland was led by jolly Mayor McCheese and a ubiquitous clown named Ronald. The most threatening character in the McDonald's commercials was the bumbling Hamburglar. The court record does not show that any young children were consulted for this case.

49. *Roth Greeting Cards v. United Card Co.*, 429 F. 2d 1106, Ninth Circuit Court of Appeals, 1970. See Yen, pp. 407–8.

50. According to Yen, some cases that could have fallen under the "total concept and feel" criteria but did not include *Hartman v. Hallmark Cards, Inc.*, 833 F. 2d 117, Eighth Circuit, 1987; *Berkie v. Crichton*, 761 F. 2d 1298, Ninth Circuit, 1985; and *Litchfield v. Spielberg*, 736 F. 2d 1352, Ninth Circuit, 1984. See Yen, p. 411, n. 108. One case that Yen did not list, yet that deserves fuller exploration elsewhere, is *Twentieth Century-Fox Film Corp. et al. v. MCA, Inc., et al.*, 715 F. 2d 1327, Ninth Circuit Court of Appeals, 1983. This case concerned possible infringement of the film *Star Wars* (1977) by the film and television series *Battlestar Galactica* (1978). The trial court judge complained that the Ninth Circuit, in *Krofft*, required him to submit the films to the vague test for "total concept and feel." He then rebelled and issued a summary judgment for the defendant, dismissing the copyright claim. The Ninth Circuit reversed that summary judgment and ordered a trial.

51. See Amy Wallace, "It's Lights! Camera! Lawyers?" *Los Angeles Times*, Dec. 10, 1997, p. A1 (my thanks to Kent Rasmussen for sending me a clip of this article). See *Art Buchwald et al. v. Paramount Pictures Corp.*, Superior Court for the State of California, County of Los Angeles, No. 706083. Both *Coming to America* and Eddie Murphy's first film, *Trading Places* (1983), were directed by John Landis and are variations on Mark Twain's comedy of manners *The Prince and the Pauper* (1882), which itself has antecedents in folklore. See Twain, *The Prince and the Pauper* (New York: Oxford University Press, 1996). The *12 Monkeys* case is *Woods v. Universal City Studios, Inc.*, 920 F. Supp. 62, Central District of California, 1995. The case involving *Seven*, which ended in favor of the studio, is *Sandoval v. New Line Cinema Corp.*, 973 F. Supp. 409, Southern District of New York, 1997. See Lemley and Volokh.

NOTES TO CHAPTER 4

1. Led Zeppelin, "Whole Lotta Love," on *Led Zeppelin II* (New York: Atlantic Records, 1969). In the 1994 digitally remastered release of *Led Zeppelin II*, Willie Dixon receives co-songwriting credit for "Whole Lotta Love" after Jimmy Page, Robert Plant, John Paul Jones, and John Bonham.

2. Willie Dixon, "You Need Love," on various artists, *Blues Masters, Volume 6* (New York: Rhino Records, 1993). The Dixon composition was originally released as a Muddy Waters recording by Chess Records in 1962. See Steve Hochman, "Willie Dixon's Daughter Makes Sure Legacy Lives On," *Los Angeles Times*, Oct. 8, 1994, p. F10. Also see Greg Kot, "Willie Dixon's Heavenly Legacy: Blues Heaven Foundation Aims to Smooth the Road for Other Blues Artists," *Chicago Tribune*, Dec. 17, 1993, p. 5.

3. Willie Dixon and Don Snowden, *I Am the Blues: The Willie Dixon Story* (New York: Da Capo Press, 1989), p. 223. Information on the Blues Heaven Foundation can be found on the World Wide Web at http://www.island.net/~blues/heaven.html. The troubling relationship between blues composers and their record and publishing companies is much clearer. More often than not, it was blatantly exploitative. For an account of the relationship between Chicago rhythm and blues labels and their exploited artists, see Mike Rowe, *Chicago Breakdown* (New York: Da Capo Press, 1979). Also see Robert Pruter, *Chicago Soul* (Urbana: University of Illinois Press, 1991). For a study of the cultural and social meaning of blues in Chicago, see Charles Keil, *Urban Blues* (Chicago: University of Chicago Press, 1966). For the most penetrating study of the blues aesthetic in American culture, see Albert Murray, *Stomping the Blues* (New York: McGraw Hill, 1976).

4. David Halberstam, *The Fifties* (New York: Villard Books, 1993), p. 478.

5. Nelson George, *The Death of Rhythm and Blues* (New York: Pantheon, 1988), pp. 62–64. Public Enemy, "Fight the Power," from *Fear of a Black Planet* (New York: Def Jam Records, 1990). Tricia Rose, *Black Noise: Rap Music and Black Culture in Contemporary America* (Hanover, N.H.: Wesleyan University Press, 1994), pp. 4–8. The observation about "alternative" playlists is my own, drawn from hundreds of hours of frustrating radio listening.

6. Dixon and Snowden, p. 224. The essential books about Delta blues include Robert Palmer, *Deep Blues* (New York: Penguin Books, 1982), and William Ferris, *Blues from the Delta* (New York: Da Capo, 1978).

7. Muddy Waters, interview with Alan Lomax in Stovall, Mississippi, August 1941, on *Muddy Waters: The Complete Plantation Recordings* (Universal City, Calif.: MCA Records, 1993). Thanks to Gena Dagel Caponi for insisting that I listen to this interview.

8. David Evans, *Big Road Blues: Tradition and Creativity in the Folk Blues* (Berkeley: University of California Press, 1982), pp. 113–15. Thanks to David Sanjek for suggesting this book, and thanks to a reader for New York University Press for insisting that I explore the blues ethic and how it evades the Boolean logical traps.

9. John Cowley, "Really the 'Walking Blues': Son House, Muddy Waters, Robert Johnson, and the Development of a Traditional Blues," in Richard Middletown and David Horn, eds., *Popular Music 1: Folk or Popular? Distinctions, Influences, Continuities* (Cambridge: Cambridge University Press, 1981), pp. 57–72. Also see Palmer, *Deep Blues*, pp. 4–7. Palmer refers to the various verses from "Country Blues" as "the common property of all blues singers."

10. Robert Johnson, "Walking Blues," on *Robert Johnson: The Complete Recordings* (Los Angeles: Columbia Records, 1990).

11. Waters, "Country Blues," on *Muddy Waters: The Complete Plantation Recordings*. The 1948 version, "Feel Like Goin' Home," was copyrighted by Arc

Music in 1964, with words and music credited to McKinley Morganfield, which was Muddy Waters's real name. Arc Music, the publishing company affiliated with Chess Records in Chicago, published most of Waters's and Dixon's compositions as works made for hire, giving flat fees but limited royalties to the composers. Arc was owned by Benny Goodman's brothers, Gene and Harry Goodman. See Dixon and Snowden.

12. Ferris, pp. 57–59.

13. Gena Dagel Caponi, ed., *Signifyin', Sanctifyin', and Slam Dunking: A Reader in African American Expressive Culture* (Amherst: University of Massachusetts Press, 1999), pp. 8–15. The introduction to this book is the single most eloquent distillation on the influence of African aesthetics on American culture. For the African influence on American dance, see Brenda Dixon Gottschild, *Digging the Africanist Presence in American Performance: Dance and Other Contexts* (Westport, Conn.: Greenwood Press, 1996). For the transnational consciousness that informs the African diaspora, see Paul Gilroy, *The Black Atlantic: Modernity and Double Consciousness* (Cambridge: Harvard University Press, 1993). For Africanisms and their presence in American music, see Gerhard Kubik, *Africa and the Blues* (Jackson: University of Mississippi Press, 1999). Also see Steven Tracy, ed., *Write Me a Few of Your Lines: A Blues Reader* (Amherst: University of Massachusetts Press, 1999). For an analysis of improvisation, see Albert Murray, "Improvisation and the Creative Process," in Robert O'Meally, ed., *The Jazz Cadence of American Culture* (New York: Columbia University Press, 1998), pp. 111–113. For Africanisms in American language, see Geneva Smitherman, *Talkin' and Testifyin': The Language of Black America* (Detroit: Wayne State University Press, 1977).

14. Christopher Small, *Music of the Common Tongue: Survival and Celebration in African American Music* (Hanover: Wesleyan University Press, 1987), pp. 289–312. Also see Robert Farris Thompson, *Flash of the Spirit: African and Afro-American Art and Philosophy* (New York: Vintage, 1983).

15. George Harrison, "My Sweet Lord," from *All Things Must Pass* (London: Apple Records, 1970). The account of Harrison's composition process is from *Bright Tunes Music Corp. v. Harrisongs Music, Ltd.*, 420 F. Supp. 177, U.S. District Court Southern District of New York, Aug. 31, 1976.

16. *Bright Tunes Music Corp. v. Harrisongs Music, Ltd.*

17. Sidney Shemel and M. William Krasilovsky, *This Business of Music*, 5th ed. (New York: Billboard Publications, 1985), pp. 265–66.

18. *Bright Tunes Music Corp. v. Harrisongs Music, Ltd.*

19. Robert Palmer, "Today's Songs, Really Yesterday's," *New York Times*, July 8, 1981, p. C21.

20. John Fogerty, *Centerfield* (Burbank: Warner Brothers Records, 1985). See George Varga, "A Good Moon Rising: Legal Troubles behind Him, Fogerty Takes Back His Own," *San Diego Union-Tribune*, August 13, 1998, p. E4. Also see

Hank Bordowitz, *Bad Moon Rising: The Unauthorized History of Creedence Clearwater Revival* (New York: Shirmer Books, 1998), pp. 202–6.

21. *Fantasy, Inc. v. Fogerty*, 664 F. Supp. 1345, Northern District of California, 1987. Also see *Fantasy Inc. v. Fogerty*, 984 F. 2d 1524, U.S. Ninth Circuit Court of Appeals, 1993. Also see Katherine Bishop, "A Victory for the Creative Process," *New York Times*, November 11, 1988, p. B5.

22. See Shemel and Krasilovsky. For the history of the development of this "bundle" of rights, especially the rise of ASCAP and BMI, see Russell Sanjek (updated by David Sanjek), *Pennies from Heaven: The American Popular Music Business in the Twentieth Century* (New York: Da Capo Press, 1996).

23. Rose, pp. 21–26.

24. Schoolly D, "Signifying Rapper," from *Smoke Some Kill* (Philadelphia: Zomba Recording Corp., 1988). For an example of the "Signifying Monkey" tale, see Langston Hughes and Arna Bontemps, eds., *Book of Negro Folklore* (New York: Dodd, Mead, 1958), pp. 365–6. Also see Roger Abrahams, ed., *Afro-American Folktales: Stories from Black Traditions in the New World* (New York: Pantheon, 1985), pp. 101–5. For the transgressive and political potential of "signifying" during African American slavery, see Abrahams, *Singing the Master: The Emergence of African American Culture in the Plantation South* (New York: Pantheon, 1992). For an account of the urban twentieth-century uses of both the practice of "signifying" and the "Signifying Monkey" tale, see Abrahams, *Deep Down in the Jungle: Negro Narrative Folklore from the Streets of Philadelphia* (Chicago: Aldine Publishing, 1970). Also see John W. Roberts, *From Trickster to Badman: The Black Folk Hero in Slavery and Freedom* (Philadelphia: University of Pennsylvania Press, 1989). For a theory of the transgressive and unifying functions of tricksters, signifying, and the "Signifying Monkey" in forging an African American literary tradition published the same year as Schoolly D's "Signifying Rapper," see Henry Louis Gates, *The Signifying Monkey: A Theory of African American Literary Criticism* (New York: Oxford University Press, 1988). For an introduction to the Afro-Caribbean roots of the Signifying Monkey, see Thompson.

25. Theresa Moore and Torri Minton, "Music of Rage," *San Francisco Chronicle*, May 18, 1992, p. 1.

26. Until late 1991, there were no sampling cases brought to trial, although many had been filed and settled out of court, according to James P. Allen Jr., "Look What They've Done to My Song, Ma—Digital Sampling in the '90s: A Legal Challenge for the Music Industry," *Entertainment and Sports Law Review* 9 (1992):181.

27. Juan Carlos Thom, note in the *Loyola Entertainment Law Journal* 8, no. 2 (1988):336.

28. David Toop, *Rap Attack 2: African Rap to Global Hip Hop* (London: Serpent's Tail, 1991), pp. 29–34. This is an updated version of his original book, *Rap Attack*. It includes more on the rise of Def Jam and its artists, and on the rise of

and controversy between Los Angeles and Miami-based rappers. Toop also writes, "No matter how far it penetrates into the twilight maze of Japanese video games and cool European electronics, its roots are still the deepest in all contemporary Afro-American music" (p. 19).

29. Toop cites Otis Redding's "Tramp" as an early dissing influence on rap pioneer Afrika Bambaataa. Toop, p. 115. Many rappers pay their debt by quoting from these masters of soul and funk. Digital Underground even named an album in honor of George Clinton's P-Funk, *Sons of the P.*

30. Mark Costello and David Foster Wallace, *Signifying Rappers: Rap and Race in the Urban Present* (New York: Ecco Press, 1990), p. 25. Also see Toop, p. 17. Many of the backing tracks to early rap hits were lifted from 1970s disco records such as Chic's "Good Times," or classic James Brown and Funkadelic riffs. It was not unusual to hear some stranger stuff, such as television theme show choruses or Kraftwerk spinning in the background. Strangely, one of the most often used and cited backing tracks was "Apache," by the Incredible Bongo Band. It was written and performed by a British instrumental group, the Shadows, and became a hit in 1960. The Ventures also covered it. Eventually, the Sugarhill Gang recorded an entire song called "Apache." See Toop, p. 114.

31. Toop, p. 66. Bambaataa was hardly alone in this practice. One of his "old school" contemporaries who tried to make a mid-eighties comeback, Kool Moe Dee, laid down a repetitive track of Paul Simon's "Fifty Ways to Leave Your Lover." Stevie Gabb's snare drum roll would introduce Dee's ominous baritone voice warning that he had "fifty ways . . . to get ya."

32. For a full exploration of the improvisational history of basketball, see Nelson George, *Elevating the Game: Black Men and Basketball* (New York: Harper-Collins, 1992). Also see Caponi. For the be-bop/hip-hop connection, see Toop, p. 18.

33. Ruth Finnegan, *Oral Literature in Africa* (London: Oxford University Press, 1970), p. 9. Oral traditions that sprout written traditions handle questions of authorship and originality in a complicated manner. While the British romantic tradition runs from influence, the American oral-written tradition revels in it, and uses it with wit and style. This aesthetic is most closely studied and clearly explained in the African American oral and literary traditions. In *The Signifying Monkey*, Gates identifies how the anxiety of influence affected opinions of African and African American expression. Gates notes that David Hume and Thomas Jefferson both accused blacks of being merely imitative rather than creative. Orally based literatures are likely to be heavily informed by immediate audience response, and the valorized storyteller must react to what has been told before and to what is going on around him. The storyteller has an important role, one of demystified authorship. Yet there is no overriding concern for originality as a substantive function, merely a stylistic one. Zora Neale Hurston took it upon herself to demystify the Anglo-Saxon author, and she expressed

ideas similar to those Mark Twain wrote to Helen Keller: "It is obvious that to get back to original sources is much too difficult for any group to claim very much as a certainty. What we really mean by originality is the modification of ideas. The most ardent admirer of the great Shakespeare cannot claim first source even for him. It is in his treatment of the borrowed material." See Hurston, "Characteristics of Negro Expression," in Robert O'Meally, *The Jazz Cadence of American Culture* (New York: Columbia University Press, 1999), p. 304. In *The Signifying Monkey,* Gates outlines tropes that determine the "blackness" of black texts. These tropes recognize the aesthetic of oral transmission and show up clearly in the written antecedents. Gates calls these tropes tropological revision, the speakerly text, and the talking texts. Gates is clear about his motive for defining the blackness in texts textually instead of biologically: to open his model to texts written by whites. For Gates and others who study African, African American, and American art, music and literature, repetition and revision are fundamental to the forms. As Gates writes, "Whatever is black about black American literature is to be found in this identifiable black Signifyin(g) difference." In other words, Gates's goal is to trace a history of distinct and conscious influence—what he calls "tropological revision"—throughout a literary tradition. Gates defines tropological revision as "the manner in which a specific trope is repeated, with differences, between two or more texts." It is important to realize that Gates's questions can and should apply to texts and traditions that few would easily call "black" or "African." So it is revealing to subject Twain and his work, as it arises out of the American and African American oral traditions, to Gates's analysis. Gates's work is about much more than African American literature. It explores how the vestiges of oral traditions survive and thrive in written literature. In cultures that are primarily oral, and within modes of expression that remain oral but operate within postoral or literate cultures, originality is a matter of style, not substance. According to Walter J. Ong, twentieth-century scholarship of oral literature has shown that repetition and revision are essential to the cognitive processes that enable communication and the transmission of meaning. Without a recognizable vocabulary of repeated expressions, an audience cannot follow a story and a storyteller cannot organize the narrative. Orally transmitted stories must be formulaic, and thus "less original," if we define originality substantively, as we do for linear, written narratives. While written cultures reward its "originators" for "making it new," oral cultures reward stylistic daring, performative excellence, improvisation, and audience participation. Doing the "same thing" better is better than doing a "new thing" the same way. See Walter J. Ong, *Orality and Literacy: The Technologizing of the Word* (London: Routledge, 1982).

34. Dick Hebdige, *Cut 'n' Mix: Culture, Identity, and Caribbean Music* (London: Comedia, 1987).

35. Hebdige, p.12.

36. Hebdige, p. 83.

37. Hebdige, p.84.

38. Hebdige, p. 137.

49. Hebdige, p. 137.

40. Hebdige, p. 137.

41. Toop, p. 60.

42. Hebdige, p. 138.

43. Daisann McLane, *New York Times*, Aug. 23, 1992, p.22.

44. The Beach Boys' breakthrough hit, "Surfin' USA," released in March 1963, relied almost entirely on Chuck Berry's "Sweet Little Sixteen," and its lyrical concept was not unlike that song's or that of Chubby Checker's "Twistin' USA." After Arc Music, Berry's publisher, sued Capitol Records, the label settled out of court and gave Berry an undisclosed monetary award and writer's credit on the label. The artistic significance of this event is that "Surfin' USA" established and popularized the Beach Boys' harmonies, vocal styles, and production techniques that would set a high mark of creativity with the *Pet Sounds* album. For a full history of this breakthrough song, see Steven Gaines, *Heroes and Villains: The True Story of the Beach Boys* (New York: New American Library, 1986), pp. 100–101.

45. Famous recorded versions include a 1958 single hit for Lloyd Price, a 1963 cut by the Isley Brothers, several by Dr. John, and a brief Cockney version by the Clash on *London Calling*.

46. Roland and Yamaha began marketing digital samplers in the United States in 1983, at a cost of up to $20,000. These days, they cost as little as $2,000. See David Sanjek, "'Don't Have to DJ No More': Sampling and the 'Autonomous' Creator," *Arts and Entertainment Law Journal* 10, no. 2 (1992): 612.

47. Allen, p. 181.

48. Hammer freely admits his dependence on other artists for his danceable beats. He is paid for his dancing and rapping, one of which is impressive. Hammer was quoted in *People* magazine saying, "Right after I did the song, I said, 'Hey, I gotta pay Rick for this.' I didn't need a lawyer to tell me that." See Peter Castro, "Chatter," *People,* July 30, 1990, p. 86. Hammer frequently bases his most catchy jams on popular hits, and some of them are not old enough to be called classic. His hit "Pray" was laid down over riffs from Prince's 1984 hit "When Doves Cry," from the album *Purple Rain*.

49. Whitney C. Broussard, "Current and Suggested Business Practices for the Licensing of Digital Samples," *Loyola Entertainment Law Journal* 2 (1991): 479.

50. "Ice Ice Baby" was certified platinum on Oct. 9, 1990, when its sales exceeded one million. After the success was certified, the original artists, record company, and publisher all sought compensation for the use of the sample. The matter was settled out of court for an undisclosed amount. See *Harvard Law Review* 105 (1992): 728.

51. Greg Tate, "Diary of a Bug," *Village Voice*, Nov. 22, 1988, p. 73.

52. Run DMC, "Walk This Way," from *Raising Hell* (New York: Profile Records, 1986). This was the first rap hit to get extensive play on MTV and more "mainstream" rock radio. It had a profound effect on those of us who grew up during the 1980s in suburban America. When we heard that three Adidas-clad men from Hollis, Queens, were down with mid-seventies rock like Aerosmith, it showed us that rap might just have something to say to us, or at least some fun to offer us. For an explanation of how "discursive communities" create meaning, see Stanley Fish, *Is There a Text in This Class?* (Cambridge: Harvard University Press, 1980).

53. George Lipsitz, "The Hip Hop Hearings: Censorship, Social Memory, and Intergenerational Tensions among African Americans," in Joe Austin and Michael Nevin Willard, eds., *Generations of Youth: Youth Cultures and History in Twentieth-Century America* (New York: New York University Press, 1998), p. 405.

54. John Leland, "Singles," *Spin*, August 1988, p. 80. Urban hip-hop is not the only subculture assaulting the foundations of creative ownership. Cyberpunk theory frequently pushes the notion of the end of proprietary information. Cybermusician Lisa Sirois of the Boston band DDT says: "We're no longer playing instruments, we're programming. We sequence music on a computer, store it on a hard disc, and then record it onto digital audio tape. Then, when we perform, we supplement it with live drums and keyboards. We're live and on tape. We play on an electronic stage." See Nathan Cobb, "Terminal Chic: Cyberpunk Subculture Swimming Closer to the Surface," *Boston Globe*, Nov. 24, 1992.

55. The 1915 case *Boosey v. Empire Music Co.* indicated that lifting six notes or more may be a violation. The 1952 case *Northern Music Corp. v. King Record Distribution Co.* indicated that as little as four bars of music may be a violation of a work. But *United States v. Taxe* in 1974 complicated any such formulas. The defendant recorded hit songs and electronically altered their speed and pitch. Strange noises were added throughout. The court was not persuaded that the defendant's works were simply "derivative," and ruled that the very recapturing of another's sound is a violation. For an explanation, see Allen, p. 190.

56. Sanjek, p. 609.

57. Note, "A New Spin on Music Sampling: A Case for Fair Play," *Harvard Law Review* (Jan. 1992): 726.

58. Allen, p. 102.

59. "A New Spin on Music Sampling," p. 729.

60. Broussard, p. 502.

61. Richard Harrington, "The Groove Robbers' Judgement," *Washington Post*, December 25, 1991, p. D1.

62. Biz Markie, "Alone Again," from *I Need a Haircut* (New York: Cold Chillin' Records, 1991). Since the lawsuit, this original version of the album has

been very hard to find. Printings after 1991 do not contain "Alone Again." Warner Bros. ordered all record stores to return copies of the album after the settlement. I searched used record stores for five years to get a copy so I could hear the song in question. Fortunately, in the fall of 1998, I discovered that Wesleyan University student Kabir Sen owned a copy of the original pressing. He lent it to me so I could complete this section.

63. Harrington. Also see Susan Upton Douglass and Craig S. Mende, "Hey, They're Playing My Song! Litigating Music Copyrights," *New York Law Journal* (July 14, 1997): S1.

64. *Grand Upright Music, Ltd. v. Warner Bros. Records*, 91 Civ. 7648 (KTD), United States District Court for the Southern District of New York, 780 F. Supp. 182 (1991).

65. Chuck Philips, "Songwriter Wins Large Settlement in Rap Suit," *Los Angeles Times,* January 1, 1992, p. F1. Also see David Goldberg and Robert J. Bernstein, "Reflections on Sampling," *New York Law Journal* (January 15, 1993): 3.

66. Douglass and Mende, p. S1.

67. Public Enemy, "Caught—Can We Get a Witness?" on *It Takes a Nation of Millions to Hold Us Back* (New York: Def Jam/Columbia Records, 1988).

68. *Campbell v. Acuff-Rose Music, Inc.*, 510 U.S. 569 (1994). See Mel Marquis, "Fair Use and the First Amendment: Parody and Its Protections," *Seton Hall Constitutional Law Journal* (1997).

69. *MCA, Inc. v. Wilson*, 677 F. 2d 180 (2d Cir. 1981). In the ruling for the case *Fisher v. Dees*, 794 F. 2d 432 (1986), the court wrote,

> In *MCA, Inc. v. Wilson*, the court held the doctrine of fair use inapplicable in the case of a song called "Cunnilingus Champion of Company C," which closely tracked the music and meter of the 40's standard, "Boogie Woogie Bugle Boy of Company B." The composers of "Champion," which was created for performance in the off-Broadway musical *Let My People Come*, admitted that the song was not originally conceived as a parody of "Bugle Boy." Rather, they had copied the original because it was "immediately identifiable as something happy and joyous and it brought back a certain period in our history when we felt that way." 677 F.2d at 184 (quoting uncited trial record). Central to the court's holding was the determination that "Champion" was not a parody of "Bugle Boy"; in copying "Bugle Boy" almost verbatim, the composers' purpose was simply to reap the advantages of a well-known tune and short-cut the rigors of composing original music.

Also see *MGM v. Showcase Atlanta Cooperative Productions*, 479 F. Supp. 351, 357 (1981). Also see *Hustler Magazine v. Falwell*, 485 U.S. 46 (1988); *Cliffs Notes, Inc. v.*

Bantam Doubleday Dell Publishing Group, 886 F. 2d 490, 493 (2d Cir. 1989); For the solidification of parody protection, see *Fisher v. Dees,* 794 F. 2d 432, 434 n.2 (9th Cir. 1986). Also see Anastasia P. Winslow, "Rapping on a Revolving Door: An Economic Analysis of Parody and Campbell v. Acuff-Rose Music, Inc.," *Southern California Law Review* 69 (1996).

70. *Benny v. Leow's, Inc.,* 239 F. 2d 532 (9th Cir. 1956).

71. *Berlin v. EC Publications, Inc.,* 329 F. 2d 541 (2d Cir. 1964).

72. *Elsmere Music, Inc. v. National Broadcasting Co.,* 482 F. Supp. 741 (S.D.N.Y), add'd, 623 F. 2d 252 (2d Cir. 1980).

73. *Fisher v. Dees,* 794 F. 2d 432 (9th Cir 1986).

74. *Campbell v. Acuff-Rose.*

75. Souter's ruling, however, came a couple of years too late for two other parodists who were denied relief by federal courts. For the painful ordeal that the avant-garde music group Negativeland had to endure when Island Records filed suit against the group and its label for a sampled parody of the Irish rock group U2, see Negativeland, *Fair Use: The Story of the Letter U and the Number 2* (Concord, Calif.: Seeland, 1995). Just as painful, artist Jeff Koons designed a sculpture that parodied a photograph postcard of a rural American couple holding a litter of puppies. Art Rogers, the photographer of the original, sued Koons and won. *Rodgers v. Koons,* 960 F. 2d 301 (2d Cir. 1992). See Vilis Inde, *Art in the Courtroom* (Westport, Conn.: Praeger, 1998). Also see Rosemary Coombe, *The Cultural Life of Intellectual Property: Authorship, Appropriation, and the Law* (Durham: Duke University Press, 1998). The culture industries and their lawyers still seem to resist the idea that parody is fair use. See Alex Kuczynski, "Parody of Talk Magazine Upsets Disney," *New York Times,* July 19, 1999, p. C10.

NOTES TO CHAPTER 5

1. Herbie Hancock is now committed to closing the "digital divide." He founded the Rhythm of Life Organization in 1996 to fund technological programs for underprivileged communities. For information on Herbie Hancock's Rhythm of Life Foundation, see http://www.imhotech.com/rolo/.

2. http://www.net.org/html/history/detail/1983-midi.html.

3. Al Willis, Nicole Hampton, and Adam Wallace, "MIDI: A Beginners' Guide," http://www.mtsu.edu/~dsmitche/rim419/midi/HTMLs/MIDHIS~1 .HTM.

4. Herbie Hancock, "Cantaloupe Island," *Empyrean Isle* (New York: Blue Note Records, 1964). Us3, "Cantaloop," *Hand on the Torch* (New York: Blue Note Records, 1993).

5. Paul Goldstein, *Copyright's Highway: The Law and Lore of Copyright from Gutenberg to the Celestial Jukebox* (New York: Hill & Wang, 1994), p. 197.

6. For a brief account of the controversies over software patents, which became available only in the late 1980s, see James Boyle, *Shamans, Software, and Spleens: Law and the Construction of the Information Society* (Cambridge: Harvard University Press, 1996), pp. 132–34. also see Andrew Chin, "Computational Complexity and the Scope of Software Patents," *Jurimetrics* (Fall 1998): 17–27. Among the best work on software patents and the idea of a *sui generis* area of "intellectual property" for software is Pamela Samuelson et al., "A Manifesto concerning the Legal Protection of Computer Programs," *Columbia Law Review* 94 (1994).

7. John Perry Barlow, "The Economy of Ideas: Everything You Know about Intellectual Property is Wrong," *Wired,* March 1994.

8. For an account of Richard Stallman's influence on the "Open Source" or "Free Software" movement, see Peter Wayner, *Free for All: How Linux and the Free Software Movement Undercut the High-Tech Titans* (New York: Harper Business, 2000). Also see the Salon Free Software Project at www.salon.com.

9. Richard Stallman, "The GNU Manifesto," at www.gnu.org/gnu/manifesto.

10. Stallman, "What Is Free Software," at www.gnu.org/philosophy/free-sw.html.

11. Stallman, "What Is Copyleft," at www.gnu.org/copyleft/copyleft.html.

12. Goldstein, pp. 199–236.

13. "Intellectual Property and the National Information Infrastructure: The Report of the Working Group on Intellectual Property Rights," September 1995. See Boyle, pp. 132–43. Also see Pamela Samuelson, "Legally Speaking: The NII Intellectual Property Report," in *Communications of the ACM,* December 1994.

14. For an explanation of the Madisonian intentions for copyright law to encourage free and rich speech, see Neil Weinstock Netanel, "Copyright and Democratic Civil Society," *Yale Law Journal* (November 1996): 292–386.

15. For a brief outline of the three treaties, see Eric Schwartz, "International Outlook: Impact of the Two New WIPO Treaties," *Intellectual Property Strategist* (January 1997): 1. For an in-depth examination of how both dangerous and unnecessary the database treaty is, see J. H. Reichman and Pamela Samuelson, "Intellectual Property Rights in Data?" *Vanderbilt Law Review* (January 1997): 49–166.

16. Jukka Liedes, "Copyright: Evolution, Not Revolution," *Science,* April 11, 1997, p. 223.

17. See Julius Marke, "Database Protection Acts and the 105th Congress," *New York Law Journal* (March 18, 1997): 5. For a brief summary of Moral Rights, see Goldstein.

18. *Campbell v. Acuff-Rose Music, Inc.*, 510 U.S. 569 (1994). For the "Chicago

School" or "Law and Economics" critique of parody and fair use, see Richard Posner, "When Is Parody Fair Use?" *Journal of Legal Studies* 21 (1992).

19. Susan Nycum, "Protection of Electronic Databases," *Computer Lawyer* (August 1997): 12.

20. Carol Levin and Don Willmott, "Is It Mine On-line?" *PC Magazine*, February 4, 1997, p. 30.

21. John Dewey, *Individualism, Old and New* (New York: Capricorn Books, 1962), p. 154. My thanks to Neil Netanel for tipping me off to Dewey's influence on how intellectual property intersects with democracy. See Netanel, p. 349.

22. U.S. Constitution, art. 1, sec. 8.

23. For an introduction to the fascinating world of Pac-man, see www .gamecenter.com.

24. *Atari, Inc. v. North American Philips Consumer Electronics Corp.*, 672 F. 2d 607 (7th Cir. 1982). For the legal background to the Pac-man disputes, see Lawrence D. Graham, *Legal Battles That Shaped the Computer Industry* (Westport, Conn.: Quorum Books, 1999), pp. 25–32.

25. Graham, p. 80.

26. Graham, p. 81.

27. *Apple Computer, Inc. v. Franklin Computer Corp.*, 545 F. Supp. 812 (E.D. Penn. 1982), rev'd, 714 F. 2d 1240 (3d Cir 1983). For histories of Apple Computer, Inc., see Jim Carlton, *Apple: The Inside Story of Intrigue, Egomania, and Business Blunders* (New York: Times Business, 1997); Michael Malone, *Infinite Loop: How the World's Most Insanely Great Computer Company Went Insane* (New York: Doubleday, 1999); Owen Linzmayer, *Apple Confidential: The Real Story of Apple Computer, Inc.* (San Francisco: No Starch Press, 1999). For a history of the Macintosh computer, see Steven Levy, *Insanely Great: The Life and Times of Macintosh, the Computer that Changed Everything* (New York: Penguin, 2000).

28. For an account of the Revolutionary developments at Xerox PARC, see Michael Hiltzik, *Dealers of Lightning: Xerox PARC and the Dawn of the Computer Age* (New York: HarperBusiness, 1999).

29. Levy, pp. 77–103.

30. For a history of Microsoft, see James Wallace and Jim Erickson, *Hard Drive: Bill Gates and the Making of the Microsoft Empire* (New York: John Wiley and Sons, 1992).

31. *Apple Computer, Inc. v. Microsoft Corp.*, 709 F. Supp. 925 (N.D. Cal. 1989); 717 F. Supp. 1428 (N.D. Cal. 1989); The appellate decision is *Apple Computer, Inc. v. Microsoft Corp.*, 35 F. 3d 1438 (9th Cir. 1994). See Graham, pp. 53–61.

32. See Julie Cohen, "Lochner in Cyberspace," *Michigan Law Review* (November 1998): 462–562. Also see Siva Vaidhyanathan, testimony at the anticircumvention hearings of the Copyright Office, http://lcweb.loc.gov/copyright/ 1201/hearings/.

33. OpenLaw forum, "DVD/DeCSS Forum Frequently Asked Questions (FAQ List," March 6, 2000, www.iag.net/aleris/dvdfaq.txt.

34. *Universal City Studios, Inc., et al. v. Shawn C. Reimerdes et al.*, 111 F. Supp. 2d 294, 2000 SDNY, August 17, 2000, decided. According to this federal court decision, distributing DeCSS code is illegal in 2000.

35. Neil Postman, *Technopoly: The Surrender of Culture to Technology* (New York: Vintage Books, 1993), pp. 71–72.

36. Lawrence Lessig, *Code and Other Laws of Cyberspace* (New York: Basic Books, 1999), p. 135.

37. See www.billboard.com. The user license is available at Secure.telescan.com/bblicense.asp.

38. *A&M Records, Inc. v. Napster, Inc.*, 114 F. Supp. 2d 896, August 10, 2000. See Siva Vaidhyanathan, "MP3: It's Only Rock & Roll and The Kids are Alright," *Nation*, July 24, 2000, http://www.thenation.com:80/issue/000724/0724vaidhyanathan.shtml.

39. Friedrich von Hayek, *The Road to Serfdom* (Chicago: University of Chicago Press, 1994).

40. See http://gnutella.wego.com/. The Free Software Foundation has expressed some doubts about whether Gnutella is actually "open source" or "free software." As Richard Stallman writes,

> Gnutella is not actually GNU software, and we cannot be sure it is actually free software. In fact, it is extremely difficult to find information about the program at all. Perhaps the original developers picked the name because they wanted it to be GNU software someday, but their employers stamped out the project, and it does not seem to have been released as free software.

See http://www.gnu.org/philosophy/gnutella.html.

41. For information on the Secure Digital Music Initiative, see http://www.sdmi.org/.

42. Michael Learmoth, "AOL and Intertrust: 'A Legal Napster,'" *The Industry Standard*, July 3, 2000, www.thestandard.com/article/display/0,1151,16564,00.html.

43. Robert Wright, "Rock 'n' Roll Heaven," *Slate*, July 31, 2000, Slate.msn.com/earthling/00-07-31/Earthling.asp. Also see Wright, "Tuesdays without Morrie?" *Slate*, August 4, 2000, Slate.msn.com/earthling/00-08-04/earthling.asp. A similar string of discussion about "the end of copyright" occurred on a forum called the Coalition for Networked Information back in 1993. See www.cni.org/hforums/cni-copyright/1993-01/0246.html.

44. Peter Jaszi, "Is This the End of Copyright As We Know It?" a talk given at the Nordinfo Conference, Oct. 9–10, 1997, in Stockholm, Sweden. The text is available at webserver.law.yale.edu/censor/jaszi.htm.

NOTES TO THE EPILOGUE

1. Lijntje Zandee, "Martha Graham and Modern American Dance," http://www.let.uu.nl/hist/ams/xroads/dance.htm.

2. See http://cyber.law.harvard.edu/eldredvreno/index.html.

3. Brenda Dixon Gottschild, *Digging the Africanist Presence in American Performance: Dance and Other Contexts* (Westport, Conn.: Greenwood Press, 1996), pp. 47–49.

4. Sarah Kaufman, "Dances in the Public Domain? Graham Works May Lack Copyright Protection," *Washington Post*, July 28, 2000, p. C1.

5. Alex Kuczynski, "Parody of Talk Magazine Upsets Disney," *New York Times*, July 19, 1999, p. C10.

6. Todd Gillman, "Studio Seeks to Ground Kirk's Ads," *Dallas Morning News*, April 27, 1999, p. 16A.

7. "Cost of Swiping the Punchline: Lawsuit," *New York Post*, Aug. 17, 2000, p. 35.

8. See FreeRepublic.com at http://www.freerepublic.com/. Thanks to Yochai Benkler for alerting me to this incident. Benkler's analysis of it is in Benkler, "Free As the Air to Common Use: First Amendment Constraints on Enclosure of the Public Domain," *New York University Law Review* (May 1999): 357. For information on the Copyright Clearance Center, see http://www.copyright.com/.

9. Pia Pera, *Lo's Diary* (New York: Foxrock, 1999), p. ix.

10. Rosemary Coombe, *The Cultural Life of Intellectual Properties: Authorship, Appropriation, and the Law* (Durham: Duke University Press, 1998), p. 128. Also see Henry Jenkins, *Textual Poachers: Television Fans and Participatory Culture* (New York: Routledge, 1992).

Index

About the Author

SIVA VAIDHYANATHAN has written for the *Nation,* the *Chronicle of Higher Education,* the *Dallas Morning News,* the *Austin American-Statesman,* and the *Fort Worth Star-Telegram.* His work has been profiled in the *New York Times* and on National Public Radio. Vaidhyanathan is an assistant professor of Information Studies at the University of Wisconsin at Madison.